In the Best Interests

Intrigue and Payback in Papua New Guinea

John and Elisa Mendzela

Mendhurst

Published by Mendhurst
Contact: www.mendhurst.com/inthebestinterests

This book is based on true events, but some names and incidents have been changed to protect individuals' identities.

A catalogue record for this book is available from the National Library of New Zealand.

ISBN 978-0-473-74814-2 (paperback)
ISBN 978-0-473-74815-9 (EPUB)

All images are from the authors' collection, unless otherwise noted.
Cover design by Jeroen ten Berge, jeroentenberge.com

Contents

To those who risked their futures and sacrificed their own welfare in the best interests of others: our students, our colleagues and most of all our dear friend Gus Gale.

And to the Papua New Guineans of today who refuse to let the bad overwhelm the good.

Introduction

This is a true story. The names of most of the people involved are changed. But the roles they played are not. All of the events portrayed can be fully validated from reports, letters, photos, notes and newspaper clippings.

This story relates past events. But abusive behaviour by individuals and public institutions, and harassment suffered by 'whistleblowers' who try to stop that behaviour, continue to this day. We believe publication of the Keravat story is in the public interest. We hope our story will encourage anyone in a similar situation to act 'in the best interests' of those they are responsible for and challenge those who would abuse their official positions to exploit others or suppress the truth.

We have recorded events and recreated actual conversations from authentic documentation and have done so to the best of our knowledge and recollection. We recognise that other people's memories of the events related in this book may in good faith be different. No damage, hurt or invasion of privacy is intended to any person living or dead.

Technological and social change happens fast. Many everyday activities were performed quite differently in the 1980s, before mobile phones, electronic files and the internet. That was also a time when sexual abuse was mostly a hidden secret and people with power could often act with impunity. The scandals of physical, psychological and sexual abuse of young people that were to engulf religious orders, charitable institutions, government, political parties and the entertainment industry still lay in the future. And the typical psychological impacts of such abuse that can lead victims to blame themselves and not to expose perpetrators were not yet well understood.

Sexual terminology was different too. The word 'gay' was widely used only within homosexual society. For most people, 'homosexual' was a neutral description. 'Queer' was considered a pejorative term for male homosexuals that liberal people mostly avoided using.

Keravat operated as a two-year government academy to prepare small numbers of top secondary school graduates for potential tertiary education. We felt Keravat's formal designation as a 'national high school' could mislead readers outside Papua New Guinea about its institutional nature, while more descriptive titles such as 'sixth-form college' would be clumsy and unfamiliar to PNG readers. To avoid confusion, we have used the terms 'Keravat College' and 'Colleges Division' throughout.

To this day, there are several alternative spellings for the location of the college. We have used 'Keravat', the spelling prevalent during our time there.

All images are sourced from the authors' own collection, unless credited to another source.

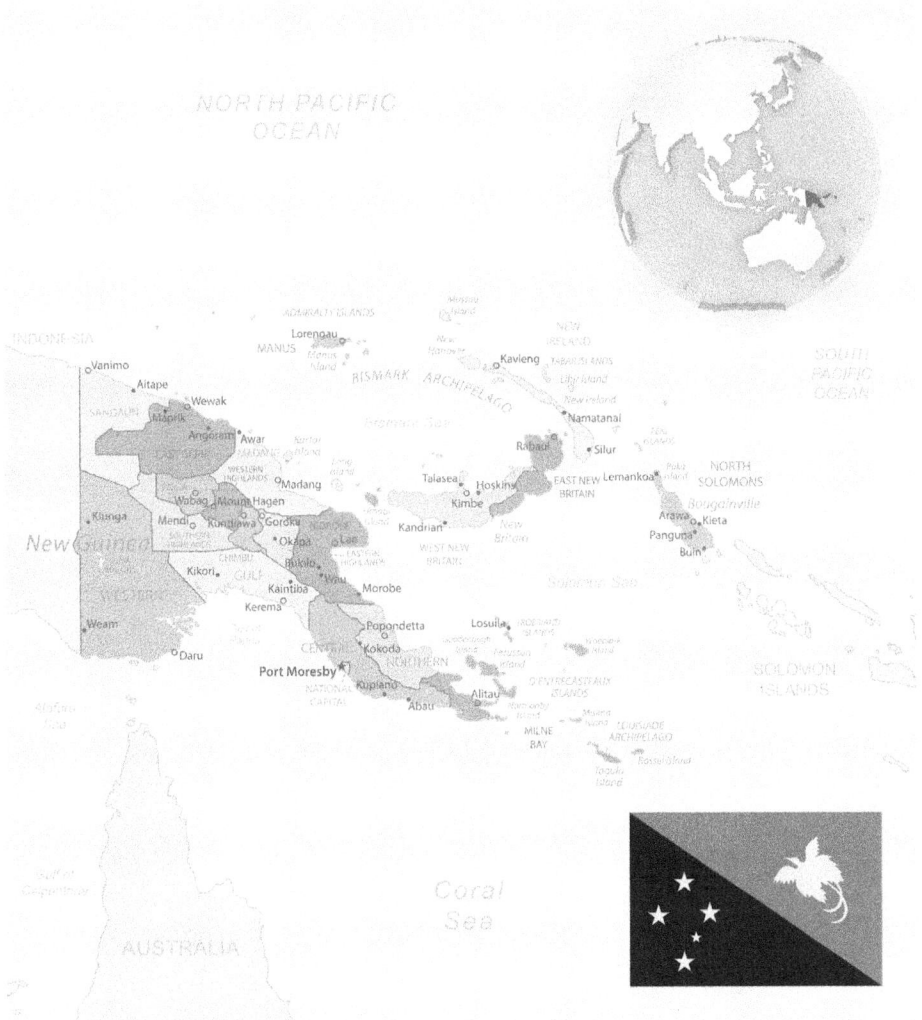

PNG lies between northeast Australia and the Pacific Ocean

1. Curious Encounters (John)

'OH LOOK!' exclaimed Martin. 'There's one of the students. Pull over, Chris.'

The wide commercial street was lined with dusty shops and offices, all closed on Sunday. Few people were around. Two teenage boys were walking quietly along one side of the road. They hadn't seen us yet.

Martin rolled down his window, leaned out, and called a name. One boy stiffened, then slowly turned around to face the car. He didn't look happy.

'Come over here,' Martin urged. 'I haven't seen you in ages.'

Martin was the inspector responsible for professional standards at the college where we would work. In fact, he was responsible for those standards at all four of Papua New Guinea's colleges. We felt thrilled that such a senior officer had personally come to the airport to meet us, in a private car and on Sunday. While his friend Chris drove us from airport to hotel, Martin told us about the colleges, the students and his own role. He explained that indigenous Papua New Guinean staff were generally referred to as 'nationals'. Teachers from overseas like us, usually referred to as 'expats', made up almost all college teaching staff and still played leading roles in most secondary schools. Other expats held senior roles throughout the economy and government.

We felt hot. The lightweight business clothing we had donned for the flight into PNG (as everyone called the country) had turned out to be far too warm for the intense afternoon sun.

Our hosts were dressed more sensibly in colourful short-sleeved tropical shirts and light slacks. Both were handsome men in their thirties. Martin was lean, with blond hair, fair skin and penetrating eyes. Chris was darker and stockier.

Everything so far had been friendly and novel. Martin was an enthusiastic informant, more like a knowledgeable tour guide than a senior official. It seemed only natural that he would take an opportunity to casually greet and talk with a college student.

The young man, a striking dark-skinned national, walked slowly towards us. His friend hung back. When the young man reached the car, Martin stretched out through the open window, took his hand, and held that in his own hands all the time they talked.

Martin introduced us as new college teachers who had just arrived. He asked how the young man was getting on and how his friends were doing. The boy answered only in quiet monosyllables. He seemed embarrassed and barely looked at us. Martin stroked his hand, then let go and said goodbye.

The car pulled off. Surprised by what we had seen, we were silent. Sensing our discomfort, Martin explained that Papua New Guineans often behaved quite differently from people in Western countries. For example, boys and men often held hands, just as friendly behaviour. And most nationals were shy with strangers, especially people from overseas.

Conversation resumed. We soon arrived at our hotel. Martin advised that a driver would collect us straight after lunch tomorrow to start our induction programme at Education Department offices. We unloaded our luggage, said goodbye and thanks, and checked in.

The hotel was decidedly basic. Our room and its sparse furnishings didn't rate a single star, let alone the advertised two. The ceiling fan operated a 'go-slow' and made little impact on the oppressive heat. The walls of our room were thin, unpainted plywood partitions. Their lowest section comprised only metal poles linked by wire mesh, leaving our room open to the corridor near floor level. Our only illumination was whatever dim light seeped through that wire mesh.

Two slim single beds with threadbare linen and rock-hard pillows squeezed a small table. Opposite stood a single upright wooden chair and a crude plywood cupboard with a clothes rail but no hangers. The bathroom was down the corridor. But the place was clean and the staff obliging. And we were determined to remain upbeat and positive. After all, we could hardly expect a developing nation to offer luxury accommodation to mere college teachers.

After a long flight, we would have enjoyed a walk. But Martin and Chris had told us that 'Moresby' (as everyone called Port Moresby, PNG's capital) was not safe to move around in, especially at night. Barred windows and wire fencing around the hotel confirmed that advice. With darkness falling tropically fast, staying in seemed wise.

The lobby boasted a telephone for guest use. While Elisa unpacked, I called Gus to confirm our arrival. Gus lived 800 kilometres away on the Keravat College campus where we would work.

I knew telephone calls were expensive, so I didn't plan to talk for long. Gus had written that he was in fact lucky even to have a home phone. But after updating Gus on our journey, I couldn't help relating our experience with Martin. Wasn't his behaviour with that student odd?

Gus didn't mince words. Yes, Martin was homosexual. So were some of the other expatriates working for the Education Department. More conservative college staff didn't like that, and there were rumours about teachers and Education Department officers behaving unethically with students. No proof had emerged though. PNG was by law and belief strongly Christian, and sex between males was illegal. So homosexuals needed to be careful. Martin was a lively character who was probably just showing off where it seemed safe.

We agreed we were liberally minded people with no aversion to homosexual relationships between consenting adults. Neither of us wanted to dwell on that topic, so talk turned to our future at the college. 'Remember life is different here,' Gus signed off. 'It's often hard to get things done. Pushing hard does no good. Just be patient and friendly and try to develop a practical solution to any problem that comes up.'

After a basic but healthy breakfast next morning, our first priority was to buy local currency. We were directed to a bank just around the corner. A young national man came to the counter to assist us. He had a warm pleasant manner but seemed unfamiliar with the calculations needed to convert our foreign currency. When the young man finished counting out PNG money and presented a paper for signature, I checked the result. He had made a mistake. I pointed that out, in a friendly way. The young man first looked upset. Then he dropped out of sight below the counter! We stood surprised and waited for him to come back up. He didn't.

What was going on? After some moments I stretched over the counter to see. No one there. The young man must have crept away, keeping out of sight.

Unsure what to do next, we waited again. After a few minutes someone else came over — an expat this time, who acted like a supervisor. After our explanation, he apologised for the mistake, corrected the paperwork and counted out the correct sum of money. I stressed that we hadn't minded the mistake but wondered why the young man had hidden from us and crept away. Did he fear punishment of some sort? The man laughed. 'No,' he said. 'Just embarrassed that he made a mistake and too ashamed to face you after that. You'll get used to it.'

It was still mid-morning, but already hot. No wonder PNG business dress meant short-sleeved shirts with shorts or light slacks for men, and loose summer dresses for women. Armed with our new currency, we set out to buy suitable clothing. We found most of what we needed in a cluttered shop a few blocks from our hotel, run (like most shops, we found out later) by a Chinese woman. While she packed our purchases, we told her that we had walked to her shop. She was dismayed. 'Not safe here!' she declaimed. 'Too many rascals. Don't walk around!'

We left cheerfully with our packages. 'Rascals' didn't sound too menacing. What did she mean? Perhaps she was joking with us. But to be on the safe side, we decided to take her warning seriously and warily retreated to the hotel for lunch and our scheduled pickup.

Our car materialised well after the promised time. The driver spoke little English. After we arrived at the Education Department, we asked our 'instructors' for the week — two young national men — if anything had gone wrong. No, it was just 'PNG time'; don't expect things to happen punctually. How was the hotel? Fine, we said. Did we have everything we needed? We described our shopping trip, and the joke about 'rascals'. 'No joke!' they quickly explained. 'Rascals' were not the mischievous but harmless characters that English word suggested — they were aggressive criminals, often violent and sometimes armed. We were learning fast.

The first day of the induction programme — a broad orientation — proved fascinating. Explanations, handouts and a documentary film explained the history and geography of this newly independent nation. Landforms, people and cultural practices were incredibly diverse. Airstrips, not roads, linked the few real towns. Many places remained several days' hard walk from any sign of 'civilisation' and millions of villagers had little contact with the outside world.

In fact, PNG was almost a last frontier. As late as 1930, much of the country was still unknown to outsiders. Sovereignty came in a rush in 1975, hastened by a politically embarrassed Australian colonial administration. Famously, flag-raising ceremonies failed in some towns where locals felt unready for national independence and defiantly hoisted the Australian flag back up.

Independence found the new nation flush with generous aid funds but lacking qualified and trained people in almost every field. Many able officials and businesspeople from colonial times had left. Government administration relied on a mix of expatriates who had stayed on, new recruits like us, and inexperienced locals.

We learned about Melanesian culture. Collective membership of a clan or tribe shaped people's behaviour. Everyone was expected to help any member of their group who asked for food, money or favours. 'Payback' for perceived wrongs committed by a different tribal group — meaning revenge, often violent and sometimes fatal — was another key cultural trait. And that payback could be legitimately inflicted on any member of the offending group, even someone unaware of the original incident. To our Western eyes,

PNG seemed strange, colourful and dangerous. It would certainly be different from anywhere else we had lived.

Our students would be different too. Two universities were only just getting started, along with a few technical institutes. A mere 800 secondary school graduates, 16 or older, were chosen by competitive examination each year to attend four two-year colleges where all instruction proceeded in the English language. Localisation — replacement of expats by trained nationals — was an aspiration, not a reality. In every professional and technical field, including higher education, PNG still depended heavily on expats.

But unlike in many ex-colonies, here nationals generally felt positive towards expatriates and valued their contributions. Our professional challenge would be to transfer our skills and knowledge to highly motivated students and novice teachers. So not just a teaching job, but a great opportunity to participate in positive change and development. We felt good about that.

At the hotel that night, Elisa and I reflected on the six years since we met at Leeds University as leaders of ecological groups. We had soon married and enthusiastically started work in education. But teaching in northern England in the 1970s frustrated us. Many students showed little interest in classroom learning. Quality of life in a crowded island felt constrained, while the British economy struggled under high inflation and frequent industrial disputes.

Young, well-qualified and adventurous, we wanted to travel and work overseas. Convinced that ecological catastrophe would punish a careless human race, probably sooner not later, we looked for somewhere remote, thinly populated and able to feed itself. And somewhere that needed qualified English-speaking teachers. Not many places met all those criteria. An advertisement in the overseas section of *The Times*

Educational Supplement seeking a pair of teachers just like us turned out to be for the Falkland Islands, which seemed a little too remote!

Another advertisement from the New Zealand High Commission sounded more enticing. A prompt interview in London proved decisive. We eagerly accepted their offer of a fresh start in an uncrowded country with a positive reputation. But to our surprise, we found the teaching environment not much different from England, while the New Zealand economy struggled with the same high inflation and frequent industrial disputes. Worse, many cultural facilities we had taken for granted in England didn't exist in Invercargill (the remote small city we were posted to). Everyone was friendly enough, but they had extended families, local interests and long-standing social networks. As a childless couple in our energetic twenties with unconventional habits like cycle-touring, we felt out on a limb.

I didn't like my job much either. The headmaster started the year by advising the staff where to buy new canes to discipline misbehaving boys and announced that all male teachers would be expected to coach a Saturday rugby team. I had never even played rugby, and I wasn't keen to cane anyone. I ended up as the supervisor for small-bore rifle shooting —something new that I had to learn about — and decided that on principle I wouldn't buy or use a cane.

Another new recruit from England arrived at my school. Gus Gale was introduced at a Monday staff meeting as an experienced science teacher and (probably more impressive, for the headmaster at least) a former rugby lock. He looked tall, formidable and distinguished. We shook hands briefly at tea break.

That Friday, it was time for 'in-service training'. Deputy headmaster Jim Smithers had roped me in for a series of lunchtime sessions at which novice teachers (we had three first-years on our staff) would share experience and ideas. 'John, I know you've been teaching for several years already, but you are new to our country. And Gus Gale has agreed to participate. So how about it?' I didn't want to lose my lunch break, but I couldn't say no.

We crowded into Jim's office — the three first-years, Gus, me and senior mistress Dorothy Pearson. Jim did a quick round-the-table introduction and we discussed general topics for a while. Jim suggested we close the session with a practical challenge, and fired off a question to one of the novices. 'Sally, here's the situation. A boy is talking and being disruptive while you're trying to explain something to the class. You've told him to be quiet twice now, and he's still carrying on. What will you do?'

Sally looked embarrassed. 'I'm not sure, Mr Smithers.' She bit her lip.

Jim let her off the hook. 'Mr Gale is the most experienced teacher here. What would you do, Gus?"

Gus spoke authoritatively, in a smooth English baritone. 'I would open the door to the corridor, go over to the boy, pick him up by the ears, carry him to the door, put him outside, close the door and resume my explanation.'

Quiet prevailed for some moments. Senior mistress Dorothy broke the silence. 'Mr Gale, you can't do that at our school. It's not legal.'

Gus spoke calmly. 'It most certainly is.' He began quoting court decisions on that very point, centred on the concept of using reasonable force to counter disruption to the learning of others. The new teachers stared at him, dumbfounded. Jim was looking unhappy. I was enjoying this!

Dorothy wasn't giving up. She drew herself up primly. 'I'm sorry Mr Gale; you can't do that here. Violence against pupils is not acceptable at our school.'

Gus stayed calm. 'I understand that caning boys is a normal practice here, Miss Pearson. Isn't that violence against pupils?'

Dorothy was outraged now. 'That's different!'

Gus gazed at her steadily. 'What's different about it?'

Dorothy sputtered for several moments. Then the solution came to her. 'We write it down. In a book.'

I couldn't help laughing out loud. Two of the novices started giggling. As deputy headmaster Jim finally opened his mouth to speak, the bell ending the lunch break rang out. Jim spoke with relief. 'Oh dear, we've run out of time. Thanks all, great session today.' Everyone hurried out.

Gus and I weren't asked to attend in-service training after that.

I invited Gus and his wife June around for dinner that weekend. The four of us clicked from the start. Unlike us, Gus had a New Zealand connection — his parents and brother lived at the northern end of the country. But, like us, they were childless and enterprising.

Fifteen years older, Gus and June had wider life experience. Gus had a diverse background in industry, the military and even politics (as mayor of a small town in England). June, his second wife after a failed early marriage, was an experienced English teacher. They met in Singapore and then drove 9000 miles overland back to England in their van, overcoming many dangers in Asia and the Middle East. Their move to New Zealand was another adventure.

We shared good times over drinks and enjoyed walking, hunting and fishing together in the spacious outdoors of southern New Zealand. But after only a couple of school terms, Gus told me he didn't intend to stay in his current teaching job for long. Quite understandable — I didn't either. I felt that a career in New Zealand education wasn't a good match for me. I had already decided to begin business studies in the evenings the following year and continue to teach maths only as an interim measure.

But we were dismayed when Gus abruptly resigned at the start of the next school year. His brother Arthur had recently taken up a senior role in technical training in Papua New Guinea. Arthur had impressed his new employers with wide capability and a 'can-do' attitude, and quickly got Gus a contract offer to teach at a college there.

That would be a real adventure! Impulsively, Elisa and I wondered whether we should be going too. At our farewell dinner with Gus and June, we asked Gus to put in a good word for us if things worked out well for them.

They did. Gus's letters bubbled with enthusiasm about working in PNG. Pay was good, his location was attractive, and work was fun — teaching bright young people who were keen to learn. June soon obtained a contract there too, and Gus told us that two teachers with no children was a package the authorities liked. Go for it, we decided.

Six months after Gus had flown off, we received a letter offering both of us jobs in the college system. The college where Gus worked had vacancies in our subjects, and we could expect to be posted there. Contracts had a standard timeframe of three years. At the end, I would still be only 30 years old — young enough to finish business studies and change careers.

We checked the short and simple contract carefully. Attractive remuneration included a low-tax gratuity. Furnished housing would be provided, travel expenses would be paid, and there were fair and reasonable provisions for other matters. But the contract also included one worrisome feature. The Public Service Commission as our employer could terminate the contract without notice 'in the best interests of Papua New Guinea'. 'What did that mean?' we asked our lawyer. Who would decide what was 'in the best interests'? And how?

Our lawyer thought that was just a 'saving' clause that needed to be there in case things didn't work out in some unexpected way. We shouldn't feel concerned. After all, the PNG authorities were making an investment and wanted the contract to succeed. And any contract termination without notice would trigger payment of all accrued gratuities and closing benefits, plus six months' extra pay — not bad given the three-year timeframe. Reassured, we signed and dispatched our contracts, put our house on the market, and started packing.

And now here we were.

Induction week passed quickly. We learned about the curriculum, the examination system and other professional topics. Apart from the top man (an Assistant Secretary for Education), the senior officers in Colleges Division were all expats who had stayed on after independence instead of 'going finish'. Bruce Hawthorne, in charge of administration, was a fit and assertive Australian in his late forties. He sported a safari suit and a military-style crewcut. Ross Johnston, the Australian in charge of curriculum, was a tall, thin and untidy man with a timid and effeminate manner who seemed close to retirement age. Thomas Smith, a chubby and more youthful Australian who introduced himself as the division's 'projects' man and legal adviser ('I'm not a lawyer though!') felt a bit slippery and insincere.

Thursday was excursion day. We traded the comfortable and air-conditioned, but rather alienating, concrete office blocks of administrative Waigani for expansive sea views and hot streets busy with a colourful mix of people: wider-faced and lighter skinned Papuans, leaner and darker curly-headed folk from distant coastal regions, and stocky Highlanders wearing hooped woollen caps despite the searing sun. Few were much taller than Elisa's five-foot-zero, and at five-foot-ten I was a giant. We toured the impressive national museum, strolled through a stilt village built over the water, and climbed an authentic treehouse in a small national park. Lunch was an adventure too — grilled crocodile steaks at a country hotel.

On Friday morning Bruce confirmed we had been posted to Keravat College and booked on the early Saturday morning flight to Rabaul, the nearest airport. And as a send-off, the Education Department would treat us to dinner at Port Moresby's new upmarket hotel on Friday evening.

The inspector joined us in the afternoon for a closing discussion. How had everything gone? How did we feel? Did we have any questions? Everything had gone well, we looked forward to getting started, and we had no questions. 'Great!' Martin said. 'But let me remind you things are different here. Give me your hand.'

Martin took my hand and stroked it. He looked directly into my face as he did that. I blushed but resisted the temptation to pull away. After a few seconds, we both laughed and Martin let go. He had made his point.

Dinner was fun. Our host was the College Divisions' head, Assistant Secretary for Education Mr Tavitai, a quiet, slim and youthful national. The hotel delivered excellent food and service. Wine flowed freely. Martin (who presided like the actual host) was entertaining and attentive. We invited him to visit us for lunch when he next came to Keravat.

We chatted happily with several other new recruits. All envied us our posting to Keravat, especially a Brit named Derek who had been assigned to Kiunga High School in remote Western Province. 'Lucky you,' he groaned. 'Rabaul is a beautiful coastal town with amenities. Me, I'll be living deep in the jungle, stuck in the pouring rain with mosquitoes and crocodiles!'

Back at the hotel, we went to bed in a glow, ready to continue our adventure.

2. Tropical Paradise? (Elisa)

GUS HAD WARNED us to expect a dramatic approach to a small airport. He wasn't joking! Our 40-seat propeller plane skimmed over fabulously steep mountains and even between them, within spitting distance it seemed. Finally, it made a tight turn and dropped inside a circle of volcanic cones for the final approach into Rabaul. With a few bumps and jumps we touched down on a short runway *inside* the huge volcanic crater that comprised the harbour. John and I descended the plane's fold-down steps with exhilaration and relief. We had arrived!

Gus and June were waiting. It was great to see them again. After hugs all around, they explained how they had made everything ready for us. The college term wouldn't start for another week, so we would have plenty of time to settle in. What's more, they had chosen a fully furnished house on the college campus for us and found a home help (a 'hausboi') who would do our cleaning and washing for a moderate fortnightly payment.

We climbed into Gus's four-wheel-drive vehicle and stowed our luggage. Only the two front seats faced forward. John and I sat on sideways benches in the back, under a soft fabric top that buttoned down onto the chassis. The only 'air conditioning' blew in around the edges of the fabric. Gus apologised that we would suffer an unfortunate side effect of sucking in road dust as well. However, he assured us, that was better than suffocating with the heat. He told us not to expect a smooth ride. 'Outside town, it's all dirt roads, bumps and dust — when it's not muddy. The college is about 50 minutes' drive from here. And there's not much suspension in vehicles like this.'

He wasn't wrong. As our vehicle bounced over corrugations and dropped in and out of potholes, we held tightly to handles fitted to the roof. Soon we felt brittle and starchy in our new coats of grey dust. For once I was glad not to be tall like John. He kept bumping the canvas roof, which retaliated with additional dust clouds. We didn't mind though — all part of the adventure! Children waved and shouted enthusiastically as our military-green 4WD car sped past. Waving back while bumping along, I felt like the Queen.

Rabaul with smoking volcano (Wikimedia)

June explained private cars were a luxury few nationals could afford. People either walked long distances or paid fares to ride in trucks and utility vans known as PMVs (Public Motor Vehicles). And the children in the villages dotted along the dirt road who looked poor to us were, in fact, affluent by national standards. Unlike people living in remote areas, most village families here could sell surplus produce for cash in Rabaul to supplement their subsistence farming.

The village houses boasted wooden frames with attractive plaited-fibre panels and thatch (or occasionally iron) roofs. They were quite lovely and certainly tidy. Gardens looked impressively fertile and people walking along the road (lots of them) seemed healthy and happy — despite the dust from passing vehicles.

When we passed a coastal strip, sizeable fishing canoes were evident. Tropical vegetation with endless coconut palms and many bright flowers presented a vivid backdrop. Novel aromas drifted in with the dust. All new and fascinating, and so different to the temperate or urban landscapes we were used to.

In less than an hour we were driving through Keravat 'township'. Gus pointed out amenities as we drove through: the Catholic church and primary school, a small police station (complete with flagpole and parade ground), the 'trade store' (a tiny general store), the 'aid post' (a basic medical facility), and the electricity generator (throbbing loudly). The road through Keravat was sealed for a full kilometre. Then a turnoff accessed the college campus via a gravel drive.

Compared to the villages we had seen, the utilitarian and standardised fibreboard buildings of the campus looked orderly but bland. The gravel access road first passed the girls' dormitories and ran alongside a sports field. Then Gus took us on a circular route around the classrooms and boys' dormitories and pointed out the 'back entrance' to the campus from a dirt track we had passed when driving through the township.

Most college buildings and staff houses were raised on stilts and reached by individual flights of stairs. Gus explained how frequent earthquakes and regular heavy rains made raised buildings a practical necessity. 'Don't worry when a quake hits. Everything sways back and forth and the electricity usually cuts out for a while, but it's perfectly safe.'

Our new home on the ridge and in the trees

To complete our tour, we returned to the main entrance and followed a short dirt track along the other side of the sports field to a dead end. Gus parked the car there and we walked up a steep flight of earth steps to a small building perched on a ridge overlooking the sports field. This fibreboard bungalow with its wooden veranda would be our new home. Behind the house, a small flat grassed area led to a steep slope down to a stream. On the far side stretched a sumptuous mass of jungle, like nothing we had seen before. Two identical dwellings, spaced about 10 metres away on either side, occupied the rest of the ridge.

The interior was simple and functional: a small kitchen, a roomy living area and two tiny bedrooms. A cramped bathroom had toilet fittings, a sink and a shower box. 'Don't expect hot water. There isn't any. Anyway, in a tropical climate you'll be too hot most of the time and won't need it.' Gus turned out to be half right — the water wasn't *too* cold, and on a hot afternoon its coolness could be welcome.

Furnishings were basic to an extreme. Iron beds offered only simple metal springs topped with thin foam-rubber mattresses. Worse, those mattresses were stained dark brown with dirt and dust, and they felt warm and sticky. Equally brown and tacky foam pillows headed each mattress. Ceiling-to-floor louvre windows in every room promised ample ventilation but no privacy.

John on our veranda, with neighbouring house in background

The shiny plastic-topped dining table had a curious shape. Like a banana, it sloped inwards where the particle board had sagged with damp. Plates and anything else placed on the table would migrate towards the centre. And we found no lounge furniture as we knew it, just a few basic cupboards with shelves and several individual wooden chairs with rigid arms, a slightly inclined back and square foam cushions — also stained brown. 'Those are your easy chairs,' Gus explained. 'Easy to make that is, not easy to sit in. And we've put together some sheets, towels and kitchen stuff for you.'

Despite their kindness, I was feeling uncomfortable about hygiene, especially the sticky and stained foam mattresses. June tried to cheer me up. She explained that simple housewares like sheets were readily available in town, and we could run up curtains and covers on her sewing machine. '*And* we managed to snaffle a washing machine for you — one that works. They're hard to get because they break easily and no one can repair them.' I looked at the small semi-automatic twin tub with dismay. I had heard about such machines but never used one.

'What about the "home help" you mentioned?' I inquired. 'I'm happy doing my own housework. I'm not sure I want a bloke around to do cleaning and laundry.'

Gus took a firm line. He explained that we would be very well off by PNG standards. Paying someone to do housework was an expected way to share some of that affluence. Local women had their own children, households and gardens to look after. So, it was men who earned cash from housework. Most were single and aging former plantation workers with no other livelihood. June chipped in, explaining that they had provisionally engaged for us a friend of their own reliable hausboi. Our helper would live in a nearby village and do our housework during the day while we were out at the college. I reminded myself that things were different here and agreed to go with the flow.

We settled in over the next week. Dirt and mould were passive opponents I could overcome and control. But we faced mobile enemies too. Mosquitoes were not just a nuisance but a serious health risk as carriers of malaria and other diseases. They took advantage of any briefly opened door or any small hole in window screens, making mosquito coils an essential night-light for the first few days. Large moths and beetles, attracted by light from our curtainless windows, frequently startled me with loud bumps (though they were harmless). Small lizards roamed the walls and ceilings at night, stalking the abundant insects. Watching those geckos hunt their prey and sometimes each other soon became an evening entertainment we could think of as 'PNG television'.

Cockroaches were the worst pest — bold, massive, numerous and evasive. I refused to accept their presence and declared war. Ecologically minded, we were reluctant to use sprays like everyone else, and decided vigorous cleaning plus plastic traps should be enough. On the fifth evening of battle, I entered our dimly lit kitchen and extracted two cups from my freshly cleaned cupboard. As I was spooning in my coffee, an especially large and repulsive cockroach crawled out of the cup. I couldn't help screaming! Idealism defeated, we again went with the flow and brought the enemy (mostly) under control with a regular spray programme.

Our Monday trip into town to open bank accounts and purchase groceries, fabrics and other household necessities was easy and fun. Rabaul offered a good range of amenities: two banks, two hotels, two small supermarkets, a thriving daily market with haphazard piles of fruit and vegetables tended by large ladies in colourful and voluminous 'meri blouses', and a small Chinatown with a few restaurants and many we-sell-everything 'trade stores'.

Buying transport was harder. Having only owned bicycles before, we were unfamiliar with cars, let alone four-wheel-drive vehicles. We took Gus's advice on everything and let him negotiate a deal for us. We bought the same medium vehicle Gus owned, a green 2.5-litre diesel Daihatsu. But (learning from experience) we bought the hardtop version with a solid roof and sliding windows that might keep out much of the dust.

We headed home in convoy, me proudly driving our brand-new 4WD wagon. It had been years since I had driven a car much, let alone anything more exotic. Our procession soon became less than triumphant. On a particularly narrow and steep dirt incline with deep corrugations, I braked too hard. Losing momentum, the car slid slowly sideways into the ditch. Fortunately, Gus had a winch and we were soon back on the road. 'Don't worry,' he reassured me. 'You'll soon learn how to bounce through the corrugations at speed.'

Elisa in our new four-wheel drive car

Next morning our hausboi arrived. Aipat didn't speak English, but his PNG pidgin (plus our phrase book) made simple communication possible. We agreed on the standard fortnightly hausboi wage, even though he was new to the job. Aipat was willing enough, and he soon scrubbed the house from top to bottom to repel mould and insects.

It didn't take long to run up curtains and cushion covers on June's sewing machine. John showed surprising aptitude for that task. The twin-tub washer soon saw plenty of action too. By Friday, we were able to host Gus and June to a thank-you dinner and sit around with drinks in our none-too-comfortable 'easy chairs'.

Gus introduced us to our colleagues as they arrived for the start of the new college year, and to other local characters like Father Luke (the lanky Australian priest for Keravat's Catholic church and parish). Our fellow teachers were keen to meet new colleagues. Many were Aussies who worked on contracts like our own or had historical connections to PNG. Most had been here for a year already, some longer.

Our principal and new boss James Beckham was a lean and handsome Aussie in his thirties who had worked in PNG for several years. He seemed capable and energetic. Like us and several other couples, he was half of a husband-and-wife team who both worked at the college. Deputy principal Isobel Barnes, of similar age, was a single lady from Australia.

There were also some real outliers: Mark Hoban was an African missionary who had left the priesthood to marry and raise a family, while Gabriel was a self-proclaimed 'African revolutionary' who had escaped from Rhodesia's racist regime to England. And Bohdan Doubek was a Czech musician who had defected from that Communist regime during a concert tour to the West. He had been sponsored to New Zealand as a refugee and soon became a brilliant linguist. While working two jobs, Bohdan had graduated with a master's degree and landed a teaching post in PNG. Like us and many others at Keravat, he was a world away from his roots.

Last to arrive for the new year was Graeme Drysdale, head of Expressive Arts department. A single Australian, he was rumoured to be homosexual. But to everyone's surprise, Graeme returned from leave claiming to be 'just married'. And he wasn't joking — a statuesque, beautiful and exuberant African woman arrived a few days later to join him. Graeme and Christine made handsome newlyweds.

We felt quite at home in our small but diverse society, and keen to start work.

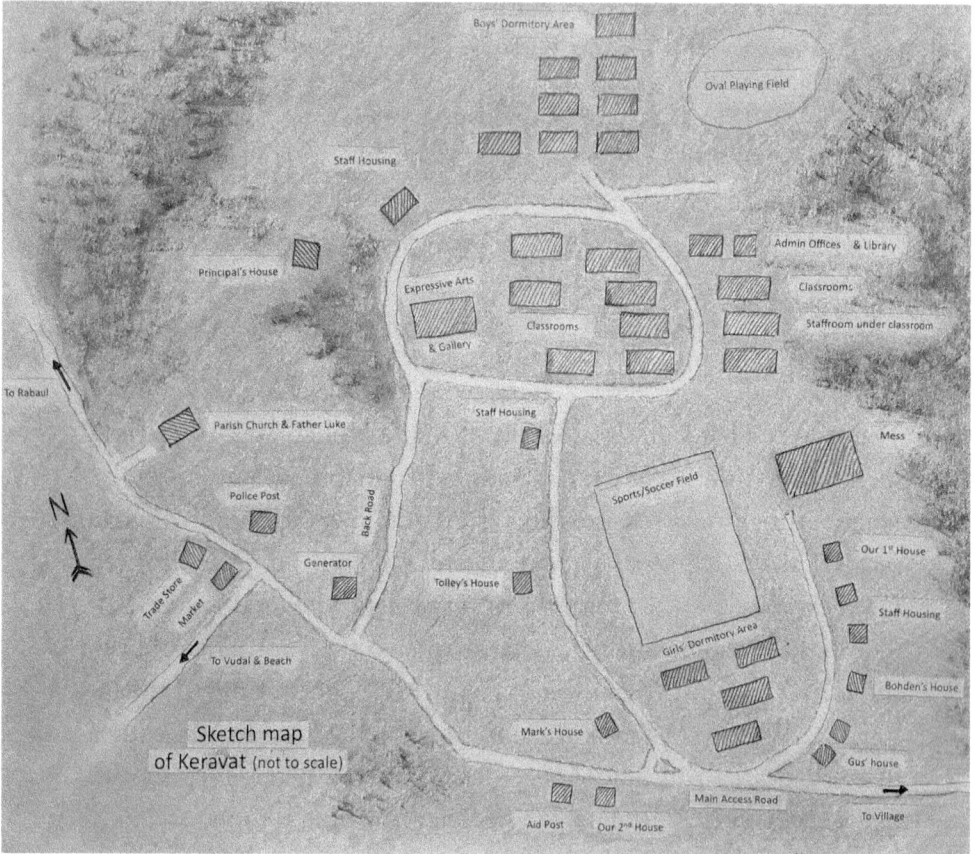

Boys' Dormitory Area

Oval Playing Field

Staff Housing

Principal's House

Expressive Arts
& Gallery

Classrooms

Admin Offices & Library

Classrooms

Staffroom under classroom

To Rabaul

Parish Church & Father Luke

Staff Housing

Mess

N

Police Post

Back Road

Sports/Soccer Field

Our 1st House

Generator

Staff Housing

Trade Store

Tolley's House

Bohden's House

Market

Girls' Dormitory Area

To Vudal & Beach

Gus' house

Sketch map
of Keravat (not to scale)

Mark's House

Main Access Road

To Village

Aid Post   Our 2nd House

Sketch map of Keravat town and campus (not to scale)

3. Enjoying Work (John)

KERAVAT WAS like nowhere we had worked before. Situated almost on the equator, day length varied hardly at all. Seasonal change was equally absent. The standard joke was that we had two seasons: the wet season and the wetter season. Lush tropical vegetation surrounded us and the heat and humidity often felt oppressive.

Our 400 students were boarders, flown in and out annually by government for a two-year stay. Most lacked the funds to visit home during the year and stayed on at college between the four terms. Each student slept in a large male or female dormitory, used communal showers and washrooms, made do with rationed toiletries and a small cash stipend, and dined in a spacious but bare mess hall. Meals were basic but healthy: tinned meat and fish, rice and sweet potatoes, local greens and seasonal fruit.

Our work logistics were basic too. A cramped admin block housed small offices for the principal and deputy, two telephones, a photocopier and a 'mailroom' where staff received notices and postal mail in their individual pigeonholes. Most teachers had their own personal classrooms equipped with wooden double desks and a small attached office and storeroom. A staffroom with wire-mesh walls sat under the stilts of one classroom block, furnished only with the ubiquitous 'easy chairs', a water boiler and a tiny refrigerator.

Students worked hard. Every weekday, classes started promptly after a dawn breakfast, while morning cool still prevailed. Classes continued with one break until early afternoon, when it grew too hot to concentrate easily (despite ceiling fans). Lunch in the mess hall was likely to be followed by 'work parade': cleaning, gardening and other campus maintenance duties. Students then enjoyed a few hours of personal time and ate dinner in the mess before two hours of compulsory study back in classrooms. Much of that 'personal time' was consumed by chores such as washing clothes and bedding in the ablution blocks. Their day ended with a final hour of personal time before it was back into the dorms and lights out.

Weekends and some weekday afternoons allowed time for sport, music and individual interests. But the college still expected students to keep up personal study schedules and behave decorously. Drinking alcohol was a serious offence. Male and female dormitories were located at opposite ends of the campus and sexual relations with other students qualified for prompt expulsion. All official conversations were in English (though pidgin was often used informally amongst students or humorously amongst staff).

Students met strenuous expectations. Only a few came from comfortable urban homes. Most had done well at a village primary school to qualify for secondary school and then worked hard as boarders there to qualify for college. Drawn from the top two percent of their age group, they felt thankful to be at Keravat with a chance to qualify for a good job or apply for university study.

For tuition and administration, students were organised into mixed-sex classes of about 30. Each class and dormitory elected captains to organise the activities that kept the college running. Individually, captains upheld disciplines like keeping dorms tidy and ensuring no exits between lights out and the morning bell. Collectively, they constituted a Student Council that could consider student concerns and voice suggestions about college administration. Male and female college captains, elected by majority vote of all students, led that council and the overall student body.

We felt humbled to watch these responsible teenagers in action, especially by comparison with their typical peers in 'advanced' countries. Of course, our students were still young people and not flawless. One part of the food plantation — the 'banana patch' — was a well-known romantic destination, and a few dubious personalities broke other rules at times. But more typically students spent their limited free time constructively. All attended church services and many engaged in charitable activities. Energetic sports were often self-organised. The college truck drove into town for supply trips several times a week, and students could book a seat on the back. Our students showed a marvellous ability to simply be happy in the moment. Their spontaneous and tuneful singing, often for no apparent reason, was another novel experience for us.

Keravat's 24 professional staff worked hard too. Teaching timetables were full-on, more like school than college. The curriculum aimed to build a solid foundation of basic knowledge for students who would either take up professional jobs or go on to university. It offered no choices or specialisms. Instead, four core subjects had equal time allocations: English, Maths, Science (rotating physics, chemistry and biology) and Social Studies (rotating history, geography and civics). Lesser time was allocated to 'Expressive Arts'. Teachers tested students internally to measure progress, but national examinations held simultaneously across all four colleges at year-end delivered most of their final grades.

Students enjoying an excursion with us

Staff without higher administrative duties had pastoral responsibilities. Elisa and I each took on a 'guidance class' of new students, who would work and play together under our oversight throughout their two years at Keravat. Our class captains did most of the related work and showed great maturity in all they did. But young men and women living away from home sometimes wanted to discuss individual problems with someone older, and we helped whenever we could. At weekends we often took small groups out in our car to the nearby swimming beach or into town.

The college system consciously tried to build a national identity that could transcend traditional tribal or regional affiliations. Students were deliberately drawn from all areas of the country. With intermarriage between tribes and regions still rare, differing physical characteristics usually made it easy to tell where a student came from. Islanders looked more Polynesian while Highlander students had stockier builds; Papuans had lighter skin colours while Bougainville students had jet-black skin. Males substantially outnumbered females, reflecting typical social norms. Guidance classes were structured so that each new student found himself or herself with a regional compatriot of the same sex, while most of his or her classmates were diverse strangers from an ethnic cross-section.

Teaching maths — my degree qualification — was a breeze. The subject matter was familiar, useful teaching materials had been accumulated, and students were keen to learn. Their enthusiasm was contagious and even dry topics often became great fun.

I hadn't expected more than my standard rank as a college teacher, classified and paid as 'Level 2'. After all, Gus was far more experienced than me and only had that rank himself. So I was surprised to find Grant Riddell, the 'Level 4' Subject Department Head for maths, was a young Australian barely older than me and less qualified. Regardless, I respected his two years of previous experience at Keravat and we got on fine. Ex-priest Mark and two other maths teachers were not specialists, but they could handle the curriculum well enough. As in most teaching situations, we blended professional collaboration with healthy inter-class rivalry.

Elisa, as an English specialist, faced greater challenges. Teaching materials were scanty, the previous year's exam results had been poor, and the English department needed improvement. Bill Tolley, her Subject Department Head, was an unknown quantity. Fresh from a renowned private school in Britain, Bill was new to PNG. Elisa's other colleagues were a mixed bunch: June was a qualified English specialist, former musician Bohdan spoke and wrote English as a second language, and Luther Tomba was the college system's first and only national teacher of English.

Bill Tolley turned out to be a great talker — inside and outside class — but not much of a doer. He showed little skill or will to run a department, develop teaching materials or mentor staff. His favourite personal teaching technique seemed to be storytelling, not structured learning. Bohdan and Luther, not native English speakers, struggled at times. Eager to help, Elisa gave Bill several ideas for practical improvements. He effusively thanked her, then ignored them.

Out of necessity, Elisa and June routinely carried more than their share of the English department workload. They developed and shared new teaching aids and better ways to teach the syllabus effectively. Elisa loved the students and her work, and she even started a regular extra class in her own time to help students who were struggling. But students inevitably became alert to the discrepancies between their English teachers, and those not in a class taught by Elisa or June probably felt unlucky.

The Science department had only one specialist for each discipline: Ray Curtis led physics, Ed Manson was overall head of science and covered chemistry, and Gus headed biology. Those specialists necessarily did all the second-year work while many first-year classes made do with less qualified staff. As a new boy, I was expected to be a utility player and taught several physics classes.

Fortunately, the technical physics content was familiar and within my capability. Unfortunately, experimental work wasn't. I knew what to do in theory but struggled with practicalities. Frequent power blackouts and chronic low-voltage 'brownouts' didn't help.

One morning I rushed into the lab to prepare an electrical experiment and connected a voltmeter to check the power voltage. Everything seemed fine, so I asked my class to file in. Absentmindedly, I disconnected the voltmeter by pulling plugs out of the meter instead of the wall socket. The plugs dropped onto a metal part of the benchtop, created an arc of sparks and bounced into the air! Then the plugs dropped back onto the metal, and the dramatic display repeated. Several cycles later, one plug finally dropped onto woodwork and I could safely disconnect the electricity. My students watched the show with amazement. I doubt they believed my story about the need to demonstrate electrical safety. Luckily, the only damage was scorch marks on the metalwork.

Next time I wasn't so lucky. The experimental process seemed simple enough: pour paraffin from a 5-litre bottle into a beaker, and then into a small tin where it could be lighted to heat a miniature boiler that would in turn impressively power a model steam engine. Physics specialist Ray — who had heard about the voltmeter — supervised a private test run. He started me off with the tin of paraffin and made sure I knew the next steps and could talk credibly about how everything worked. Sadly, Ray assumed too much. Teaching by myself next day, I foolishly poured paraffin straight out of the heavy bottle into the tin, with no intermediary beaker. Paraffin spilled unobtrusively over the workbench. When I lit the tin, a flash fire engulfed the bench, steam engine and boiler. Again, my students watched with amazement. The fire wasn't dangerous and soon expired, but it melted beyond repair the plastic controls for the steam engine. Ray was not amused. But he did accept my penitential offer to analyse test results for a curriculum symposium later in the year — something I *could* capably do.

Teaching and guidance classes weren't the only staff duties. We all had extra responsibilities to lead work parade projects, operate the rudimentary sick bay, or be duty staff during night hours and term breaks. Elisa and I soon made 'Lights out dorm 5!' an in-joke for our own bedtime.

I decided to reclaim for agriculture an overgrown part of the college plantation and worked with male students to chop down trees and hitch them to a tractor for extraction. Elisa led a female team to brighten up dormitories and banish the mould that quickly encroached upon every neglected surface. We also helped with student clubs: I tutored chess and Elisa coached string bands.

Gus worked especially hard. Most evenings found him in his laboratory preparing equipment and experiments. Outside teaching, Gus was in constant demand amongst students and staff for his terrific mechanical skills with trucks, generators and anything else with moving parts. In our humid tropical environment where typewriters quickly rusted and even a photocopier required special air conditioning, there was always plenty for him to do. And as a natural leader, Gus was unanimously elected to represent staff on the college's Governing Council.

We didn't miss TV or other past distractions. Evenings became a pleasant time when the air cooled and we could catch up on marking, read, write letters or just chat over a drink. Once a week we drove into town for our weekly shopping, followed by dinner in Chinatown. Occasional dances at the local social club and student-generated entertainments on campus varied the mix. We were busy and we were happy.

· · ·

At a staff meeting halfway through term one, principal James announced that the first of several official visits from the inspector for the college system — our recent acquaintance Martin Simpson — would occur early in term two. Education Department regulations required that all teachers who had not yet been officially evaluated be inspected and given a 'rating'. That rule might not be fully enforced this year, because the inspector would focus on staff up for contract renewal. But regardless, any member of staff could volunteer for inspection and receive a rating. James presented that idea as an opportunity that was important for contract renewal and could deliver other benefits including recommendation for promotion. He noted several staff had already taken up that option and invited further volunteers to come forward.

No one seemed interested. Instead, a sullen attitude was evident. James was visibly disappointed. After he left the staffroom, we heard some hostile muttering about inspections.

That bemused Elisa and me. An inspection visit didn't worry us. Teacher inspection and rating was a necessary feature of most educational systems. Everything seemed positive here and capable professional staff surely had nothing to worry about. In fact, Elisa and I had discussed the rating system with Gus and following his lead we had already volunteered for inspection.

That evening I asked Gus what the negativity was all about. 'It's more personal than professional,' he explained. 'Martin's a recent appointment as inspector, who went around acting superior and egotistical during his visits last year. And some of the more conservative staff disapprove of his homosexuality. James sucks up to him — not surprising, since it was Martin who recommended him into the principal's job. They act like a clique, holding parties with outsiders and the Expressive Arts head Graeme Drysdale, without inviting other college staff. And a couple of staff who spoke up about those things last year — good people who were specially funded by an Australian aid agency — didn't get their contracts renewed.'

But that wasn't the worst of it, Gus explained. Martin also tended to hang around the students more than was appropriate, which inevitably generated suspicions about potential unprofessional behaviour. Father Luke as local parish priest and school chaplain had received complaints about 'expatriate homosexuals' from town pursuing boys from the parish. And Drysdale, the staff member James had chosen as adviser to the Student Council, was rumoured to be personally involving himself with our own male students — the previous year he had even thrown a lavish birthday party for one of them.

I was taken aback. 'That's awful Gus! You wrote to us that everything was great here. Why didn't you mention any of that?'

Gus wasn't apologetic. 'It didn't seem important in the greater scheme of things, and we didn't want to put you off coming to Keravat. Anyway, Simpson will only be here a few days. He did inspection reports on several staff last year and they were all rated favourably. Let's give him the benefit of the doubt, get our inspections out of the way and focus on the positives.'

4. Local Learning (Elisa)

UNDER OUR CONTRACT, the Education Department paid to ship our household goods to Keravat. Their allowance was reasonable too, since our accommodation was basically furnished. So we had sold our house in New Zealand, put our heavy furniture into storage, and packed everything else we owned into shipping crates. A holiday on the way to PNG would give our cargo several weeks' lead time.

As planned, the first term was only a few weeks old when our ship came in — literally. A message from the college office told us our cargo had arrived and was stored at the port under customs bond. We eagerly visited the shipping agent to arrange customs clearance. John filled in the old-fashioned import declaration form by hand, the agent checked the declaration, a customs official approved it, and we arranged delivery by truck the very next day.

It felt great to have a wide selection of linen, clothing and kitchenware again. And we were delighted to recover our books, music tapes and other personal effects. Some items, like hiking gear and a tent, we would probably never use here. And some items we had forgotten about, like John's .22 rifle from the rabbit-shooting expeditions we had enjoyed with Gus back in New Zealand. Never mind — we soon got everything sorted and made ourselves comfortable.

But that .22 rifle became a problem. Next trip to town, we visited the police station to check if John needed a firearms licence. Indeed, he did. But no worries — all the police needed to issue one was John's overseas firearms licence and approved import declaration. John, well-organised as usual, had those handy. The police officer cheerfully scanned the documentation but then frowned. 'There is no firearm on this import declaration. I cannot issue you with a licence.' John frowned too. 'What's the problem? I answered all the questions on the declaration. None of them asked about a firearm.'

The policeman checked again. 'Oh, I see why. This is an old form. The law changed two years ago to require that all firearms be declared on arrival. Your firearm has not been properly imported, so I cannot issue a licence without further information.' What could that be? 'You need a proper reason to own a firearm. And you need to be a landowner or have permission from the person who owns the land where you live. Bring that information to me and I can issue you with a licence.' The policeman wanted to help, but he was firm about the rules.

We left frustrated. We shared our problem with Gus, who suggested that the college principal was probably the 'landowner'. Sure enough, James was happy to give us a letter stating that, as manager of the government property where we lived, he was happy for John to hold a .22 rifle at our house. We went back to the police station the next week and met the same policeman. He photocopied the letter and gave John a licence application to fill out. 'Just put a proper reason where it says "reason for owning firearm",' he advised.

But what might a 'proper' reason be? Hunting was probably out of the question, since all land was owned by someone, and we didn't know any local people. And we could hardly claim that a college teacher needed a firearm for work. 'How about target shooting?' John suggested. 'I used to coach students in that, and I can follow that hobby here with the local gun club.'

'Yes, that would be fine,' the policeman agreed. 'Just bring me a membership card signed by the club president.'

We left with that goal. But enquiries around Rabaul revealed that the local gun club had disbanded years ago. We went back to the policeman, who was sympathetic but adamant. 'You *must* give me a proper reason before I can issue you with a licence.'

'What if I can't?' John asked. It was the policeman's turn to get frustrated.

'Maybe if you will never use it then you should not worry about getting a licence. Officially this firearm did not even enter our country. I should not even know about it!' He wasn't trying to trap us — he just wanted the problem to go away. We thanked him and left.

We were unhappy though. I felt that an unlicensed firearm might somehow become a source of trouble. We again shared our problem with Gus. A few days later, he came to the rescue. 'Take this to the police,' he said, throwing us a faded government pamphlet.

John read the title aloud: 'Collecting Botanical Specimens'. He looked puzzled.

Gus grinned. 'Look at page 37.'

Sure enough, page 37 offered the solution we needed. It explained how the best way to collect botanical specimens from canopy trees was to use a light rifle to shoot down branches. Next time we went into town, John visited the police station again with a completed licence application. His reason for owning a firearm? Obvious — 'collecting plant specimens'. Happy to resolve the impasse, our policeman (almost a friend by now) issued a licence with that unique

notation. A tribute to Gus's approach to getting things done here —
be patient and friendly and develop a practical solution. Problem
solved.

PAPUA NEW GUINEA   P 30

Firearms Registration Act 1963-1970   ORIGINAL/~~RENEWAL~~

APPLICATION FORM

REGISTRATION CERTIFICATE HIGH-POWERED FIREARM/~~LOW-POWERED FIREARM~~ No.............
(Delete type not applicable)

I,......**John Marion Mendzela**..............................Age..**27**.........Occupation...**Teacher**......

Residential Address..**Keravat National High School (House 203)**..Phone No...**926219**....
Business Address (NOT P.O. Box No.)....**Keravat National High School**........Phone No...**926219**....
Postal Address......**Keravat National High School, Private Mail Bag, Keravat, ENBP.**
make application for a Certificate of Registration/~~Licence~~ for the under-mentioned weapon.

Make....**Brno**..............Model...**452**.....Calibre/~~Gauge~~...**.22**....

No. of Shots..**Bolt action (5-shot magazine)**..Manufacturer's Serial Number...**240,659**....
I require the firearm for the following purposes:—

1) **Smallbore rifle target shooting**

2) **Collecting plant specimens (see Botany Bulletin No. 2, Department of Forests)**

page 20

John's firearms license was issued for "collecting plant specimens"

Having all our personal possessions again gave Aipat a lot more to do.
In the hot humid climate, *everything* needed regular and vigorous
cleaning to combat mould. Books were the worst, and we had a lot.
Aipat couldn't read, so at first we found many books replaced upside
down after cleaning. But to our surprise, Aipat soon learned to use
the shape of the titles on the spine to work out which way was up. A
few books still finished upside down, but only because the title direction on their spines was reversed.

Laundry gave Aipat bigger problems. We lost several garments to
scorching by the electric iron. Aipat always apologised, explaining
that he was a 'nupela man' (new to the job that is). The washing
machine was even tougher. John demonstrated, with the aid of his

clumsy pidgin, how to use the machine: put the clothes in, turn the water on, start the agitation, add the powder, etc. Aipat learned fast, and our clothes came out clean enough. But everything felt stiff, as if starched. Meanwhile washing powder disappeared at a prodigious rate, far beyond the minor pilfering that many houseboys indulged in. I came home unexpectedly at lunchtime one day and solved the mystery. Aipat wasn't plugging the tub! Instead, he just ran water continually, regularly pouring in more powder to generate fresh suds. There was never any rinse at all. After further explanation amidst much hilarity, washing powder consumption moderated and our clothes felt normal again.

Pidgin still gave me problems at times. It was a while before I found out why Aipat always grinned when I told him to be sure to 'raus olgeta kakaruk' (get rid of all the cockroaches). 'Kakaruk' was actually the word for chicken; a cockroach was a 'kokoros'. And after one morning's instruction to 'kilinim antap' (wipe down the mouldy ceiling I pointed at), I returned home to find him outside working on the roof instead.

Elisa with hausboi Aipat (dressed for a singsing with his friends)

Spectacular mountain and beach scenery encouraged John to explore local tracks in our new 4WD. I wasn't keen, but I usually went along for the ride. On one occasion a wide and rocky watercourse brought us to a sudden halt. John's map — once an accurate military record, but now 40 years old — told us the track crossed the stream and continued. Sure enough, a dirt slope rose from the opposite bank about 30 metres downstream. And the water looked quite shallow, on our side at least. No problem to ford, John decided. Overruling my protests, he set off in lowest gear. We rumbled steadily across. 'See,' John purred, 'no worries.' But as we neared the other side, the car dropped sharply. We both hit the roof, hard! Water started pouring in under the doors. John managed to keep the engine roaring, and the car somehow scrambled out. Unsurprisingly, we then found the 'continuing road' long over-grown. 'What did I tell you?' I said pointedly. It took hours of low-gear meandering to pick our way through regenerating forest to a track that could take us home.

I decided that was the last straw. We would at least install seatbelts! Our car dealer had never seen or ordered anything like that before, but eventually two seatbelts arrived. Fitting them puzzled his mechanics at first, but finally we could strap up at the start of every drive. Just in time too. A few days later we followed a gravel road at speed through a coconut plantation. With a sudden loud bang, the entire windscreen disappeared amid a shower of glass! John ran the car into a ditch, but our seatbelts kept us in place and clear of the worst glass. We had nearly suffered 'death by coconut' — a not uncommon fate locally, when a coconut fell from a great height onto someone. Impressed by our survival story, the dealer ordered a supply of seatbelts that soon sold out!

At the end of term one, the college tested second-year students in all their subjects. Students directly competed for top marks, while staff naturally hoped their own classes would score well. Test compilation was shared out so that every staff member prepared some questions and no particular class had an advantage. To ensure consistency, heads of department marked all the test papers for their subjects.

Mostly, no surprises emerged. But the published English department results dismayed me. The classes June and I taught did worse than the class taught by our department head Bill, and no better than the other classes. The individual student scores on the handwritten list for my classes mostly met my expectations — it was only my low averages that disappointed me. Then I noticed something strange. The handwritten numbers for the class averages looked as though they had been altered. I asked John as an independent maths colleague to check them on his calculator. Sure enough, the originally correct averages had been overwritten, and clumsily at that. The average for Bill's class had been raised from 58 percent to 62 percent. John carefully recalculated the results for June's classes and my own. Our results had been lowered by several percentage points.

I tackled Bill privately about this. Had he adjusted the scores in any way?

'Of course not!' he protested.

I showed him the correct averages, and the alterations that had been made. 'Oh, that's what you're worried about,' he soothed. 'Maths isn't my strong suit. I made some mistakes calculating the averages and then corrected them.' I persevered — it wasn't the original figures that were wrong, but the 'corrected' class averages that had been released to students. Bill grew flustered. 'Well, class averages aren't important. The individual student results are correct and that's what matters.' At our department staff meeting the next day, I outlined how the class averages had been misleading. Bill angrily ruled discussion out of order, demanding that we work as a team and not focus on differences between classes. Furthermore, he advised us, subject department heads were accountable directly to headquarters for curriculum and testing, not to their staff or even to the college principal. So he wouldn't change anything.

That evening, I talked the situation through with John. Bill clearly felt threatened. As the department's professional leader, his behaviour was indefensible. What should I do? Or should I do nothing?

We decided that Bill's alteration of the class averages was not a major issue, but also not something that should be ignored. Next steps posed difficulty though. Our principal James seemed quite friendly with Bill, and his deputy Isobel seemed distant from specific departmental matters. They might regard me as a pedantic troublemaker, not a concerned professional. In any case, Bill had claimed that a direct channel to headquarters should operate on such matters.

We decided on a roundabout approach. When the inspector visited, John would show him the altered averages as something he had accidentally noticed through his guidance class. He would leave me out of it altogether and put the matter confidentially in the inspector's hands.

The one-week break between terms flashed by. Our boarding duties gave us no holiday time as such, but the break did create a refreshing new daily routine, plus more social time with our guidance classes. A day at the beach was a highlight. Everyone went into the water — even the Highlanders who at first feared the open ocean they had never experienced. John and I were the only bathers with swimsuits. The students frolicked in the waves in their everyday clothes, laughing prodigiously. After drying out, they gathered wood and built an improvised BBQ. Class captains took charge to carefully grill sausages over the fiery contraption, and everyone agreed they had rarely tasted anything so delicious.

All too soon, teaching duties resumed as term two began.

5. An Inspector Calls (John)

EARLY IN TERM TWO, Martin Simpson arrived to conduct his week-long inspection programme. I was pleased to see him and get my inspection report under way. I also planned to confidentially show him the altered class averages for English tests. And because we had committed ourselves to returning his hospitality in Moresby, I would invite him to lunch at our house at the end of the week.

Martin's visit to evaluate my teaching passed quietly. I explained the inspector's role to the class. Martin sat at the back, watched the lesson and made notes.

Martin shared his notes with me afterwards. They were mostly favourable and made minor but useful suggestions that I could apply in future. Martin advised that he would of course get a formal report from my head of department as part of the inspection process, but he was already impressed with the quality of my work and how quickly I had adapted to teaching PNG students. Was there anything else I would like to discuss at this stage?

I said there was, though not something that directly concerned my teaching. I gave him copies of the lists with the altered English test averages, explaining that I had checked the data as a guidance teacher and maths specialist. I related how Elisa had failed to obtain any professional explanation of the changes that her head of department Bill Tolley had made. Instead, she'd been told that his accountability on academic matters was to headquarters, represented by the inspector in the first instance. But Elisa didn't want to make a direct complaint that might damage the department's unity and morale.

'So,' I concluded, 'I decided I should tell you about the problem informally instead.'

Martin looked at me thoughtfully. 'You were right to confidentially bring this matter to my attention.' He paused. 'You've analysed the numbers. What's your explanation?'

I was ready for the question. 'Based on what I know about the English staff, I think Bill altered the class averages to protect his own reputation, not to build staff teamwork. Specifically, he pulled his own class average up, pulled Elisa's and June's down, and left the others (still the lowest) alone. It's really just about the implied comparison between the teaching capability of Bill as head of department and the capabilities of Elisa and June. Of course, student results can vary for many reasons, and the individual results haven't been distorted. But surreptitiously altering the class averages was professionally wrong.'

Martin thanked me for the information. 'I agree. It's not a major concern, but it is an error of judgement that shouldn't be ignored. Bill's still new to his role, so I'll follow up with him privately, and not with Elisa or with the English department as a whole. I'm sure you understand why.'

'Fully,' I said. 'But I hope there won't be too much negative impact on Bill.'

Martin looked stern. 'Well, as he's a subject department head new to PNG, he's on my list of staff to be inspected. And I will need to look hard at how the English department progresses and especially at their test results. But don't feel concerned; it won't be a major issue.'

The campus was a small place with most classrooms and offices openly visible. Elisa and I could observe for ourselves that Martin spent considerable time in private discussion with Bill. But Martin also visited department heads who were not being inspected and spent a lot of time with James (mostly at the principal's house, where Martin lived while on campus). We didn't know what had been said about the altered class averages. But we felt satisfied that we had taken discreet professional action and could now forget the whole affair.

I didn't talk with Martin during the rest of that week. Elisa had her classroom visit from him, followed by a positive individual discussion similar to mine. Bohdan (who wanted his contract renewed at year-end and had volunteered for inspection) and Gus had their own visits and discussions too. Everything seemed to have been professional and constructive.

Over a drink one night, I asked Gus how his classroom visit had gone. 'Fine — but I'm unhappy with our inspector for other reasons.'

He explained why. Working late in his laboratory, Gus had several times noticed Martin chatting with individual students near the dormitories, *after* lights out. Our lights-out regime was strictly enforced and students needed a good reason to leave their dormitories. Gus mentioned his observations to Kevin Maitland, the week's duty teacher. It turned out Kevin had stopped two students outside the night before, only to be told that 'the inspector' wanted a private talk with them to ask about their teachers. Kevin had conveyed concern about that dubious behaviour to James and Isobel, who said they would 'look into it'.

Gus paused for a moment. 'And that's not all. Simpson, as inspector, met with the student council to discuss general matters affecting the overall student body. All right and proper. But he didn't stop there. Kevin Maitland's class captains complained to him — unofficially — that Simpson started asking the council members about individual teachers. They didn't think that was right. And it's not. Kevin's contract comes up for renewal at year-end, so he doesn't want to personally take things further. And the students are too wary about risking their own futures to write up the matter. But Kevin thought that as staff representative on the Governing Council I should know. In that capacity I passed on the information to James, along with my personal observations of Simpson breaching our lights-out rule.'

On the last day of his visit, Martin convened a staff meeting to informally outline inspection outcomes. His visits to individual teachers had gone very well. He had also talked with the student council about college studies and living conditions, and everything appeared fine. But he was disappointed that 'some teachers' (he didn't mention names) were trying to prevent the confidential discussions with individual students that were essential to his role as inspector. James chipped in to say that as principal he fully supported the inspector in doing that part of his job.

A silence descended. Then Gus spoke up. 'Inspector, I don't think anyone here is concerned about you having discussions with students. There's plenty of time for that — but during the day, not after lights-out. And I'm sure you'll agree that discussions with the student council shouldn't include asking about the work of individual teachers — certainly not without a good reason and under proper professional protocols.'

Martin turned red in the face and raised his voice. 'And I'm sure *you'll* agree that neither you nor anyone else in this room should be telling *me* how to do my job!'

James quickly intervened. 'Let's leave that topic — maybe Gus and Martin can chat informally this afternoon. Are there any other questions?' There were not. The meeting closed awkwardly.

Coming immediately after that staffroom exchange, our lunch with Martin was not a success. He was still angry, and Elisa and I were feeling less than friendly. On our way home, we had overheard one of our colleagues refer to us as 'arse lickers'!

In hindsight, lunch with the inspector had been a thoroughly bad idea. But somehow we got through it, chatting about the weather like distant cousins at a family wedding. Our parting with inspector Martin Simpson was cordial but reserved.

That afternoon, I saw Gus walk across the campus to the principal's office. Over a beer at his house in the evening, he told us why. 'James asked me to go and see Simpson there.' He paused for a moment. 'James was there too of course. At first, they were very friendly and told me they were greatly impressed with my work. I could expect to receive an outstanding inspection report, and I was "more than ready for promotion".' Then Simpson looked straight at me and said, "As you know, Ed Manson is on his last year of contract as head of science here, and he's decided not to renew. Would you be interested in becoming Head of Science?"

'I told him I would certainly consider that. Then came the punchline from James. "Naturally, a lot of extra responsibility would come with that job. And it's important that senior staff support one another, here and at headquarters. For example, they shouldn't publicly raise questions that challenge the judgement of superiors and undermine the system, like you did today in the staffroom. That's not in the best interests of your career here."'

Gus paused.

'What happened then?' Elisa asked.

'We went around the houses for a while. I said that at a residential college everyone had to take extra care not to do anything that might look unprofessional or improper. They said of course that was so, but there wasn't anything wrong with the inspector taking 'informal soundings' on various matters and bending college rules a little for that purpose. They waffled on about trusting one another's integrity. I said that appearances mattered too. Simpson just glowered at me after I wouldn't back down, so James did most of the talking. In the end I made an excuse and left. They weren't happy!'

Gus paused again. 'The whole discussion was a rerun of one last year, when I questioned how science funding was spent and made what I thought were constructive suggestions. Instead of listening, they got defensive and angry that time too. So I dropped my suggestions. Simpson's an egotist who doesn't like being challenged on anything, and James just goes along with him.'

June interrupted. 'Instead of hanging around the dorms, why doesn't Simpson do something about the English department? We've got real problems with a lack of good teaching materials and a new head of department who does nothing to support his less experienced staff. And I've overheard students grumble to each other about Bill's own teaching — he just tells them stories from his personal experiences, with no relevant focus. *And* he doesn't mark their workbooks.'

I looked at Elisa. She nodded for me to go ahead. I recounted how I had disclosed the altered class averages to Simpson, and how he had responded. 'Maybe we should give the inspector the benefit of the doubt on that topic. We know he had several discussions with Bill. Let's see if the English department improves.'

We decided to be grateful inspection week was over, with positive results for our personal reports. The inspector had departed. It would be back to business-as-usual next week.

But dissatisfaction with Simpson's inspection visit didn't die down. First, several students complained to their guidance teachers that the inspector had embarrassed them with questions about individual teachers. And that had happened in the evening when they should have been in study hall or dorms.

Then several staff who weren't even being inspected found out that the inspector had been asking their department heads about them. A meeting of department heads confirmed that had occurred and that Simpson had also asked leading questions about the individual teachers who were being inspected — 'not for their formal reports you understand'.

Grumbling about Simpson's sly and unprofessional approach came up at staff meetings several times. James made strong efforts to play down the issues. 'Alright, let's move on. The inspector's got a tricky job to do, and it's easy to misunderstand and criticise. I'll take up your concerns informally with him before his next visit.'

6. Colourful Days (Elisa)

THE ENGLISH DEPARTMENT didn't improve. Bill no longer held department meetings ('a waste of time,' he proclaimed). Bohdan and Luther sometimes floundered, despite encouragement and informal help from June and me. Bill's students grew subdued and fatalistic about their poorly structured lessons and unmarked workbooks. I tried to stay cheerful and professional despite the chronic problems that Bill refused to tackle.

Partly because of shared frustration with the English department, John and I became especially friendly with Bohdan. Now approaching 30 and no longer a musician, Bohdan was an energetic 'party animal' with a talent for identifying accents. More than once, he wowed onlookers by successfully betting a visitor that he could guess his origins and the main places he had lived just by listening to him for a few minutes. Bohdan was keen on qualifications too. He soon persuaded me to take up some further university study by correspondence and signed up all three of us for a correspondence diploma in English as a Second Language.

Social activities refreshed the daily routine. After work parade we often drove over a bumpy coral-aggregate road to a nearby bay for a refreshing swim in the sea and a walk on the lovely beach that fronted local coconut plantations. John was his usual systematic self, swimming a regular course to 'keep fit' despite his nagging suspicion that crocodiles might still lurk in the vicinity. My efforts were more haphazard. Often, we crammed six students into the back of the vehicle. The fun of a trip beyond campus would trigger a metamorphosis. The usually quiet and serious students would unlock their inner selves as they sang songs and hymns, improvised beach volleyball competitions, or ran races into the water whooping for joy.

We found sporting outlets for our energy too. Gus fixed the broken floodlights for the college tennis court so we could play there in the cool of the evening. Teaching students to play tennis was great fun, and some were soon a match for us. John discovered a squash court at the agricultural college, a 15-minute drive away, and developed an intense rivalry with our African friend Gabriel. I watched them compete fiercely and sweat copiously in a humid concrete furnace, and occasionally I played a bit myself.

John's competitive spirit shone again when the college organised a day trip for students to climb the tallest volcano overlooking Rabaul harbour. The mountain — known locally as 'Mount Mother' to distinguish it from smaller surrounding 'child' volcanos — rose many hundreds of metres from the starting point at sea level. Most of the staff struggled just to walk up, but John almost ran to the top and finished a worthy seventh in a race with the students. Arriving breathless with the main body, I found the stunning 360-degree view well worth the effort.

I enjoyed my weekly visit to Rabaul. The intense aroma of coconut would waft into the car as we passed the copra-processing plant on the outskirts of town, and then that scent would give way to the fragrance of the frangipani flowers Rabaul was famous for. From the colourful open-air market, papaya, 'kaukau' (sweet potato), rambutan and other tropical fruits and vegetables entered our diet to supplement the more familiar fare from supermarkets. On one memorable occasion I bought a bundle of live crabs tied loosely together. Having no idea how to cook them, I asked Aipat for advice. To his great wonder and delight, I gave him most of the claws in exchange and kept all of the much larger bodies for us. That night we discovered the reason for his surprise, when the crab bodies turned out to have no meat inside.

One way or another, our weekly town trip usually extended well into the evening. We often enjoyed drinks at one of the hotels or a dinner in Chinatown. John went running — and drinking — several times with a mainly expat group of Hash House Harriers. We even found a personal connection with another English couple. Amazingly enough, we had known their parents quite well in the UK and a post-card to those faraway friends generated an unexpected dinner invitation.

We enjoyed glimpses into local tradi-tions. We had admired Gus's kundus: tall carved wooden drums with an hourglass shape, topped with lizard skin and beaten loudly at celebra-tions. We soon bought two kundus for ourselves from his favourite tradi-tional carver Isaac.

On several occasions our drive into town was delayed by a procession behind a 'dukduk man' walking to a local ceremony. Dressed in leaves with a painted conical headdress, a

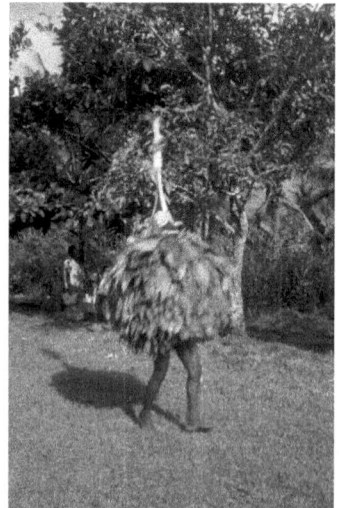

Dukduk man on a mission

dukduk man resembled a verdant traffic cone precariously balanced on two spindly legs. And we heard about, but never saw, the similar-looking but more secretive and dangerous 'tumbuan'. We were told that a tumbuan would mysteriously appear at the door of miscreants to warn them to cease their wrongdoing or face severe penalties up to and including a mysterious death.

That wasn't the only cultural novelty we encountered. Many Papua New Guineans chewed 'buai' (betel nut) as a mild intoxicant to replace or supplement cigarettes. The 'chew' — highly acidic even after lime was added — had to be spat out. And it was, staining pavements, walls and even road signs with bright red blotches to create an unsightly health risk. Thankfully buai was strictly banned at the college.

And buai certainly didn't displace the imported vice of excessive alcohol consumption. Aipat cheerfully explained to us how he got 'spak' (drunk) every fortnight, immediately after we paid him. He and his friends, all men from the same province living in a small hamlet, operated a roster. One or two would use their wages to buy enough rice and other food to supply the entire group for the next two weeks, and everybody else would use their wages to buy beer for communal drinking. 'Drink until it's gone' was the norm, and it wasn't wise to drive after dark on the fortnightly 'pay Fridays' when entire villages could be partying. Laying out an unconscious celebrant on the road might be considered a great joke. In stark contrast, other villages might collectively join a strict religious denomination and go entirely teetotal.

Staff social activities could get out of hand too. John was elated when one supermarket started selling canned Guinness. Chilled for our climate, it tasted much better than the PNG and Australian beers on offer. Bohdan, who often took our two national teachers out on the town, enthusiastically adopted this novelty. He laughed off John's warning that Guinness was a lot stronger than local beers and might have unexpected impacts. One midweek morning I noticed that neither Bohdan nor Luther had turned up to teach their English classes. Garemo, the national teacher who taught Expressive Arts, was missing too. I asked John to check what was wrong. As he later explained, 'I could hear the snoring from outside Bohdan's house, even 20 metres away. There they were, lying on the floor surrounded by empty Guinness cans, dead to the world. I had a huge struggle to get them up and back at work before too many people found out.' They all (apart from John) firmly swore off Guinness after that.

Despite English department hassles and the staff unease about inspection activities, we continued to enjoy life at Keravat. We tried hard to maintain good relations with all our colleagues, even Bill Tolley. In fact, outside work Bill was a live wire, full of vivid stories and exciting initiatives. He had already started a programme of occasional bridge evenings when we could enjoy some mental exercise in the company of expats from outside the college.

Early in term two, Bill suggested a group of staff could form a convoy and drive hundreds of kilometres around the coast to the other end of New Britain during a term break. 'Look, this relief map shows a vehicle track right around, with several plantations on the way. With a few four-wheel-drives helping each other through the worst bits, I'm sure we could make it.'

I was dubious. Asking around, I learned there would be steep mountain slopes to master and wide unbridged rivers to cross. And the 'plantations on the way' were actually all isolated farms supplied by sea not land. The line on the map showing a vehicle track was (like many government claims) an aspiration, not a reality. So much for that idea.

Bill's next proposal — charter a boat to visit the Duke of York Islands midway in the wide Bismarck Strait between New Britain and New Ireland — sounded more realistic. Bill enthusiastically promoted the excursion and soon recruited enough takers, including several complete families, to make the per-head charge modest. Arriving at the wharf early one Sunday morning, we discovered a solid and heavy workboat. Normally used to collect copra from isolated locations, its 18-metre length, crew of three and ancient engine did not inspire great confidence. But just one hour's chugging through smooth seas brought us to the islands. We threaded vivid coral reefs amid stunning green water to reach a superb white-sand beach. Several relaxing hours ensued as we swam, snorkelled and watched village children dive acrobatically into the water from coconut trees. Everyone congratulated Bill on his splendid initiative.

As one o'clock came and went, the boat's captain grew visibly anxious to leave. But our happy party was reluctant to hurry, and Bill assured us that the captain probably just wanted to get home early. We lingered over lunch before reboarding well after 2 pm.

Emerging from the shelter of the island reefs, we faced a stormy sea. Strong winds drove a hostile swell that our craft could make no headway against. Forced to run before the waves on a long looping course, our boat seemed likely to capsize at any moment. The motor belched black smoke and sounded ready to collapse. We huddled in the dark and lurching engine room while spray crashed over the roof, breathing acrid fumes of burning oil combined with the sickly-sweet smell of copra. Several passengers grew seasick and added pungent new ingredients to the olfactory mix. Two children began screaming: 'Mommy, I don't want to die!'

After three full hours of struggle by a remarkably calm and capable crew, we reached Rabaul harbour as darkness fell. And contrary to Bill's lame excuses, we soon ascertained that the seas in the strait *usually* became violent during the afternoon and 'anyone organising a trip out to the islands should know better'. Bill found few takers for his recreational proposals after that.

Gus Gale with two of his "Highlanders United"

As term two ended, the campus buzzed with preparations for Kapti (Cup-of-Tea) Day. Our students would organise themselves into ethnic groups, dress in beautiful traditional costumes and showcase fascinating songs, dances and artefacts. This colourful annual event was popular with everyone at the college, and far beyond. Local notables and expatriates attended keenly, and many other townspeople and villagers came along too.

Formal competition was not part of the format. But naturally each ethnic group was keen to promote its own unique talents and traditions and outdo the other groups. Students bustled about to collect materials, prepare intricate costumes and plan colourful body art. For the last week, work parade was suspended to make way for boisterous practice sessions.

The preparations enlisted staff too. Gus with his practical skills was in great demand. To everyone's amazement, he managed to persuade all the students from the normally factious Highlands tribes to combine into a single dance group. With unprecedented unity and contrast, their fierce show was sure to be a star attraction.

Highlanders ready for the arena

John was our usual family photographer. However, he would be away for several days at a science curriculum symposium in Lae on the mainland and would reluctantly miss Kapti Day. I took extra responsibility to help John's class as well as my own prepare for their performances and planned to capture on film as much of the show as I could.

Kapti Day dawned bright and beautiful. A large crowd arrived, and the festivities didn't disappoint them. In theory, groups entered and left the 'arena' (the college sports field) in a timed programme. In practice, some groups arrived late while others grew too enthusiastic to leave when their scheduled time was up. But the disorganisation was amiable and each

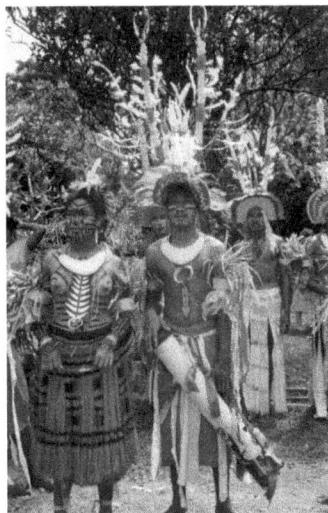

Mekeos from Papua await their turn

act was great fun. It startled me to see our normally shy, tidy and modest students parading publicly in not much more than colourful body paint, loudly singing or ululating as they danced vigorously.

Principal James's wife Sue was in charge of official portraits. Operating a makeshift photography studio, she did a roaring trade with students keen to take away a personal memory and visitors intent on colourful souvenirs. I bought several stunning photos myself. Official proceedings ended in the late afternoon. But lively activities continued around the campus into the evening as staff and students socialised with outside visitors. Everyone had enjoyed a spectacular display of colourful tradition.

Gus Gale with "Mudmen" from Asaro, "resurrected" to battle their enemies

7. Mysterious Events (John)

OUR WEEKLY TRIP to town usually began at the bank to present a cheque for cash. One Friday afternoon, as I stood inside writing out the cheque, I noticed a local man watching me carefully. I spoke to him in a friendly manner, but he didn't answer. His dress suggested he was not a town-dweller, but a 'bushman' who didn't understand English.

Bushman or not, he did understand what money was. And he wanted some. Still watching me closely, the man unfolded an empty cigarette packet and used the bank's countertop pen to make some marks on it. I went to the teller and exchanged my cheque for cash. Then the man went up to the counter and offered his cigarette packet. The teller laughed and waved him away, smiling at me. I smiled back, unobtrusively to avoid seeming rude. But as I left, I reflected that *my* actions were strange, not his. After all, if one person can make a mark on paper and exchange that for money, why can't someone else do the same?

Crashed bomber with two boys and two million mosquitoes

During World War II, Rabaul had served as a fortress for the Japanese military. Their abandoned defences and equipment exerted an inevitable fascination. We could visit a headquarters bunker beneath the town with a small battle tank above. Superb snorkelling beckoned at 'Submarine Base' where coral reefs dropped abruptly into deep water and submarines had cruised right up to the shoreline. A forbidding track up a steep hill led to a pillbox where a large naval gun had commanded approaches to Rabaul harbour. A crashed bomber in a swamp near the airport boasted the world's densest concentration of mosquitoes. Hidden firing posts that opened backwards and could only be activated *after* invaders had bypassed their occupants gave tangible insight into Japanese defence psychology.

One Saturday, Gus organised a rare opportunity for the two of us to explore extensive man-made caves that had been bomb shelters for Japanese stores, factories and even a hospital. The villagers who owned that land didn't enter the caves themselves, perhaps feeling they were taboo. They normally kept strangers out too, but made an exception for us because of kinship connections with one of our students. The landowners still set strict conditions though — only men allowed, and we must remain under the care and oversight of village guides.

By torchlight, we explored musty caves still littered with equipment, bottles, clothing and medicines from the war. We also discovered curious cave creatures. One large invertebrate had eight legs like a spider but antennae like an insect (Gus's later research identified it as a rare species that pre-dated both). And we were astonished by a physical demonstration of root pressure within plants. One of our young guides casually chopped into a large tree root buried at least 20 metres underground, and sticky white sap sprayed like a fountain out of the cut.

John's expedition to the caves, about to go underground

Inclined towards claustrophobia, I found the trip through the caves hard going. Some chambers were already blocked by landslips and I feared even a small earthquake could seal us off. After four hours underground, I felt relieved to finally emerge into daylight.

In most places, an earthquake — known locally as a 'guria' — would be a remote contingency. But at Keravat we lived in one of the most geologically active regions on the planet. Perceptible earth tremors were frequent. Stronger movements led to electric power going out and books falling out of shelves as the whole house swayed. One evening a snake dropped out of a tree amongst a group of students who were leaving the mess hall, just as the lights went out. Screams and laughter erupted. On another notable occasion, a severe quake at dusk sent us scurrying onto our front porch that overlooked the college sports field. To our amazement, the field was visibly rippling — land waves!

A volcanic eruption was no remote chance either. Rabaul town was overlooked by four large volcanic cones. The last major eruption, which had forced the town's hasty evacuation, had occurred only 50 years earlier. A small cone in the middle of the harbour still regularly emitted gas and often added a tinge of sulphur to the air. One night we attended a bridge evening hosted by PNG's top vulcanologist. His home, located just below one of the harbour's cones, was accessible only by a steep and unlit four-wheel-drive track. A tropical storm with dramatic thunder and lightning made that evening memorable even before a card was dealt.

Not all our local excursions proceeded smoothly. One afternoon Elisa and I took four students to a rarely visited scenic spot along a river, not far from the regional prison. To get there, we endured a tough drive through swampy ground with no real track. After a refreshing swim, Elisa and I relaxed on a woven mat. The students, more energetic, went for a walk in the jungle.

Local boys play soldiers with real (if rusted) guns

I dozed off in the heat — and woke with a start to find an unkempt man in a ragged uniform standing over me. He held a machete! Rising on my elbow, I saw several other men behind him, all similarly dressed and all holding machetes (known locally as 'bush knives'). Abruptly I recalled Aipat's excited news a few days ago that a group of six convicts had escaped from the prison. I counted the men. There were six! I went cold with terror. Were we about to be murdered?

I looked at Elisa, lying down in only her bikini. She was thinking what I was thinking, if not worse. I sat up, trying to look unworried, smiled at the man, and said hello. He smiled back and explained in pidgin that he was leading a work party to collect some of the pandanus vegetation around us. I spotted the reassuring presence of an armed guard not far away. Whew! We planned our excursions more carefully after that.

.   .   .

Health was an ongoing concern. We debated how best to manage risk. Should we hazard getting malaria or take pills that could protect us against that but might cause organ damage? We took the pills. Should we boil all our drinking water or rely on the college chlorination facility? We didn't boil the water.

Some health risks ambushed us. A sandfly bite on my calf seemed to quickly heal over but somehow still felt a little soggy. A doctor in town cheerfully reopened the wound and extracted a lump of decaying flesh that looked like a cigarette with several tentacles. 'You don't know about tropical ulcers? They just keep on growing and eventually even rot through bone. Don't worry, I'll swab the hole thoroughly with EUSOL — that's short for Edinburgh University solution. It's a great antiseptic — just use it daily until the hole closes up.' Thankfully, he was right.

Our house on the ridge sat on the opposite side of the campus from student dormitories. Nights were usually cool. We slept under just a sheet with all the louvre windows open. Only thin cotton curtains and a flyscreen separated us from the outside air. And we slept soundly, until one Saturday night...

I woke abruptly, feeling alarmed and fearful. Instinctively, I remained silent and turned quietly to Elisa. She was already awake, and equally still. I could see Elisa clearly because our bedroom was brightly lit. But not by us. Light streamed through the curtains *from outside*! We could see every blade of grass around the house illuminated clear as day. The intense light seemed to originate *above* the house, as if from a giant flashlight. But no flashlight could be that bright. An eerie silence prevailed too — none of the normal frog calls or gecko barks.

We slipped noiselessly out of the bedroom and headed for the front door. As we cautiously opened the door and stepped onto the porch, the light snapped out. Suddenly it was pitch black, as usual. And the eerie feeling had snapped out too. Normal night noises resumed.

What on earth had happened? A flashlight tour around the exterior and surrounds — we even studied the roof — turned up nothing unusual. We talked through the logical possibilities. There simply were *no* potential light sources nearby that might be strong enough to explain what we had experienced. The ridge was accessed only by a footpath with steep steps on the campus side, and it fell sharply away into a river and dense forest on the other side. Any heavy equipment would struggle even to get here and would certainly have left traces. We could just about envisage a helicopter hovering with a powerful floodlight — but not silently.

We weren't keen to start a rumour about flying saucers. We went back to bed and slept uneasily. Next day Elisa separately approached the single male colleagues who lived in the other two houses on the ridge. Had they heard or seen anything strange in the night? No. Both had slept soundly, perhaps sleeping off a night out. With no evidence or testimony to back our story, we decided to say nothing to anybody unless something similar happened again. It never did (or at least not to us).

The inspector's second visit to the college late in term two and his final visit early in term three had been brief and wary. Simpson kept a low profile, focused on formalities, and avoided staff meetings. He spent most of his time with James and subject department heads, and that suited the rest of the staff. If after-hours meetings with students continued, they weren't obvious.

Two weeks after the inspector's final visit, tragedy struck my guidance class. Lucius, my male deputy class captain, was a handsome and responsible young man with a quiet and almost self-effacing personality. So I was surprised when two of my female students came to see me to complain about him. 'Lucius jumped around in the mess hall like in a kung fu movie, swearing and shouting at the girls. He says he hates girls now and they must not come near him. He hit one girl who was close by him.'

Somewhat disbelieving, I took Lucius aside. He looked at me sullenly. 'Yes, I hate girls now.' I pressed for an explanation. 'Mr Mendzela, this is something private for me. I do not want to talk about it. I am learning kung fu now.' Patiently, I explained that he could learn kung fu if he wanted to, but he must be restrained and polite with his fellow students, both male and female. Otherwise, he could not continue as deputy captain. 'I do not care about that anymore,' Lucius retorted. Stymied, I asked him to go away and think about his behaviour.

Returning home from town next afternoon, I found several of my students waiting on our porch. 'Oh Mr Mendzela, it is terrible! Lucius went crazy. The police took him away!'

Shocked, I rushed to the administration block and found James still in his office. 'I'm sorry, John, but that's correct. With no warning or cause, Lucius began lashing out at girls in the mess hall. He hurt one girl quite badly. He seemed to be having a fit of some sort. No one could talk to him or restrain him. Finally, we called the police, and they arrested him. I had no choice but to expel him immediately.'

Still in shock, I asked several witnesses about what had happened. The duty teacher shook his head. 'It was a horrible sight. Lucius was throwing himself around and yelling incoherently. He actually foamed at the mouth! In the end the police threw him into a cage and took him away to town. They will put him on a plane first thing tomorrow morning, with a guard. And before you ask, he's been expelled from the college into police custody, with no visitors allowed. The police have agreed not to press criminal charges, provided he goes back to his village and never returns to the college.'

Our students often faced conflicting academic, social and cultural pressures. Unreal influences like kung fu movies could confuse or frighten them. It wasn't rare for a student to break down, run away, or be sent home. In fact, to 'go longlong' — behave crazily without being mentally responsible for what occurred — was an accepted cultural phenomenon. But this breakdown didn't feel right, especially the sudden hatred for girls. I knew that Lucius had been keen on Expressive Arts, the department headed by Graeme Drysdale, and spent some of his free time helping in the gallery there. I couldn't help thinking that some type of sexual interference, somewhere along the line, had caused him to go berserk. But there was nothing more I could do for him now. My male students sadly elected a new deputy captain.

To distract them, I asked for volunteers to build a carport for our 4WD car below the steps to our house. That would give them a small practical project to grapple with and a chance to earn some pocket money. The resulting roof of branches and leaves wouldn't keep out all the rain, but it would offer some shelter to anyone arriving or leaving in a downpour. Helped along by cups of sweetened tea and snacks from Elisa, my students enjoyed the physical work. Soon after completion, we were amused to hear a constant slight crunching as insects energetically chewed away at the structure. Untreated timber wouldn't last long in the tropics, but our new carport had contributed a helpful diversion.

8. The Postman Knocks (Elisa)

MIDWAY THROUGH TERM THREE, Gus came to our house after work parade. Late afternoon was usually a time for rest not socialising, but I quickly offered coffee. 'No thank you, I'm here on business and won't stop.' He handed John a pile of the shiny grey papers that our library photocopier produced. Sounding mysterious and formal, Gus asked us to look at those papers and 'develop your independent professional views' about what should be done. 'I'll come around tonight to hear what you think.' He left without saying anything more.

Bemused, John sat down to read through the papers while I did other things. I saw him look startled and sit back hard in his chair. Then he read slowly, quite unlike his usual speedy style. After finishing the last page, John looked thoughtful.

'What's the problem?' I exclaimed. 'What's all the mystery about?'

'You read the papers yourself first, while I go for a walk and think about it. Then we'll talk.'

I sat down and began reading what turned out to be someone's private mail. The papers were photocopies of handwritten letters to someone working at Keravat, written by various friends in PNG and Australia. They described in colourful language — and disturbing detail —homosexual relationships and abusive activities. Occasional parties where young men new to the group were given drink and drugs and 'initiated' seemed to be a highlight for the expatriate organisers and participants. Despite the use of nicknames, some identities were obvious. Our inspector Martin Simpson was prominently referred to. Other participants apparently worked in the PNG education system too. And at least some of the young men being 'initiated' were clearly current or former college students.

I could guess whose letters they were. And I could guess who copied them. Christine, the African woman newly married to our Head of Expressive Arts, Graeme Drysdale, had taken a post as assistant librarian at the start of the year. Overseeing the college library was part of June's English department duties. She had been pleased with Christine's work and became her friend and confidante. And June, with Christine's permission, had shared some of those confidences with me.

Some weeks ago, June found Christine crying bitterly. What was wrong? Tearfully, Christine explained her distress. She had wanted to stay in Australia after finishing studies there but had no legal or economic basis for doing that. Then she met Drysdale through a mutual friend. They soon became lovers. When he proposed marriage, she accepted. Apart from apparently mutual attraction, their marriage gave her precious Australian residence rights. His motives — affection for her and a desire for children — seemed sincere.

But as everyone at Keravat had thought, Drysdale was homosexual or bisexual. Christine discovered his inclinations for male partners only after they were married and living at Keravat. She had been horrified. An angry confrontation led to a stand-off. Christine told her new husband that she refused to tolerate any further activities of that nature in her home. Drysdale told her he would do whatever he liked. And if she tried to make trouble for him, she would be sorry.

Then Drysdale had started pressuring Christine to leave the country. James, good friends with Drysdale, helped him arrange telephone calls to Christine from the Education Department. Christine was told that if her husband didn't want her to live with him, she would lose her work permit and her job, and must leave PNG. With no one else to turn to, Christine had confided in June, who encouraged her to reject that threat and seek a legal route out of her situation. With Gus's help, Christine had quietly engaged a local lawyer to defeat any administrative action and plan divorce proceedings. That would take a while. In the meantime, I had promised to maintain confidence about it all and hadn't even told John.

What I was reading now must have been collected by Christine as evidence of her husband's abusive behaviour. Incoming mail for college staff was sorted by a secretary and placed in open individual pigeonholes in the mailroom. It would have been simple for Christine to purloin her husband's letters, steam them open, photocopy them at the library, and replace them in his pigeonhole.

Gus and June came round that evening to discuss the situation. June confirmed the origin of the letters and added fresh information. After the inspector's latest visit, Drysdale had started making more concrete demands. Christine would be expected to tolerate and keep secret her husband's extramarital sexual activities and even host parties at their home. If she refused, Drysdale would force her to leave PNG, and she would lose her Australian residency too.

Frightened and angry, Christine had copied several of his letters and passed them on to June. And now all four of us had read them.

Christine needed help with her personal situation, and June and Gus would continue with that. But the content of the letters we had read took matters much further. We now had evidence that Drysdale, Simpson and others in the PNG education system were abusing their professional positions to encourage college students into sexual activities with expatriates. All four of us felt we had a professional responsibility to stop that abuse if we could. We should at least bring our evidence to the attention of the proper authorities. Gus confirmed that Christine was happy for us to do that.

The compromising letters were strong evidence. But what action would be effective? Some of the 'proper authorities' who should investigate wrongdoing seemed to be directly involved in it themselves. We didn't know who — if anyone — at Education Department headquarters could be trusted. Locally, our own principal, James, seemed to sympathise with Drysdale and strongly support Simpson, so we couldn't rely on that 'proper authority' either. Going to the police was unlikely to generate a skilled investigation, and the people involved might have connections even there. Local PNG media — two small daily newspapers, a pidgin weekly and the monopoly government radio — were worthy enough but probably wouldn't respond. And if they did the publicity would be damaging for everyone, not least the unfortunate students who had been abused.

After long and sober discussion, we decided to keep the letters secret for now and continue working quietly in our usual roles. But we would also pursue two lines of action. Gus would see if church networks could identify a path to top officials or government ministers who would reliably act on the problem. Meanwhile John would look more closely into Simpson's activities as inspector and try to find administrative rulings that could justify his dismissal for professional reasons. With luck, we could engineer the quiet removal of Simpson and the others involved. We could at least make it harder for them to abuse students.

We adjourned for Gus and John to do that initial research. June and I would keep our heads well down to help cover our tracks, and make sure Christine did the same. The four of us would meet a few nights later at Gus's place to exchange information and plan next steps. To avoid arousing suspicion, Christine wouldn't join us.

9. First Moves (John)

Our next meeting was optimistic. We were making progress!

To help develop church contacts, Gus had enlisted the local Catholic priest, Father Luke. That hadn't been easy. Gus learned that Father Luke had already tried to obstruct the activities of expatriate men prowling around Keravat township and displaying sexual interest in young males, but his Catholic hierarchy had sternly ordered him to drop the matter and focus on his parish duties. Also, none of us were Catholics ourselves. So Gus had brought another of the Keravat staff into the secret, to vouch for our good intentions. Mark Hoban was a devout Catholic who was himself a former missionary priest. As an older man with a wife and young family to support, Mark wanted to avoid any direct involvement. But he had convinced Father Luke that our evidence of Education Department officers abusing students could not easily be ignored and should be taken up through the church.

On the administrative side, I had studied the various official manuals and circulars on inspection procedures. As I expected, they required an inspector to form judgements on individual teachers based on his own observations, supplemented by test results and written reports from the teacher's head of department. In fact, the official 'secretary's instructions' explicitly stated that student views on individual teachers should *not* be sought except in special circumstances. And naturally enough, inspectors should rigorously respect the rules of the institutions they visited.

Measured against those requirements, Simpson's approach was improper on multiple grounds. First, several students had complained to staff about how he had embarrassed them and led them to break college rules by questioning them after lights-out. Second, Simpson had used his routine meetings with student leaders to question them about their teachers' competence. Simpson also had a documented history of soliciting additional *oral* comments from Keravat's department heads and then quoting those comments selectively and out of context. And despite James playing down concerns expressed about Simpson's unprofessional activities, bad feeling amongst the staff justifiably ran high.

And it wasn't just Keravat. At the national curriculum symposium, I had heard that staff at Aiyura College complained to their principal about similar problems with Simpson there. Following up by phone with contacts from that event, I learned how their principal (unlike ours) had backed his staff. Conflict escalated to the point where Aiyura's principal and staff refused to cooperate with Simpson and forced him to curtail his last inspection visit. Both sides complained to headquarters, and the college had formally requested a different inspector. An uneasy compromise had been reached where Simpson returned to complete his work under the supervision of another accompanying inspector. And Aiyura's principal and staff wouldn't accept Simpson back next year. Now, we had independent corroboration of Simpson's improper approach to his job.

A practical plan took shape. My documentation of Simpson's improper professional actions at Keravat, supported by multiple witnesses here and corroborated from another college, should more than neutralise any support he might get from our principal James. Meanwhile Gus was a mature and respected professional who sat on the Governing Council and could not be lightly ignored or quieted. So even if the authorities in Moresby were inclined to treat the personal behaviour they would hear about through the church as 'off the job', they would surely be forced to discipline Simpson and Drysdale and curb their access to students. In the meantime, to keep the focus on professional issues and avoid leaks, we would not disclose our intentions to Christine (a talkative lady). She would know only that we had action under way.

I felt uneasy though. After all, we came from countries where homosexuals had often been persecuted. I played devil's advocate against our plan. Could we justify using intercepted personal correspondence to take professional action? Might Gus, as leader of our group, perhaps be taking things too personally based on his conflicts with Simpson and James? Was there any 'halfway house' we should consider before taking action that would ruin professional careers?

I knew Gus well enough to put him on the spot: 'Gus, are you taking a stand on this because it's the right thing to do, or for personal motives?'

Gus thought carefully before replying. First, he worked us through all the professional issues again. 'Let's be clear,' he concluded. 'We're not bigots targeting homosexuals. If these were expat men exploiting female students, would we hesitate to take action? If we were back in England or New Zealand, would we ignore what we're seeing here? Would the Education Department there just do nothing about it? I don't think so! These guys are using their professional positions and the great respect that nationals show for expats to abuse students placed under their care. Students who look up to them and trust them. That's not just wrong. It's appalling!' And then he answered my underlying question. 'I'm doing this because it's right — and maybe a little bit for me too.' He looked around. 'Does anyone think we should stop?'

No one did.

Over the next few weeks, we got to work. Simpson's inspection reports on us arrived. They were all strongly positive. Gus's report spoke of his 'maturity and experience to carry a position of senior responsibility'. I had a 'very promising career'. Elisa was an 'excellent and enthusiastic teacher with a real care for her students'. But to retaliate for the staff challenges to his authority and methods, Simpson had also inserted a few barbs about personality: Gus 'could produce tension', I sometimes lacked a 'sense of proportion', and Elisa could apparently be 'somewhat sharp in criticism' (Bill Tolley's input, no doubt). But James, and everyone else we showed the reports to, said our reports were amongst the best they had ever seen. The rating system gave only a simple pass or fail. 'Satisfactory' ratings would be a mere formality.

It came as a surprise to most people when I tabled official manuals and circulars at the next staff meeting. I declared that several of us intended to object to the procedures the inspector had used to compile our reports. I also related the similar events at Aiyura College, and the outcome there.

Animated discussion broke out. Even staff who actively disliked Simpson's approach to his job worried that it might be unwise to alienate the inspector. James pointed out how our objections might seem unreasonable to the 'Ratings Conference' of all inspectors that would evaluate and rate the reports. He warned that staff who challenged their inspection reports might be rated 'Unsatisfactory', which could have serious consequences for them. At best, more inspections would follow. At worst, their contracts might be cancelled. So as our principal, he strongly advised against any official objection to the reports.

I replied that we were not objecting to the reports themselves, but to the improper activities of the inspector at this college. Gus and Elisa echoed those views and confirmed their intention to object too. Then Bohdan spoke up. 'If his professional procedures are improper, then we should show unity and object to them. Certainly, I will.'

Mark Hoban took up the argument: 'We should take a collective stand as a staff, not just leave it to the individuals being inspected.' Several other speakers concurred. The meeting overwhelmingly passed a motion to record the staff's 'professional concern' about improper inspection procedures and seek a response from headquarters.

A response came swiftly. James approached me brightly one morning. He told me our inspector was naturally upset by the 'negative feedback' he had received. Mr Simpson denied any improper behaviour and was sure that there had been a misunderstanding. Would I, as the lead objector, talk with him by telephone? Maybe we could straighten the whole thing out, so that the objections we had attached to our inspection reports and the expression of concern from the wider staff could be withdrawn?

I couldn't reasonably refuse. But I felt wary about any undocumented conversation with Simpson. 'Sure, James, let's do that. And to avoid any possible confusion about facts and technicalities, can we arrange for you as principal and Mark (as a staff member who has not been inspected) to listen in on the extension?'

'Certainly!' said James. 'I'll make all the arrangements for morning break tomorrow. Just come along then.'

Mark and I proceeded to the admin block next morning. James awaited us. Soon we were connected long-distance to Simpson at headquarters. After James confirmed we could all hear one another, I set the scene. 'Mr Simpson, I understand you wanted to have a conversation with me about your inspection procedures and the objections about them that I attached to my inspection report. Is that correct?' Simpson said it was. 'Well, I'm here for that, with James and Mark listening in on an extension. Please go ahead.'

Simpson spoke smoothly. 'Oh, I thought we would just have an informal personal chat to clear everything up. I don't want to proceed in that unfriendly way. Let's just talk it through by ourselves.'

I explained that we would be discussing important professional concerns, so it was essential to avoid any later debate about what was said. Simpson paused for some moments. Then he spoke petulantly: 'In that case, we won't talk at all.' He hung up.

James emerged red-faced from his office, saying he didn't know what had gone wrong. Mark emerged behind him, trying to stifle laughter. That ended informal negotiations.

A few days later, James brought a letter from Simpson to the weekly staff meeting and read it aloud. Simpson strenuously denied any improper conduct during his inspections and expressed his dismay that such misunderstandings had arisen. No one bothered to comment. James waited awhile. Then, looking pained at the silence, he moved to the next agenda item.

The days raced by. Term three would soon end. The deadline for returning inspection reports loomed — it was 'put up or shut up'. With just two days left, I checked the deadline with James. 'Why not forget the whole thing?' he cheerfully suggested. Then he added, in a darker tone, 'You don't *really* want to get into trouble, do you?'

DEPARTMENT OF EDUCATION

TEACHER'S PERSONAL REPORT

TO BE COMPLETED BY TEACHER:—

Personal File No. 292502

Name .... GALE .... BRIAN PHILIP
Surname   Christian Names

Substantive Rank ... E.O. 2 .... Date of Promotion/Appointment. MAY 1979

Posting ... KERAVAT N.H.S. .... Position SUBJECT MASTER ... H.D.A. to ... -

Date Commenced Present Posting ... MAY 1979 .... Dates of Inspection. JULY 31 - AUGUST 7 1980

You have devoted a great deal of time and enthusiasm to your various extra curricular activities in particular your care of motor vehicles, lawn mowers and other machinery on the campus. You are patron to the Highlands Club and have organised occasional weekend cricket fixtures. You are also dormitory advisor and a class tutor and staff representative on the Governing Council as well as acting Secretary to that body. You are very conscientious in the performance of all these responsibilities.

You do not perform boarding school duties.

You are a **very** conscientious and competent teacher with many years of experience. You have good relations with the students and a real concern for them and a good knowledge of them. You are meticulous in your preparation and in the quality of work that you produce. You are a respected and valued member of staff and have the maturity and experience to carry positions of responsibility.

Gus Gale's inspection report, full of glowing praise

That did it. Not to be intimidated, we all wrote up our individual paperwork. Each of us was careful to avoid any comment about the *content* of our respective reports (which in every case was accurate and mostly favourable). Instead, we expressed professional concern about the *procedures* Simpson had applied at the college and added a copy of the meeting minutes recording the staff's collective statement of professional concern. Then we signed the inspection reports and our supporting documentation.

The staff's collective professional concern didn't include Bill Tolley. When I asked him what he was doing, as the head of English department who should be supporting Elisa and Bohdan, I got evasive waffling. Naturally, he couldn't discuss his own role in the inspection process — that was professionally private. But as a senior member of staff, he had to take a responsible position in relation to higher administration, and so he wouldn't join our 'protest'. Mildly, I said I could fully understand his position. After all, internal test scores demonstrated he was delivering better student results than anyone else in the department. No doubt he wanted to fully support the inspector. Bill turned away, red-faced and sheepish.

I took the full package of our documents to James. 'Who at headquarters should I send this to?' I asked.

James glared. 'Mr Simpson, of course.'

I shook my head. 'I'm sorry, James, I won't do that. He's the subject of our objections.'

James smirked. 'It doesn't matter who you send it to. It will end up on his desk regardless.'

I left to consult Gus. We decided that he, as staff representative for Keravat's Governing Council, would write to Mr Tavitai, the head of Colleges Division. Gus would enclose all the signed reports with our objections, plus the staff meeting minutes.

```
I would point out to you that M▇▇▇▇▇▇▇ has written a most
favourable report on you in which he has very much minimised
the troubles you have stirred during your time at Keravat.
It is unfortunate that you have failed to take notice of his
advice in the 2 May letter - "The writing of such letters will
inevitably have a damaging effect on your career."

You are strongly urged to consider the implications of your actions.
```

Headquarters tries to intimidate us. We didn't back down.

A response came fast, not from Tavitai but from his superior the Deputy Secretary for Education. Gus read it to us. 'The inspector has given you a most favourable report in which he has very much minimised the troubles you have stirred during your time at Keravat. It is unfortunate that you have failed to take notice of his advice. The writing of such letters will inevitably have a damaging effect upon your career. Furthermore, objections regarding procedures should not be attached to individual inspection reports.'

More intimidation!

We persisted. Checking on what would happen next, we discovered that our objections had somehow been 'lost' at headquarters and hadn't been sent to the Ratings Conference at all. We promptly dispatched copies of our objections directly to the Conference by air cargo to ensure they couldn't deny receiving them.

Term three was ending. With the administrative battle under way, it was time to open our second front.

10. Gus Blows the Whistle (Elisa)

FROM MY OFFICE WINDOW, I watched Gus and Mark enter the principal's office. They would give James a copy of just one of the letters that linked Graeme Drysdale and inspector Martin Simpson to sexual activities with students. Gus would explain that Christine had found the letter, copied it, and brought it to him as the staff representative on the Governing Council. Mark would participate in the process only as a respected witness who was not otherwise involved.

We believed James would have no choice but to initiate some official response, against Drysdale at least. And Drysdale — not likely to be heroic— would probably turn 'state's evidence' against Simpson.

After about 20 minutes, Mark left James's office. Ten minutes after that, Christine went in. Five minutes later she came back out. A few minutes after that, Gus emerged and headed for the staffroom. What was going on?

It was hard to contain myself until the bell rang for morning break and then walk nonchalantly down to the staffroom.

Staff helped themselves to coffee and tea and settled into chairs amid the usual chatter. I caught Gus's eye. He looked uncertain. What had transpired in the principal's office?

Gus stood up and raised his voice. 'Attention please everyone! The principal has asked me to make some important and urgent announcements.' Chatter stopped.

'Two unusual events occurred this morning. Firstly, I presented the principal with evidence of improper conduct with students by a member of the college staff and a senior officer of the Education Department. Mark witnessed that. That is distressing for the college and for all of us. James will arrange an independent and impartial investigation.

'Normally that could happen without a public announcement. But not after the second event. Last night Graeme Drysdale left the college and his residence without notice. He slipped a note under the principal's office door to say that he will not return to Keravat.'

Silence was intense. Gus continued. 'You will naturally wonder whether those events are related. They are. The allegations of improper conduct with students involve Mr Drysdale. Whatever emerges from the investigation, James does not expect Mr Drysdale to return to Keravat. Isobel will make arrangements to cover his duties.'

Gus looked around. 'James will leave for Moresby immediately, to take to headquarters the information I presented to him. He asks us all as professional people to suspend judgement on these events. In particular, please don't discuss them with students or people from outside the college. Just carry on normally, in the best interests of our students and the college.'

Several staff tried to question Gus. Who was the 'senior officer' involved in the allegations? What specifically was being alleged? At the college or elsewhere? Gus quietly replied that his announcements spoke for themselves, and he was not in a position to explain further. The bell for classes rang, and staff left for their duties without any further official discussion. But people being people, I knew that unofficial speculation about the answers to those questions would flourish.

Our group of four met that evening. Gus recounted what had happened in the principal's office. 'Just as planned, I explained that I had important information to confidentially present to him and had asked Mark to come along as a witness. Then I gave James the letter, stating that it was clear evidence of improper conduct by Drysdale with college students. James just glanced at it. He didn't seem shocked or even much interested.

'Then he told me about Drysdale's surprise departure. I got the distinct impression his departure was no surprise to James. He read to us from Drysdale's farewell note: "unforgiving and uncharitable wife" ... "not prepared to understand me" ... "I couldn't take any more". James said it was all very sad. He would make an announcement at morning break and follow up appropriately. Then he thanked me for "acting properly in this difficult matter" and stood up, expecting us to leave.

'I stayed in my seat. "You haven't read the letter yet. It's not just Drysdale. It's Simpson. And others."'

Gus smiled at the memory. '*That* shook him! He sat down again and read the letter carefully. Twice. He took a few minutes to recover — you could see the mental gears churning.

'Then James regained his usual poise. He said he would call Christine in immediately "for a private discussion please".

'I wasn't having that. I told him any discussion with Christine should be witnessed. He reluctantly conceded that I could stay if I liked, but Mark should leave.

'When Christine came in, James put on his best official tone. He looked straight at her and held up the letter. "Are there more letters like this one?"'

Gus chuckled again. 'Christine was ready for that. She said, "Yes. My lawyers have them." James tried friendly persuasion, but she wouldn't budge: "I gave Mr Gale one letter so that you could act properly as principal to protect the college and students. I have been legally advised to keep the rest of the letters confidential and not give them to you or to the Education Department."'

'I kept my face straight and serious the whole time — at least I hope I did! James dismissed Christine and stayed in formal mode. He explained how "This could be a matter of national importance. I must bring this letter to the direct attention of the Secretary for Education." James told me he would leave immediately and asked me to make a brief announcement to the staff at break on his behalf, mentioning *only* Drysdale by name. He emphasised that "*only*".

'Then as I was going out the door, he asked me if I had seen the other letters myself. I looked back and said, "I'm not at liberty to answer that question." I left without saying any more. What happened at the staff meeting you already know.'

11. Opportunity Knocks (John)

TERM THREE WAS ENDING. Our second-year students would soon face national exams vital to their future. They kept staff busy with a stream of individual requests for tuition, especially on answers to examination questions from previous years. So there was not much talk about Drysdale's bolt.

James returned to Keravat after three days. He called a brief staff meeting to say that he had laid all the allegations and evidence about Drysdale before the Secretary for Education. 'We can now leave everything in his hands. Mrs Beckham will take charge of the Expressive Arts department until the end of the year.' James looked wistful. 'Whatever his personal life, Graeme Drysdale was an excellent teacher and professional colleague. I'm sorry he's gone.'

Eyebrows went up around the room. One staff member asked whether others besides Drysdale might be involved in improper activities. 'What about our inspector, for instance?'

James refused the bait. 'Let's not speculate please. I've put all the information I received in the hands of the secretary, who will take action as he sees fit. Until we hear further, I won't entertain further discussion on the topic. Let matters rest.' He sounded professional and trustworthy.

But our group wasn't persuaded to let matters rest. Informal enquiries through the secretarial network revealed that the Secretary for Education had been away during James's visit to headquarters. Who had James seen and talked to? All the signs of a cover-up, it seemed to us. And with Drysdale out of the way, that cover-up could hope to succeed.

James didn't let matters rest either. He told Christine that Drysdale had left the country, so she had no right to remain resident in PNG. Her job as school librarian and her accommodation at Keravat would have to terminate at the end of the college year, maybe sooner. But, he suggested, if she would just make the other letters available to him then he might be able to help. Christine held her ground and reiterated that her lawyers would only make those available to the Secretary for Education himself. She was frightened though — what would happen to her when the college year ended?

Time was on Simpson's side. We needed to do something more, soon. But what?

Opportunity unexpectedly knocked. We heard that Philip Manu, the Secretary for Education, would speak at a graduation ceremony at a nearby agricultural school, not long after our own graduation ceremony. And like most nationals, Manu was a practising Christian. Father Luke acted as our intermediary to senior clergy in Port Moresby who remained unknown to us and arranged a clandestine conclave. Gus, Father Luke and Christine would drive to the agricultural school in secret. After the ceremony, the secretary would meet them informally and unobtrusively.

With compelling evidence placed personally before him, the secretary would surely have to act. Gus would present all my professional material on the administrative issues, including the inspection reports with their attached objections and staff meeting minutes. And he would explain how Simpson was working with Aiyura College only under the supervision of another inspector. The secretary would have strong grounds to remove Simpson for administrative reasons and thereby resolve the bigger and more sensitive problem quietly. An optimal outcome.

Staff thoughts began turning to the future. Like us, many had contracts with further time to run and would continue at Keravat next year. A few such as our head of science Ed Manson and principal James himself would 'go finish'.

My militant squash opponent Gabriel had private plans. His year had started well when Gus organised a party to celebrate Zimbabwe becoming an independent and multiracial state. Gabriel quickly became good friends with our two national teachers and a popular figure in Rabaul town. But his 'black consciousness' philosophy had taken a few knocks. Keen to support national not expatriate businesses, Gabriel bought his car second-hand from a local dealer. Too late, he discovered serious body and engine problems that had been deliberately hidden from him. Next, his principled stance on not having a 'houseboy' backfired. Villagers saw him not as a black compatriot but as a well-paid expat who wouldn't share his wealth. On several occasions they broke into his house while he was out, pilfered his possessions or left excrement on the porch.

Gabriel sympathised with our professional concerns, but he interpreted them in a political context of 'colonialist exploitation'. The ferocity he brought to our squash rivalry sometimes seemed fuelled by the discrimination he had suffered in white-ruled Rhodesia.

As we sat exhausted after an especially demanding match, Gabriel confided that with Zimbabwe now under majority rule he would not remain in PNG. 'I'm tired of this neocolonial environment where everything is still run by corrupt or incompetent white guys who even abuse their students. I like the people here, but they won't do anything to change that. I have arranged a job for myself as a headmaster in a rural part of my own country, where I can contribute to building a truly independent nation. Don't tell anyone else please, but I won't come back next year.'

I felt sorry to lose a friend, but I could understand his feelings. Then a thought occurred. 'Gabriel, have you ever lived in a rural area?'

Gabriel shook his head. 'Actually, no. I always lived in the city, back home and in England too. That's one reason I came here, to broaden my experience.'

I persisted. 'It might be dangerous where you're going, after a war. Do you know how to protect yourself if you need to? Have you ever fired a gun?'

He looked at me sheepishly and shook his head again.

'Well, I'm sorry you're leaving. I hope you know what you're doing.' I wanted to tell Gabriel about the meeting we had arranged and what it would achieve. But I couldn't. 'Right!' I decided. 'I have a .22 rifle at home. Only James and Gus know about it, and I'm not allowed to use it except with permission from a local landowner. If you can arrange that permission, I'll make some paper targets and teach you gun safety and basic shooting, like I did for school students in New Zealand.'

Equipped with my firearms licence for 'collecting plant specimens', I bought a box of ammunition on our next trip to town. With a few sessions of target practice in a remote patch of jungle, we finished off the box and Gabriel became a passable shot. I had done what I could to safeguard my friend.

12. From Opportunity to Despair (Elisa)

TERM FOUR BEGAN. For the first-year students, it was just another term of classes. But graduating students had only two weeks of lessons, followed by a fortnight for personal study. Nationally set and securely delivered exams would then proceed through two intensive weeks. Our own professional roles would shift from sympathetic teachers to neutral (and strict) exam monitors.

Right after that would come the highlight of the college year: graduation. Exam results would arrive only several weeks later, but in the interim all second-year students would receive a certificate of course completion and be treated as graduates. A joyous occasion!

Those new graduates would then depart for distant and separate homes, and perhaps never see many of their friends again. So other emotions would run high too. And it wasn't only students who would feel loss and grief. John and I would continue with the same guidance classes for another year, but like most staff we had grown personally attached to many of the graduating students. The graduation ceremony would be an occasion of 'sweet sorrow'.

Exams passed busily and without incident. The graduation ceremony that followed was attended mainly by students, staff and local notables. A few students invited relatives who lived nearby. Most could not invite anyone because their families lived far away.

Principal James was master of ceremonies. Proceedings began conventionally enough with a blessing and an opening speech from a regional community leader. Next came distribution of certificates, with extra recognition for those students who had made special contributions to college life, as class captains or in some other way. A few more speeches followed, and then James stood up to close the event before everyone moved on to refreshments. We expected him to express a few standard sentiments of gratitude for everyone's work during the year, and we didn't expect him to mention Drysdale.

Wrong, on both counts. James first explained that, as staff already knew, he would complete his current contract and leave for Australia very soon. Next, he spoke about how the college had developed and progressed under his leadership during his time as principal. Then came the bombshell. James concluded his speech with an effusive eulogy for Drysdale. He described Drysdale's 'many fine achievements' and expressed deep sorrow that he had left the college 'for personal reasons'. No other staff member got a mention, individually or even collectively. Eyebrows went up around the staff, but it was not the time or place to comment.

The graduation ceremony convinced our group that James would no longer even pretend to be neutral. Instead, he stood firmly alongside Drysdale, Simpson and their cronies. James could and would cast doubt on anything we said. With half the students and some departing staff gone, Simpson in denial, and James backing Simpson, we would find it hard to conclusively prove that improper inspection procedures had been applied. We decided that more documentation would be helpful, while memories were still fresh.

Before they left for home, Gus asked the female school captain and vice-captain if they would give him written statements describing how Simpson had questioned them about individual teachers. He explained the professional concerns we had. Helen and Felicity were intelligent young women who understood those issues and greatly respected Gus, and both were happy to oblige. Meanwhile I drove John to the airport — he was heading away to attend Part 2 of the science curriculum symposium.

Next morning brought a surprise. June handed me a glossy magazine. 'Look at what Christine just gave me!' she exclaimed. 'She found it in Drysdale's cupboards. It's a clincher!'

I flipped through the pages. The magazine mostly reported on art exhibitions in Australia. What could June mean? Then towards the back, a familiar name jumped out — Graeme Drysdale, Head of our Expressive Arts department until his recent bolt. The photo accompanied a review of his art exhibition in Sydney the previous summer. The review described in loving detail — or from my point of view, appalling detail — the sexually based artworks he had produced at *our* college using *our* students.

The article made grim reading. One work had been entitled 'Four Choice Thighs'. Another showed 'the uncircumcised male member in various stages of erection'. Those creations had been made with the aid of 'enthusiastic natives who offered their bodies without embarrassment to the white man's body art'.

This really was a clincher! Drysdale had been foolish enough to publicise his improper activities with students, using racist language no less. We would no longer need to rely on intercepted private correspondence. Gus took careful custody of the magazine and added references to his notes for the secret meeting with the Secretary for Education — now only a few days away.

Another development emerged after lunch. In the mailroom, I found a large official envelope from headquarters waiting in my pigeonhole. John's pigeonhole held a similar envelope, and several others poked out elsewhere.

It was my inspection report, now officially stamped 'Satisfactory' by the grandly titled National Ratings Conference of Inspectors. My expression of concern about inspection procedures was still attached, but no response to it was evident. That was the cynical outcome we expected from the headquarters hierarchy — close the process off and ignore the issues we had raised. Well, we would see about that. Gus would soon meet with the Secretary for Education and rumble the whole show.

Soon after I arrived home, a frantic knock rattled the door. It was Bohdan, looking angry and worried. 'Did you get your inspection report?' he wanted to know.

'Yes,' I replied.

'Aren't you upset?' he demanded.

'Not really. It's what I expected.'

'So, you don't mind being rated "Unsatisfactory"?' he shouted, waving his inspection report.

'But I wasn't!'

'Well, *I* was.'

Bohdan's report was indeed stamped 'Unsatisfactory', with no explanation or further information.

We rushed back to the mailroom. I opened John's envelope. He had been rated 'Unsatisfactory' too. We hurried down the path towards Gus's house and met him coming up. Gus looked grimly amused. 'All *unsatisfactory* together, are we?' he asked.

I felt deeply insulted. How dare they rate me 'Satisfactory' and not the others. I felt even more angry next morning, when I aggressively tracked down Bill and found that he — the least competent and least professional of all those inspected — had not even been rated. Bill's lame explanation that the inspector had decided not to formally report on him this year 'because the English department was in a developmental phase' made no sense. Furthermore, I was sure that omission was against regulations. The entire inspection reporting and rating process had been rigged to punish those who had challenged Simpson, reward Bill for loyalty, and — by exempting me from the punishment — keep Bill's non-performance out of the picture. That was smart payback.

That wasn't all. Every staff member found in their pigeonhole a new letter from Simpson to the college staff, formally denying the use of all the inspection procedures we had objected to. The letter was dated nearly two weeks previously, and had no doubt been held back until the rating process was over to stop any staff rebuttal reaching the Ratings Conference.

Worse news came next morning. The Secretary for Education would now not attend the nearby graduation ceremony next week after all, due to 'other commitments'. Our plan was unravelling fast. Gus brought Mark and (for the first time) Bohdan fully into the picture and we discussed what to do next. There were no obvious steps to take. Feeling forlorn, all we could agree was that John, who was still away, needed to know. Maybe he would have a fresh idea?

INSPECTOR'S REPORT

For use by Primary Teachers only:—No. on Roll .... No. Present ....

| FOR H.Q. USE ONLY | You have a Cert. Ed. at King Alfred's College Winchester and are an M..I Bid.Starting in 1953 you have had a varied career in Industry, the Forces and you have taught at the equivalent of secondary modern level in the United Kingdom, Singapore and New Zealand. |

Performance Unsatisfactory
at Substantive Level

Your preparation and planning are meticulous and the work sheets, overhead projector material and handout sheets are outstanding in their quality. You have built intelligently on the material and programmes that have been developed in previous years.

You are methodical and efficient in the administrative routines for which you are responsible.
SECRETARY for EDUCATION maintain good comments and you have an intelligent knowledge of the students. You keep records of all assessments for your own information. A file is maintained on each class giving you a running record of information and work covered. Your class roll book is up-to-date and analyses have been worked out. You perform a stock check on materials maintained in your own office. Records are kept of meetings and you maintain an efficient filing system.

You have a logical and deliberate style of delivery in the classroom that is well levelled to student comprehension in terms of sentence structures and vocabulary. You make use of demonstration material and organise and supervise practical classes efficiently.

You attended the ....

Gus's report after the Ratings Conference, with "Performance Unsatisfactory" stamp added!

13. Fortune Favours the Brave (John)

THREE DAYS PASSED QUICKLY. Working creatively with my Keravat colleague Ray and teachers from other colleges to review the science curriculum and develop new teaching materials felt worthwhile. Goroka Teachers College, our venue for the symposium, was delightfully located in a hilly region at an altitude of over 1000 metres. The town of Goroka was surrounded by fertile forests and food crops. Its spring-like days and genuinely cool nights contrasted sharply with hot and humid Keravat. The air smelled fresh and scented by pines. What a pleasure to sleep under a blanket again!

But my thoughts often drifted elsewhere. Gus would meet with the Secretary for Education soon, and the results from our inspection reports and objections should emerge at about the same time. What would happen then?

Despite my distraction, I had enjoyed the opening dinner, especially the welcome address from the Catholic monk who was principal of our host institution. Brother David had spent most of his working life in PNG and regaled us with fascinating and hilarious stories from the colonial days. Not many school principals had been woken up in the middle of the night to shoot a crocodile in the flooded boys' toilets! Clearly a man of courage and integrity, David ended his discourse by exhorting us to energetically pursue our teaching work (you would expect him to say that) and rigorously fulfil our pastoral responsibilities to 'protect from harm' the students placed in our care — not an obvious phrase to use, and he didn't explain it any further.

Today was the final day of the symposium. Proceedings would end at lunchtime and participants would begin to catch their individual flights out. I had a dawn flight back to Rabaul next day, after a free afternoon.

During the morning tea break, a secretary brought me a note. Could I please phone Mr Gale urgently?

That sounded ominous. Excusing myself, I obtained permission to use a telephone and rang Gus's home. Tersely, Gus explained how our plan was fast going awry. The Ratings Conference had been carefully rigged to deliver Simpson's chosen outcomes, and — much more seriously — the meeting with the Secretary for Education would now not happen. Suddenly we — with our new 'Unsatisfactory' ratings — were in trouble, not Simpson. Did I have any fresh ideas about what to do next? Was there anyone at the symposium who could help us?

Dismayed, I couldn't say much. I explained how I had already probed the symposium participants over evening drinks. Most had heard rumours about unsavoury activities involving some teachers or senior officers or disliked the way the inspection system was run. But no one felt able or impelled to do much about it. The consensus was that if you wanted to get on in PNG's education system, you shut your eyes to some things. Anyway, they were technical people with little influence on the Education Department hierarchy.

All I could suggest was to wait until I returned next day and think carefully then. Gus sounded disconsolate when he hung up.

I felt depressed. And frustrated. And helpless. Gus's questions still echoed in my mind. So did Brother David's phrase 'protect from harm'. I should at least *try* to do something.

As the symposium broke up after lunch and participants checked out with cheerful farewells, I strode into the administration block and asked to see Brother David about a confidential professional matter.

'I'm sorry, sir. He's out for the rest of today and all day tomorrow,' his secretary told me.

I heard a voice from the office inside. His voice. The secretary heard it too. 'Oh, he hasn't left yet — but he's very busy.'

'Please tell him it's urgent and concerns serious harmful actions against college students.'

The secretary went in and returned almost immediately. I was ushered straight into Brother David's office. She left. David was packing a briefcase. 'Don't shut the door,' he said, 'I'm about to leave.'

I started to explain how his speech had impressed me, especially one comment.

David interrupted: 'I've only got a minute. Get to the point. How can I help you?'

It was now or never. I took a deep breath and looked straight at him. 'I have written evidence that senior Education Department officers are abusing their positions to encourage college students into homosexual activities. I need to get that evidence to the right people, urgently.'

David looked hard at me for a moment. Then he got up, told the secretary he must not be disturbed, closed the door, and sat down. 'Tell me the whole story, but quickly please.'

Still standing, I did my best to deliver a summary. David listened intently. When I had finished, he first looked thoughtful and then decisive. 'Everyone talks about this, but no one's had any hard evidence. Can you guarantee that what you are saying is true? About the letters, and about the administrative irregularities and payback? And about the meeting that was arranged with the Secretary for Education?'

I could, and I did.

'All right,' he said after a moment. 'Sit down.' David picked up the phone, dialled a number from memory and asked for the Secretary for Education. 'Tell him it's Brother David, and I must speak with him urgently.' There was a pause as someone spoke at the other end.

'Then he has to leave the meeting, please. I must speak with him, right now,' David insisted. I could hardly believe my ears. Could he really pull the top man out of a meeting, without notice?

We waited silently for a couple of minutes. Then David began to speak again. 'Hello Philip. I'm sorry to drag you away from the meeting. Here's the situation. I understand some people from Keravat College arranged a private meeting with you. They have information that you must personally see and act on.' He paused as the other end replied. 'No, please do *not* cancel your trip. Please promise me that you will have that meeting.' Another pause, longer this time. 'Good. You know I wouldn't ask you otherwise. You will have difficult decisions to make. I am confident you will do the right thing. Thank you, Philip. Goodbye.' He hung up.

I sat dumbfounded. Had I really lucked into someone who could go straight to the top like that? Brother David saw my expression and chuckled. 'I know what you're thinking. Yes, I do know the secretary personally. In fact, I taught him at high school. He's a good man, and he will put things right if he can. And that's not just your good luck. The Lord may sometimes move in mysterious ways, but always to a purpose.'

I was still stunned. 'Thank you for trusting a stranger,' I said. 'You won't regret it.'

Brother David smiled. 'Don't thank me, thank God. And thank yourself. We should all do what we can to improve the world, and you and your friends are doing the right thing.' He frowned thoughtfully. 'I'd heard rumours about abuse of students, but I didn't realise it was so widespread and so actively covered up. That's a worry.' David picked up his briefcase. 'I really must leave now, but feel free to phone me if you need my help again.' He dashed away with a quick handshake.

I left the administration block jubilant. What a break! I couldn't wait to tell the others. I tried to telephone Gus again. But as so often in PNG, I couldn't get a connection to his home phone. I did manage to leave a cryptic message at the college office, to confirm my arrival time next day and say that I would bring back some helpful information.

14. Bowing Out Disgracefully (Elisa)

As usual, I drove to the airstrip carefully and arrived early. And as usual, the flight arrived late. I had ample time to speculate about what John's 'helpful information' might be. I knew it must be about the battle with Simpson and headquarters. But as Gus had suggested the previous night, John had probably just uncovered another lead to follow up or met some sympathiser. We needed more than that.

So while we were glad to see one another again, I was puzzled by the big grin that kept crossing John's face as we chatted with acquaintances who were meeting another flight. But as we drove off and John related what Brother David had done, I was soon grinning too.

It would be unwise to convene our group straightaway — the campus was too small for people not to notice. We quietly did the rounds to update our team individually and arrange a meeting for the evening, when it would look more like a social gathering. And a gathering it was, with Mark, Bohdan, Father Luke and Christine joining our usual foursome.

John told his story all over again. We celebrated properly with a toast. After that excitement died down, attention turned to the magazine article. Now we had objective and conclusive evidence to add to the letters. Pornographic 'artwork' with racist overtones had been produced on college premises, with college equipment, by a member of the college staff, using college students sexually. The secretary couldn't ignore that evidence from an independent published source, no matter what James or Simpson might say or deny.

But we still prepared thoroughly. John's confidential report to the Secretary for Education explained Simpson's unprofessional conduct as Keravat's inspector, proving in detail his failure to apply the requirements and restrictions of the official 'secretary's instructions'. Those failures now included not inspecting Bill Tolley as regulations required, even after concerns about Tolley's alterations of test results were brought to his attention. Supporting documents included staff meeting minutes and the signed statements from college captain Helen and deputy captain Felicity. John's report also outlined Simpson's rejection by Aiyura College and its principal, for similar misconduct.

Gus's separate report focused on Drysdale's and Simpson's improper involvement with past and current students, as evidenced by the letter already given to James and by the magazine article. Gus had unearthed a lot more evidence too. He outlined the cronyism whereby Simpson had after his own promotion to inspector recommended his current protector James for Keravat and likely sympathisers for other roles. The report also recorded, sometimes with newspaper references, how several headquarters' officers and their appointees around the country had court convictions (in one case for homosexual assault on a school student) or serious conflicts with local people (one had been beaten up for 'spoiling a boy'). Moving the problem person elsewhere seemed to be the only action that was ever taken. Finally, Gus quoted the widespread concern he had encountered socially about the undue power and influence of headquarters officers over staff and students and the negative impact that had on the Education Department's reputation.

The third component of the package comprised letters from Christine's lawyer. One outlined her own grievances and evidence. A second letter recorded his formal opinion that the 'Unsatisfactory' trio could take legal action against the department for its administrative abuses against them. A third letter recorded assurances that the trio would instead consider those matters closed if the secretary took appropriate remedial action.

Father Luke, as a witness of unimpeachable character who was not directly involved, would hand over and explain the full package of evidence and information.

The final staff meeting of the year convened the next day. Feelings ran high. Several staff previously passive during discussions about Simpson angrily challenged James about his graduation speech that eulogised Drysdale and ignored the rest of the staff. Coolly, James claimed he had simply been preoccupied with other matters. Failing to recognise the work of other staff had been an unintentional omission. And no, he didn't think any apology was called for.

Simpson's letter of denial came next on the agenda. Gus tabled and read out the statements from our female captain and vice-captain, supporting staff claims of improper procedures. Encouraged by the two national teachers, the staff decided to collectively complain about Simpson to the association that represented national teachers at all levels of the education sector, and to send the student statements to the Ratings Conference chairman. James looked pained and said nothing.

After a few administrative matters, James reminded us that he would depart in a few days. Classes for first-year students to complete the college year would end just before he left. Isobel, as Deputy Principal, would administer the college until a new principal was appointed and would publish the staffing list for next year as soon as that arrived. It was now time for his closing words to the staff: 'It has been a pleasure to be principal here. Thank you all very much for your support, and best wishes for the future.' A stony silence ensued. The meeting closed.

Everyone was winding up their professional work for the year. Staff who were 'going finish' began their personal packing. But unexpectedly, James called one more staff meeting.

His attitude was different this time. James explained that he had organised this extra meeting in a spirit of reconciliation, looking to the future. Perhaps staff concerns were justified, and Mr Simpson had acted unwisely during his inspections, but he, as principal, had no knowledge of that at the time. He asked that staff withdraw their concerns and complaints about inspection procedures, to allow a 'fresh start' that would be in everyone's best interests.

To everyone's surprise, Deputy Principal Isobel — normally an administration loyalist — spoke up. 'James, that's not true. I told you about the problems with the inspector's procedures months ago. You told me then that you thought his procedures were unprofessional.'

Flustered for a moment, James recovered. 'I can't recall that conversation,' he said, shaking his head.

Bohdan coolly attacked: 'Mr Beckham, I have always observed that you have an excellent memory. Surely you can recall such an important professional matter. Or do you just have a *convenient* memory?'

James coloured up. 'I resent that implication. I just don't happen to recall that conversation.'

Silence descended on the meeting. James handed the chair over to Isobel and stalked out. The meeting reaffirmed its original concerns about Simpson, confirmed its intention to make further professional complaints, and resolved that a copy of the meeting minutes be sent to headquarters. Even Deputy Isobel and Bill Tolley didn't oppose that collective view.

But it wasn't quite unanimous. James Beckham's wife Sue (Acting Head of our Expressive Arts Department) stood up, yelling and tearful. 'You people don't appreciate all the hard work James put in here. You're just a bunch of jealous nobodies. To hell with you!' She spluttered incoherently for a few more seconds and then ran from the room.

Isobel displayed impressive composure. 'I think we can leave those last remarks out of the minutes. I declare the meeting closed. Thanks everybody.'

John didn't wait for the minutes. He quickly typed up a written account of the statements made by James and Isobel at the meeting and sent it to the principal's office requesting confirmation of its accuracy. James sent the document back, initialled 'OK'.

End-of-year joy and celebration concealed an undertone of anxiety. To everyone's frustration, the staffing list for next year didn't arrive. That wasn't normal. Something must be going on.

Something was. In the next mailbag, John received formal notification of a new posting to a remote high school for both of us next year. He immediately telephoned the superintendent responsible for high schools, a senior national officer. I bent close to the handset and listened in. 'Oh yes,' the superintendent said. 'Colleges Division explained that you both requested a transfer. We badly need good teachers with overseas training, so the school will be delighted to have you. In fact, as the senior head of department there you will receive an immediate promotion to Level 3!'

John explained that we had not requested a transfer. 'But I have the letter from Colleges Division right here,' the superintendent said. 'Actually, it says that there are five of you available. You two, Mr and Mrs Gale, and Mr Doubek. We have already allocated you to three different schools around the country. Mr Gale will also receive a promotion to Level 3.'

John explained that none of us had requested a transfer. Colleges Division was embarrassed about professional matters that the college staff had raised, where senior officers were at fault for improper behaviour with students. 'Did they tell you that we have been inspected and rated "Unsatisfactory", just because we raised those matters?'

'Certainly not!' the superintendent said. 'All they told us was that you are excellent teachers and in fact deserved promotions.' He paused. John waited. 'Mr Mendzela, thank you for calling me. We don't want to become involved in college disputes or accept people who are being transferred against their will. I will reply to the letter right away and cancel all those postings. Please tell your colleagues that.' John thanked him.

We were taking nothing at face value. That afternoon, Gus called the superintendent to check on his promise. The superintendent wasn't in, but his secretary knew what Gus's inquiry was about. 'Oh yes, sir, I have a letter to Colleges Division right here. The superintendent was not happy to be given wrong information. He telephoned them already to refuse the transfers, and I am just typing his formal reply.'

Our next call was to Colleges Division. John described his call to the superintendent and its outcome. Even from several feet away, I could hear the man at the other end — Bruce Hawthorne, operational head of Colleges Division — explode. 'It's too late John — the deal has been done. Don't make more trouble for yourself!'

John continued, quoting the superintendent's secretary. 'I guess you will just have to keep us all here at Keravat,' he smoothly concluded.

Hawthorne exploded again. 'Listen, you! Don't think you're so clever. And don't think you've won. Those postings were actually pretty good. Now I'll make sure you get much worse postings! And if you don't accept those, we'll terminate your contracts.' He banged down the phone.

We advised our interim principal Isobel about the latest developments. She wasn't surprised. 'I told Bruce you wouldn't go. But he wouldn't listen. They're used to pushing everyone around, and they just don't understand you guys. We'll have to wait and see what happens next.'

I resisted the temptation to tell her that tomorrow's meeting with the Secretary for Education was likely to make quite a few things happen.

15. Defeat or Victory? (John)

Gus set off next morning, ostensibly on a trip to town. Once away from the campus, he would rendezvous with Father Luke and Christine. (She had already moved out of the campus to live with friends in town.) They would proceed to the arranged meeting site to see the secretary. Our evidence was checked and ready: my report documenting Simpson's improper inspection procedures, Gus's report tracing sexual involvement with students to Drysdale, Simpson and others, and the letters from Christine's lawyer. The meeting was scheduled for early afternoon, so we expected Gus to return well before dark.

Time dragged. It was hard to concentrate on college work, or anything else. Tropical darkness fell sharply at six o'clock as usual. Still no Gus! Elisa, Mark and I gathered at Bohdan's house, feeling anxious. Finally, about 9.30, we heard the low rumble of Gus's diesel vehicle. He parked at his home and went straight inside. We heard the house door slam shut. Gus didn't emerge.

After waiting an hour, we just had to know more. I walked down the dirt road to Gus's house, my flashlight battling the intense dark of a clear and moonless tropical night. I climbed the stairs to the front door and knocked softly.

Gus flung open the door. He stood there filling the doorframe, and didn't invite me in. 'What is it? What do you want? It's late!' He seemed angry with me.

Startled, I tried to divert the conversation onto a less personal footing. 'Bohdan wanted to know how the meeting went. I know we can talk about it tomorrow, but naturally everyone's on edge.'

'Well, you and Bohdan and everyone can just stay on edge. I've had it!' Gus slammed the door shut.

That behaviour was completely out of character. I felt hurt and angry. We had all taken the same risks together and deserved to know what had happened. I reported to the others disconsolately. Our group broke up. The night wasn't happy or restful.

Next morning Father Luke explained. He, Gus and Christine had been kept at bay by gatekeepers who told them the secretary was 'fully engaged' and could not see them. They had persevered, waited many hours and sent in repeated messages. Finally, the secretary's senior minder expounded that 'it would be improper for the secretary to meet with individual teachers', who should instead send complaints through the proper channels. After further strenuous pleas, the secretary had (they were told) agreed only to receive documents 'for consideration' and only from Father Luke. Even Luke didn't get a private conversation, and we couldn't be sure the secretary would receive and read our reports and letters. No wonder Gus came home upset!

The next few days were tense. Feeling hurt, I barely spoke with Gus — and we were both too proud to heal the breach.

Principal James and his wife Sue drove away for the airport. Nobody waved them off. Most staff and all of the remaining students began to depart for holidays and home. Still no staffing list for next year arrived. Gloom prevailed amongst our group.

Finally, on the very last day of the college year, an Education Department car and driver hand-delivered a staffing list for next year. Isobel immediately posted it up. None of the 'Unsatisfactory' group or their partners appeared on it. Those positions were all labelled 'new expatriate appointee'.

Whatever our personal feelings, we had to act as a team again. With Elisa and Bohdan in tow, I went to see Gus. He chaired a hurried conference. To help him play our last card, Elisa and June went to the college admin block to keep the two college phone lines too busy to receive any incoming calls. Gus telephoned Education Department headquarters from his home phone while Bohdan and I listened in.

Gus impressively bulldozed his way through the bureaucracy. He insisted on speaking personally with the secretary about 'an emergency situation at Keravat College'. 'No, the principal isn't available. I'm a member of the Governing Council. It's imperative that I speak with the secretary right away.'

To our delight, the secretary came on the line and spoke pleasantly. Yes, he knew who Gus was. And yes, he had considered the documents 'confidentially presented to the department'. He would now 'personally rectify the situation'. All those matters would be sorted out in a few days. Would we please delay going on leave and remain on campus until then?

Gus thanked the secretary and slowly put the phone down. With a great sense of relief, Gus and I walked to the admin block together to tell Isobel the news. As we walked, the lingering tension between us gave way to shared elation. We — in truth, mostly Gus — had won!

```
Dear Mr Gale

INSPECTION REPORT 1980.

I have received your inspection report and the letters you
submitted to the Chairman of the Ratings Conference.

I find that you do not dispute the report as such and have
signed it.  The Inspection Report by itself indicates a
satisfactory performance.

Your Inspection Report has therefore been amended to read
"Performance Efficient at Substantive Level".

Yours faithfully




SECRETARY FOR EDUCATION
```

The letter from the Secretary that changed Gus's rating

That was Friday. Now it was Tuesday. The college year was over and the campus was almost deserted. A secretary excitedly summoned Gus and me to the office for an 'official phone call from headquarters'. It was Bruce Hawthorne, operations head at Colleges Division.

This time his tone was subdued. 'I'm calling to inform you that we've changed the staffing list for next year. At the direction of the secretary, all five of you who had been listed for transfer will remain at Keravat. The secretary has also changed your inspection ratings, to satisfactory. You will receive letters confirming those decisions.' We grinned from ear to ear but replied in the same neutral tone to thank him for that information and to look forward to continuing our work at Keravat next year. 'But what about the problems with inspection procedures?' I asked.

Hawthorne replied curtly. 'I've told you everything that concerns you as individual staff. Any other administrative matters will proceed in a proper manner and be announced in due course through the proper channels.' He hung up.

We weren't surprised that 'other administrative matters' would be dealt with quietly. That had been our goal all along. We felt confident that Keravat and all the other colleges had seen the last of Simpson, and that it would be much harder and riskier for other potential abusers to target college students in future. Under a new principal, Keravat would have a true fresh start.

We celebrated that night, toasting victory and joyously reliving key moments.

Bohdan departed for home leave the next day, nursing a hangover. But when an official copy of the revised staff list and individual letters to Gus and me enclosing our re-rated reports (now over-stamped 'Effective' and 'Satisfactory') arrived two days later, no letter arrived for Bohdan. We asked Isobel to enquire. She reported to us: 'Bohdan's on the staff list, just as Bruce Hawthorne advised. But the secretary reviewed each inspection report individually and felt the rating on that one should not change. That's official.'

On reflection, that wasn't a major surprise. As a second-language English speaker who had little previous teaching experience and got no help from Bill as department head, Bohdan occasionally struggled to deliver his lessons effectively. Simpson's inspection report on him had included critical but fair comment on that, so the glaring contrast between content and rating that was obvious for Gus and me hadn't applied for Bohdan. An unfortunate outcome, but not a great worry. At worst, Bohdan would be inspected again next year by someone else, under proper professional procedures.

We heard good news from Christine too. Rather than fight to stay on at the college, she had found a teaching job in a nearby high school. That qualified her for a 12-month work and residence permit.

Christine would have time to start divorce proceedings and plan her future.

Our tumultuous year had ended happily. We resurrected vacation plans that had gone on the back burner during the struggle. Like most expatriate staff, June would be travelling to her home country for a family visit. Elisa and I — and Gus — had more adventurous ideas.

16. An Unquiet Night (Elisa)

OUR CONTRACTS ENTITLED us to home leave on paid travel only every 18 months. Under the standard three-year term, that entitlement came at the end of year two and (if contracts were renewed) again at the end of year three. Most expats travelled to their home countries or some other overseas location for an annual holiday every year anyway, paying their own way when they had to. Some grumbled about that.

John and I didn't. We had come to Papua New Guinea for adventure, and six weeks' leave was a once-in-a-lifetime opportunity to see more of this unique nation. John planned an exciting itinerary — a flight to the mainland to PNG's second city Lae, travel by bus and rental car to everywhere we could reach by road from there, and an adventure cruise by river into a remote and otherwise inaccessible cultural heartland. My friend Samantha from New Zealand would join us for part of the time.

Gus had even more adventurous plans. He and his brother Arthur would fit out a small yacht in Lae and sail it to Rabaul. Few private boats attempted such journeys through the often-turbulent tropical ocean. Gus and Arthur would rely on basic marine charts and their own navigational, mechanical and sailing skills to traverse unfamiliar waters for at least a week.

Our holiday began well. Samantha arrived at Rabaul, and we enjoyed showing her the local environment for a few days. We flitted around the coast admiring the grandeur and beauty of the rugged landscape, set against hot blue skies. The town of Rabaul, skirting the sea and nestled in the caldera of an ancient volcano, exerted its many charms.

Then we flew to Lae and had several fun days with Gus and Arthur. Their new yacht, third-hand and in poor repair, needed a lot of work before it could take on the ocean. But both brothers were excellent mechanics and sailors, and good facilities were available at Lae's yacht club. They departed on a weekend trip to crew another boat and practise navigation while a specialist contractor strengthened their own boat's hull.

After waving them off, the three of us returned to Arthur's place to stay the night before our own departure the next day. Arthur's house was in a small government housing estate for national civil servants. He had been happy to let us stay at his home, but he warned us to be careful: 'Especially at night. There's a lot of crime around.'

We weren't too concerned. The small two-storey building had iron bars on its doors and windows to deter unwanted visitors. And it had a telephone.

Arthur had sent away his house-girl — a young woman from a nearby village — for the duration of his absence. His instructions to us were clear. 'You can't trust your home help while you're away. Others can put pressure on them to allow damage and stealing. If she comes around, especially with company, *don't* let her in under any circumstances or whatever her story.'

Typically for PNG, the first hours of darkness were noisy. We heard people come and go outside in the cool evening air as they enjoyed meals and socialising. Later on, things quietened down. We checked everything was locked and headed upstairs to sleep.

Suddenly the front door rattled loudly. 'Husat?' John called. It was the house-girl, pleading piteously in pidgin to be let in. When John quoted Arthur's strict instructions and made it clear we would follow them, her tone changed. She made threats, saying her friends would come and make us sorry if we didn't open the door. We decided to ignore her, and eventually she wandered off. We went to bed.

Two hours later, she woke us up by shouting and rattling the door again. No humble pleas this time. Tactics had changed. Peering cautiously from the upstairs window, we could see her companions — three burly men, armed with machetes. We also noticed silent darkness around all the neighbouring houses and realised that the inhabitants were likely to mind their own business and ignore any trouble. It was time to call the police. But picking up the receiver, we discovered the telephone was dead. Bad luck? (PNG's telephone services were notoriously erratic.) Or had they cut the wires?

We had heard enough grisly tales and read enough newspaper stories to know that robbery was now the least of our worries, especially for two young women.

The front door was solid wood with steel bars. It would hold. But it didn't take long for the men, directed by the girl, to test out the back door and the ground floor windows. Luckily, they were all barred too. No way in for them, we consoled ourselves.

Our relief didn't last long. A lean-to shed with a steep corrugated-iron roof had been built against the house at the back. It offered a difficult but feasible passage up to two of the upstairs windows, and those windows were *not* barred. We could hear the men planning how best to climb up and break in.

Now we were frightened (but tried not to show it). A quick search for weapons turned up nothing more lethal than kitchen knives and a small wooden club. No match for machetes! John sent Samantha and me to one of the front bedrooms, where we could barricade ourselves in. He stationed himself with the club near the most vulnerable window. My heart was racing. In one corner of my mind, I was kicking myself (and John!) for stupidly getting into this situation.

Whispered commands and scuffling noises signalled the assault had begun. We tensed. Suddenly we heard a great crash. Peering out a different window to avoid being seen, I saw that one man had been standing on a pile of firewood that had collapsed under him. Now he was lying on the ground surrounded by small logs, swearing loudly.

The other two men, and the girl, began laughing. Soon the fallen one joined in. They were all seriously drunk!

But also persistent. For the next hour, the three men explored various routes to the upper storey. Twice one of them actually made it onto the corrugated-iron roof, only to slide down and fall off. Hysterical laughter again but also groans. More attempts followed, all failures.

One man started yelling at the girl, who had (in rough translation, with expletives deleted) 'ruined their drinking night with her stupid ideas'. Finally, they all drifted off into the darkness. We breathed a deep sigh of relief that our assailants hadn't been better prepared and more sober!

Next morning, we left the house keys and a detailed message for Arthur at the yacht club.

17. Dangerous Roads (John)

AT THE BUS STATION — a muddy patch of bare ground next to a colourful market — we bought three passages on a PMV (Public Motor Vehicle) minivan. Its scheduled route would take us along a river valley where mining had once flourished. In the 1920s, dredges had been airlifted in to explore rich deposits of alluvial gold. We had seen historic photos of bulky metal parts dangling precariously from biplanes to assemble the dredges on site. But those big dreams had died in the Great Depression of the 1930s. Now the huge dredges stood rusting and abandoned, like prehistoric monsters being reclaimed by the jungle. We clambered around one of the marooned giants, tipping the self-appointed caretaker who lived aboard with his family.

Smaller dreams still bloomed though. Family groups of local miners panned the river flats with hand tools. We learned they could make a meagre living from what had been missed or spat out by the dredges in earlier days. A lucky group might even strike it rich and find sizable nuggets.

We stayed several days at an ecological research institute that offered hostel accommodation. The enthusiasm of the staff for their scientific work inspired us to hike in the nearby hills to view indigenous plants and animals. But we soon discovered the uncomfortable realities of tropical ecology — stifling heat and humidity, sharp grasses and tangled vines to struggle through, no animals or even birds to be seen, and aggressive insects for lunch (we were their lunch). Trudging behind our guide on a narrow path through tall grasses that I could barely see over, I felt something weigh on my foot and looked down. It was a snake! Fortunately, just a python slowly crossing the path via my foot.

We returned to Lae to meet up with Gus again. But our reunion quickly hit a snag. Arthur had changed his mind about the boat trip and gone off to Australia for the rest of his vacation.

Typically, Gus hadn't changed *his* mind. He now intended to make the trip alone. That sounded dangerous. We suggested that I might accompany Gus on the voyage, only to be firmly told 'No thanks. Without the right skills and experience, you'd only be in the way.'

Hiking in Wau, before sharing a much narrower path with a snake

The mood turned more convivial as we visited the boat and enjoyed a fine dinner at the yacht club before returning to Arthur's house. But our concerns about the voyage resurfaced when we heard Gus being sick in the night. His sallow complexion and obvious severe digestion troubles suggested health problems that would make a solo trip truly hazardous. We all three pleaded strenuously for a cancellation, to no avail. Gus shrugged off our concerns, saying that he had been to the doctor and was taking medication for a simple stomach bug.

Parting was tense. We felt seriously worried, while Gus, strongly independent as usual, resented our intrusion. 'It's my business what I do, not yours.' We managed only to extract a promise that he would see the doctor again before setting off.

We collected our rental car and drove into the mountainous interior. We had been warned about roadblocks and robberies on the twisting dirt Highlands Highway. We checked local knowledge carefully before setting out each day, and travelled in convoy with other vehicles when we could. Luckily for us, law and order held temporary ascendancy after a recent burst of helicopter-aided policing. At the few roadblocks we did encounter, rocks and logs had been pushed to the side of the road and nobody threatening was around. In fact, most villagers were friendly and cheerful, keen to sell fruit and handicrafts. Their colourful 'bilums' (string bags made from thin strips of vine) could and did expand to accommodate massive loads of food, firewood and babies.

Young people were often keen to chat with us to ask questions and test out their English. How much English they could speak, and how well, varied. One group surprised us with a strong accent and even dialect words straight out of Scotland; a Scottish missionary had been their teacher. What church we belonged to was usually an early question, and we soon learned to proclaim our nominal Catholic heritage rather than hint at any agnosticism.

On day three of our trip, we arrived in Mount Hagen — or, as we came to think of it, 'Dodge City'. It certainly felt like the Wild West. Tribesmen in native dress, armed with traditional weapons, roamed the streets. Town councillors drawn from the headmen of local tribes sported little tin-star badges of office like something out of a cowboy movie. The manager of our basic hostel accommodation, a flamboyant Hungarian-Australian, offered to take us to watch nearby tribal fighting, as though it was a soccer game. We went, only to find that the 'match' had been postponed due to a heavy police presence that weekend.

Our host was also an impresario who set up popular and rambunctious disco nights in nearby villages — and closed them at pistol point when things got too rowdy. Contrary to the conventional advice that expats should drive carefully to avoid injuring anyone, he speeded up when he saw people. 'They know my car so they get out of the way!'

Our Wild West metaphor was not far from the truth. Relations between neighbouring tribes were often confrontational and based on payback: 'If you kill one of us, then we'll kill one of you — and anyone will do.' On any given day some tribes felt in arrears and keen to score an equaliser if they thought they could get away with that. One of our students who was home for the holidays showed us local sights. He explained that people were usually very cautious when travelling outside their home village, but he would be okay so long as he was with us.

Peace-making sometimes succeeded. Not far from town we attended a 'sing-sing' that was also an armistice ceremony. Amongst much singing and dancing, two tribes in amazingly colourful body paint and costumes energetically exchanged traditional wealth of yams, pigs and artefacts. The tribes mingled freely and everyone seemed happy and friendly. Casual visitors like us were welcomed and could even take photos. The only bad temper on display came from dozens of pigs staked out with ropes, who seemed to know they were on the dinner menu. A lot of alcohol was stacked up though, so we left before darkness fell and the party would really get going.

Dressed to kill for the peacemaking ceremony outside Mount Hagen. The men are wearing wigs made from their wives' hair. The women playing kundu drums sport valuable kina shells and bird-of-paradise feathers.

Next day, we drove to Tari, terminus for the highway 'until further construction'. What looked from a distance like strange roadside trees turned out to be wonderful woven baskets and tableware propped up on sticks. A colourful market was a photographer's delight. A diminutive and shy married couple walking along the road in vivid costumes happily had their pictures taken, then held their hands out afterwards to demand 'tenpela kina' as a modelling fee that we were happy to pay.

We retraced some of our route through the highlands and drove to the beautiful coastal resort town of Madang. From there, a day trip took us up a coastline flanked by a large and ominous volcanic island. Samantha and Elisa keenly met and worked with authentic local potters, while I explored a World War II airstrip surrounded by skeletons of Japanese fighter planes, vehicles and anti-aircraft guns.

He carries an axe; she carries everything else in a string bilum
(bag). Women might have deep creases on their heads from
carrying heavy loads.

Next morning we handed in our car and boarded a small expedition cruise ship that would take us well off the beaten track in reasonable comfort. Over dinner the first evening, as the ship motored along the coast, we met the expat former 'kiap' (rural policeman) Simon who would be our guide. There were 13 other passengers: art collectors, ornithologists and adventurers, drawn from Mexico, the USA, Europe and Australia. Next morning, we woke to find ourselves steaming up the mighty Sepik River — a wide brown waterway flowing between distant walls of magnificent green jungle.

After dark, we ventured out in small speedboats equipped with searchlights to find crocodiles. 'Look out for red eyes reflecting back at you,' Simon instructed. We found none that night, but local people who operated a crocodile farm brought us some small specimens next morning. They turned those over and invited us to stroke their wonderfully soft belly skin. We hesitated at first, but then the small crocodiles went limply unconscious. Their ferocious pointed teeth gleamed like small pearls. Turned upright again, the animals snapped into terrifying action and we all jerked back away from danger. 'Now you know what to do to neutralise a crocodile if one attacks you — just turn it upside down and hold it there for a while,' Simon wryly advised.

Amazing days followed. We visited several substantial villages along the main river. Large thatched houses rose skyward on giant log stilts. Climbing ladders gave access to their dark and smoky interiors, many metres above the river. But that height was strictly seasonal. At full flood, the buildings would be accessed at water level.

We squeezed into two speedboats to travel up tributaries and reach smaller villages hidden in deep jungle, far from any road or airstrip. Their food supplies were derived mainly from hunting and gathering, supplemented by sago palms and small seasonal gardens. Local travel was by canoe or, in rare cases, motorboat. Even small children had their own individual miniature canoes.

Sepik dancers greet us as visitors to their village. Their impressive haus tambaran in the background has tilted after a recent earthquake.

Visitors were a rare event that the villagers welcomed. They dressed up to perform traditional dances and offered attractive wooden carvings and other artefacts for sale. An elaborately decorated 'men's house' was always the tallest structure. That was where carving occurred, and indeed all men were expected to express themselves through that medium. The gloomy men's houses were filled with strange shapes and smelled of exotic woods. They held the cultural and ceremonial treasures of the village (missionaries had made sure those treasures no longer included enemy skulls). The music, magic and knowledge that the men shared were for them alone; women were forbidden to enter or observe. An exemption of some sort might be made for expatriate females, but in some stricter villages only the males in our party were allowed to visit the men's house.

Of course, we were really just tourists, but it didn't feel like that. Many carvings were culturally active or sensitive in some way, and so not for sale. Those that could be bargained for were sold with an accompanying story that had to be told at great length. If the carver wasn't around to add value through his tale, prices were discounted. Some carvings even boasted charming price-tags that showed 'first prais' (story included) on the front and a lower 'second prais' (no story) on the back.

Our expedition ended hundreds of miles from the coast at Ambunti, a large village boasting the only airstrip in a seemingly endless jungle. Here the river narrowed and even our small ship could go no further. A final upriver excursion involved a long speedboat trip to a small and poor village that was rarely visited. We saw no modern dress or objects

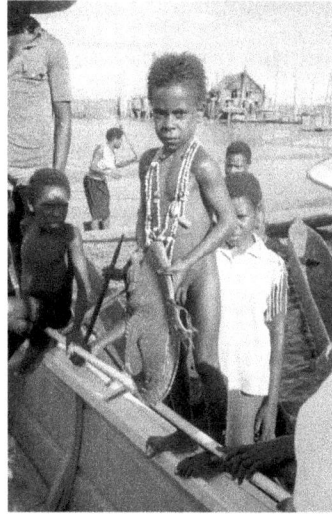

Young Sepik boy with his own canoe, keen to sell us a carving

there; everything was made of local bush materials. One house displayed a human skull outside the door — part of a respectful extended funeral rite.

Not every skull was respected though. One man offered to sell us a beautifully decorated skull, at a very reasonable price. Sensing buyer resistance, the salesman assured us through an interpreter that it was his uncle's skull and entirely without malign influences. I was tempted. Elisa wasn't. Her recollection that there was a specific law against buying human remains finally settled the question, and we bought a few less controversial items instead.

Back at Ambunti, it was time to fly out. A small propeller plane chartered from 'Mission Aviation' arrived on schedule and touched down gracefully on the grass airstrip that sloped downwards from village to river. But our tour group soon fell from grace with its pilot. Three of our fellow passengers had been booked to continue upriver in canoes. Now one felt ill, and all three insisted on flying out with the rest of us. Tasked with 18 passengers instead of the agreed 15, the pilot initially threatened to leave without any of us. After fervent negotiation by our guide, he relented. Then he carefully weighed everyone and everything on an old weighing scale from the village, and shuffled people and baggage around the crowded plane for some time. The heavier members of the party felt embarrassed but laughed off the situation. I knew enough about flying in small planes to realise that the pilot was genuinely worried.

Finally, we set off. Revving mightily, the plane with its excessive load lumbered down the grass towards the river. Propellers screamed at high pitch as our overloaded craft strained to gain enough lift to take off. The barbed-wire fence looming at the river's edge looked more and more threatening. Then with a final leap, just clearing the wire, we were airborne.

Exultation turned to dismay as the plane hit turbulent air over the river, lurched downwards and almost dropped into the water. But our pilot regained control and flew us in slowly ascending circles for an hour to gain enough height to clear the mountains. His skilful landing at Mount Hagen came as a great relief, especially to those like me who could see the fuel gauges falling towards zero.

A jeep awaited Samanatha at the airstrip to take her to a mission school run by the same religious order she worked for back in New Zealand. After a week there, she would return directly home via Moresby. After heartfelt farewells, Elisa and I left for town to spend two more nights in Mount Hagen before our flight back to Rabaul.

18. Sanctuary? (Elisa)

NEXT DAY WAS SUNDAY. John had read about a bird sanctuary located 40 kilometres away on a well-established dirt road. He wanted to visit. Against my better judgement, I agreed.

We had no trouble finding a minivan PMV heading that way at an affordable 'tripela kina wan wan' (three kina each) fare. But halfway there, our driver stopped amidst dense forest. The operator in charge, backed up by several of the passengers, demanded more money from us because we weren't nationals. 'Tenpela kina wan wan long yupela!' (ten kina each, for you). John negotiated through this opportunistic shakedown with impressive coolness, eventually paying half the demanded price as a 'Sunday premium'. Cheerful and friendly again, the operator dropped us off at our destination and promised to collect us on his return trip to town in the late afternoon.

The bird sanctuary fascinated us for a while, but we began to fret about getting back to town. We waited outside the gate for our PMV as the few other visitors dribbled away. No PMV.

The PMV crew to the bird sanctuary, after *extorting extra payment*

Afternoon was fading as the custodian locked up. His daughter spoke English and asked what we were waiting for. Her response alarmed us. 'No PMV will come at this time. Not on Sunday.' She offered a lift on her father's flat-bed utility. 'We can drop you off halfway back to town, where we turn off the main road. Plenty of traffic from there.' We accepted eagerly.

The girl and her father squeezed up to make room for me in the cab. We chatted amiably. John sat on the open back, across from another passenger — a small muscular man clad only in a belt and loincloth and armed with an axe. I watched John smile and greet him. The man made no sound and just stared stonily at him. That unnerving silence and hostile stare continued throughout the journey, despite John's efforts to be friendly.

Our drop-off point was a small village on the 'main road'. We relaxed as the locals seemed friendly. A number of women and older men lined up to shake our hands (some even came around twice). But our rescuer's promise of 'plenty of traffic' turned out to be optimistic. The few vehicles that came by, some driven by expats, ignored our greetings and wave-downs. None would stop. We started fretting again.

A group of young men gathered, unsmiling, around a nearby hut. One came over to talk. He ignored our greetings and scowled at us. 'Watpo you stap hia? Em i ples bilong mipela tasol!' (Why are you here? This is *our* place!) Before we could answer, he stomped back to his friends.

Our next visitor was a young woman who looked worriedly at that group. She kindly offered sleeping places in her family's hut if we needed them. But we knew that wouldn't provide any real protection from the young men. We tried to look cheerful, but fear was taking hold. Fifteen minutes passed with no vehicles at all. Dusk was closing in.

A huge 4WD vehicle travelling at speed materialised out of the growing gloom. We waved frantically as it roared past, to no avail. Then, to our immense relief, it abruptly stopped and reversed back to us at speed in a cloud of dust. The driver, a grizzled expat, rolled down his window and stared at us for a moment. 'I'm going to town. Get in. Quick — I'm in a hurry!' he said gruffly.

We crowded into the cab. Once away from the village, our rescuer grew more amiable. Hearing our story, he just shook his head. 'You've been really lucky. Normally people won't stop, and you can't blame them. I thought you were probably missionaries wanting me to take some sick person to hospital. That's a sure way to get into trouble — when anyone dies, it's always someone's fault.' He grinned. 'Anyway, something told me to stop. I'll get you back to town.' He pointed into the rear. 'But I have to deliver these jokers first.'

'These jokers' were two enormous fierce-looking dogs. They stood tall behind a metal mesh that spanned the back of the vehicle. 'I breed them for the plantations,' our driver explained. 'They're a cross — Dobermann and Rhodesian Ridgeback.' He chuckled. 'The rascals around here are terrified of them, especially when they find out the dogs are trained to rip off their balls!' Unsure what to say about that novel canine training, I said nothing. John kept mum too.

We detoured onto a track and reached the gate of a large compound. Our driver sounded the horn. 'Stay in the car!' he commanded us. Unseen hands opened the gate from inside. Three immense dogs bounded out and jumped at our vehicle with savage growls. Hearing a loud whistle from beyond the gate, they instantly and silently lay down. Our driver got out, extracted his own dogs through the tailgate, and strolled inside to complete delivery.

Safely back at the hostel, we toasted the end of our vacation and our lucky escapes.

We expected to fly to Rabaul next morning on the scheduled flight that we had booked and paid for. But at check-in we found a message waiting for us. Due to 'scheduling difficulties', our flight had been cancelled. And due to 'full bookings', no seats for the trip would be available to us for a week.

After a long polite-but-firm discussion, our bookings for a one-stop flight were transferred to a sequence of small plane flights with other operators. Our journey would now stretch over a long day and require six stops on the way. But no worries. Small plane veterans now, that even sounded like fun.

We still had a couple of days to wait though. With the hostel closing for Christmas, we were forced to move to the more expensive commercial hotel. Their Christmas dinner was expensive, but it came with free Australian champagne. And the cost would work out fine if we stuffed ourselves so full that we would not need to eat at all the next day.

There were plenty of expats booked for Christmas dinner, mostly Australian blokes who were not at all congenial to strangers. Scorning the free wine at the tables, rough-looking men stood around in their Christmas dinner dress — overalls held up by suspenders — and downed amazing quantities of beer. Their interactions with nationals were often aggressive and rude. No stern or disapproving looks from us seemed to make any difference. John narrowly avoided a fight when he objected to a particularly offensive and racist remark that one drunk boorishly directed at a polite and genial bartender. If this was the performance they put on for Christmas Day, how did those men manage to create any value or work effectively with Papua New Guineans, I wondered? After apologising to the bartender for them, we heaved a sigh of relief and left for the peace of our hotel room.

After our economical day of fasting, we went to bed early to prepare for our dawn flight. Our first stop, a tiny airstrip on a small plateau in steep mountainous terrain, looked like an aircraft carrier stranded on land. The pilot cheerfully informed us this airstrip could only be used early in the morning before the winds that whistled through the surrounding gorges got going for the day. The next two stops were a grass airstrip deep in the jungle and a coral-sand beach. Landing on tarmac at the small airport in the centre of Lae at lunchtime to change planes seemed downright decadent. A plaque informed us that it was from this runway in 1937 that the pioneering female aviator Amelia Earhart had set off to cross the Pacific Ocean in an attempt to circumnavigate the world, never to be seen again.

The next aircraft seemed huge by our new flying standards — two propellers not one, 30 seats, a separate cockpit and even a flight attendant! We took off late. Then problems at each of the two scheduled stops delayed us further. Recalling the drastic descent into Rabaul airport, the lack of runway lights, and the likely afternoon thunderstorms, we grew apprehensive.

The pilot comforted his passengers with a cheerful refrain after each take-off: 'Hi again folks. We're a bit behind schedule, but don't worry — we'll be fine.' The primitive intercom system made his voice high, tinny and hard to hear. We couldn't look ahead or watch the pilot fly like in a smaller aircraft, but his confident reassurances gave us comfort.

Sure enough, we hit a storm. Heavy black cloud closed in. Lightning flashed, thunder boomed, and tropical darkness was falling early. The plane bounced around unpredictably, back and forth and up and down. The squeaky voice of our pilot came over the intercom again, quite unfazed: 'Don't worry folks, we'll be fine. Just late afternoon showers!' I looked around and saw my fellow passengers wearing the same scared face I must be displaying. A few appeared to pray.

After what seemed like an eternity, we shot out from dense cloud into clear twilight. We were just over Rabaul airport. A rapid, silky-smooth approach and landing followed. As the plane taxied to a halt, a spontaneous hearty cheer went up. The pilot came on the intercom again to apologise for the rough ride. He still sounded squeaky.

As we gratefully walked down our folding steps, we saw the pilot come down his. It hadn't just been the intercom that made the pilot's voice sound high and tinny. He was a middle-aged expatriate, but only about 4 feet tall! As he waved and departed, we stared in disbelief. The flight attendant laughed and let us look into the cockpit. The pilot's seat had been specially adapted to bring it closer to the controls. The pedals had blocks of wood attached to accommodate his short legs. The colleague who met us a few minutes later laughed too. 'They say Bob Jefferson's been flying up here since he was just a kid. He's one of the best there is.' We smiled to think how Bob had overcome his handicap to become a skilled and valued professional. Only in PNG, I reflected as we drove home to the campus.

19. Fresh Start (John)

IT FELT good to be back. Elisa and I had a quiet professional week to prepare for the new college year. We also had urgent personal tasks. Each year, continuing staff played musical chairs to capture better houses and furniture relinquished by those leaving. We vacated our small house on the campus ridge for a larger and better furnished house in Keravat village.

The previous occupants hadn't been diligent housekeepers. Elisa, with help from Christine, scrubbed the decks while I, with help from Aipat, moved in our personal items. Aipat made himself useful in other ways too, gleefully stamping out a nest of mice with his bare hands. I didn't dare tell Elisa about that. Meticulous about hygiene, she was already fuming about the 'disgraceful!' state our new home had been left in.

Aipat was more pleased than anyone. 'Mi laikim planti!' He would take up residence in a 'boi-haus' in the back garden. That small concrete block building with running water and electric light gave him modern accommodation and ended his daily commute.

Students progressively arrived to occupy the dormitories. Staff drifted in, including several new expats and two further national staff (we now had four). We enjoyed meeting new colleagues and catching up with those we knew already. To my surprise, Gabriel turned up; he had decided to finish his contract and save more cash before going back to Zimbabwe. Grant Riddell for Maths and Bill Tolley for English would be the only continuing department heads. Ray Curtis took over Science, Kevin Maitland had been promoted to lead Social Studies and Practical Skills teacher Evan became the new head of Expressive Arts.

Everyone speculated about who the new principal would be. If Isobel knew, she wasn't telling. And whoever that person might be, they were in no hurry to get here.

Nobody had heard from Gus. We eagerly awaited his triumphant arrival by sea. But the news that reached us was quite different. Gus had flown in, borrowed a car, and gone straight home. We hurried around to see what had gone wrong and found him looking dreadful — gaunt, jaundiced and shaky. No, he hadn't tried to sail the boat; not up to it. He'd gone to Hong Kong for a short holiday instead. Yes, he'd seen the doctor again, who told him to go home and rest up. June would arrive tomorrow, and he would be fine by the time term started. We should just let him take it easy until then. We offered to collect June at the airport next morning to spare him the trip, but as usual Gus insisted on self-reliance.

Elisa and I called around again the next afternoon to find Gus gone. June was there, deeply distressed. Gus had met her at the airport alright, but looking terrible. He was barely conscious and in no fit state to drive home. June had taken Gus straight to a doctor, who immediately admitted him to Rabaul Hospital for assessment. June would go back to the hospital tomorrow. Meanwhile the doctor's instruction was strictly no visitors.

We felt shattered. Rabaul Hospital with its limited facilities was no place for anyone with a serious condition. What about medical evacuation, we asked?

June replied vaguely. 'I'm looking into that. It's complicated and expensive, so I hope it won't be necessary. Anyway, it's Sunday today, so I can't do anything until tomorrow.' We felt she wasn't taking the situation seriously enough but had to back off.

The days got busy as the first week of the college year got under way. We kept in close touch with June. She went to the hospital each afternoon and assured us they were doing everything possible for Gus there. His condition was now stable, the doctor said, but other visitors were still not allowed. June had contacted Gus's brother Arthur and he would fly in early next week to help out. We hoped to go to the hospital before that, perhaps at the weekend.

The new principal arrived mid-week, days later than expected. Steven Townsend was a PNG high school principal from outside the college system. The only thing any of our friends could find out about him was that he was another of the old Australian hands who had stayed on. And Townsend was, like so many of them, an unmarried man without strong professional qualifications. We had our suspicions about his fitness and motivation for the job.

Townsend created a positive impression at his first staff meeting. He opened on a firm note: 'I want to start my time as principal of Keravat College by clearing away baggage. I know there were problems here last year, on several fronts. And I know staff were unhappy with some aspects of college administration. I also know that some serious matters are still under consideration at national headquarters. We will no doubt hear more about them later.' He looked around all of us, slowly. 'I wasn't involved with any of those past matters, and I don't want to hear about them or let them colour the future. I want all of us — whether you are one of the continuing staff, or a new staff member like me — to commit to a fresh start. Let's work together as a united professional team, in the best interests of our students. Please direct all your talents and energy toward that goal.'

A fresh start sounded good. We like everyone else were willing to give the new principal the benefit of the doubt and a fair go. The meeting moved on to the many administrative matters that needed attention. Arrangements were made to cover Gus's absence until he returned to work. The college would give June time off to visit the hospital while Elisa volunteered to cover June's classes and duties.

20. Tragedy Strikes (Elisa)

IT HAD BEEN a busy week for everyone. But especially for me, as I planned tuition and organised logistics to cover for June. It was a relief to get to Friday evening.

John and I planned to go to June's house on Saturday morning to check on Gus's condition before we visited him in hospital. But before we could do that, June came to us distraught. 'Something's happened to Gus. He's worse now than at the beginning of the week. No one at the hospital seems to know what's happening. And no one will tell me anything! I wanted to stay, but they sent me away. I'm absolutely exhausted and I'm going straight to bed.'

We rushed to the hospital and demanded to see Gus. The national nursing staff bent the visitor rules that would normally keep us out. We found Gus unconscious and breathing heavily.

The hospital didn't seem to know what to do. No doctors would be available until next morning. The nurses would only shake their heads sadly and say, 'He's *very* ill...' or 'He needs to rest.'

We sat by Gus's bed for a while. His body looked discoloured, shrunken under the sheet yet swollen around the midriff. His face was a strange mixture of grey and yellow.

After half an hour, Gus regained consciousness. He recognised us and smiled. But if anything, that made him look worse.

We strained to hide our distress and talked optimistically and reassuringly for a few minutes. Gus was quiet, no doubt somewhat sedated. Then the nurses politely asked us to leave. We tried to part on a cheerful note. 'Don't worry Gus. We have to go now, but June's getting everything organised. You'll be out of here and back on your feet soon.'

Gus reacted violently. Sitting up straight with a painful effort, he glared at us. 'June hasn't got a bloody clue!' Then he fell back into an exhausted silence. The nurses ushered us out.

Panicked, we rushed back to campus. We knew that June, as spouse, would have to authorise all legal and medical arrangements. We insisted she arrange immediate evacuation, based on Gus's worsening condition. We didn't disclose what he had said. We extracted a promise that June would do whatever was necessary to have Gus flown to Australia and offered to help in any way we could. Luckily, Arthur was flying in early next morning. June would meet him at the airport. We felt confident that Arthur would take charge of the situation.

Sunday was anxious. I wanted to rush to the hospital and spend the day there. John insisted that we leave matters in the hands of Gus's wife and brother — they knew we were there to help if needed. We argued furiously for a while. In the end we didn't go.

Arthur and June didn't return to the campus that evening. Alarmed, we visited a colleague who had a telephone and called the hospital. Yes, they were there. No, we couldn't speak to them — they were with the patient and the doctor. And no, we couldn't visit — it was after hours.

We didn't get much sleep that night. We weren't surprised to find Gus's house unoccupied early next morning; driving at night was dangerous at best and there were several hotels in town. But the lack of information was disturbing. With no telephone of our own, we couldn't even stay in touch. Then Monday's classes — the first of the year — occupied us fully for the rest of the day. I reported June as on sick leave and covered her classes as well as mine.

As soon as classes were over, we rushed down the path to Gus's house. The car was there. Arthur answered the door, even before we knocked. But one look at his haggard face quenched our excitement. 'Let's talk outside,' he whispered. 'June's exhausted and sleeping.'

Out of earshot of the house, Arthur stopped. His sagging posture said it all, even before he spoke. 'There's nothing anyone can do. Gus is unconscious. His liver and kidneys have failed, and he can't be moved now. It would be a miracle if he survived. And it might be worse if he did — his brain might never be the same. All we can do is wait and hope.'

We stood aghast. Arthur continued quietly. 'Believe me, I know how you are feeling. I'm shocked too. I'll go to the hospital tomorrow and see if anything has changed. Right now, June and I need to rest. So just go home. Please explain the situation to close friends only, and in confidence. Keep them away from the house. And in the morning, tell the principal that June will be on leave indefinitely.'

Numbly, we stumbled around the campus, passing on the information and request to Mark, Bohdan and a few others. John didn't sleep much that night; I barely slept at all. My thoughts revolved in tight circles. Surely this can't be true. How could this have happened to

Gus? Why hadn't we done something earlier that week when we maybe still had a chance to save him?

Work the next day was an ordeal, but also a welcome distraction. For the first hours, managing two simultaneous classes demanded my complete attention. As I headed towards the staffroom for morning break, I saw the principal preceding me. The staffroom, with most people there already, went silent as he entered. The suspense didn't last long. Townsend quietly called for attention. 'I just received a telephone message to say that Gus Gale died in hospital early this morning. I know that many of you, and many of our students, will be deeply upset by that news. I didn't know Gus personally, but I know about how hard he worked for Keravat College and for our students. I'll issue a circular this afternoon when I know more. In the meantime, please carry on as usual.'

That was Tuesday morning. The next two days passed in a blur. College routines continued, but I barely noticed. Second-year students kept telling me how sorry they were that our good friend and their fine teacher was gone. Many were profoundly upset. Even the first-year students who had never known Gus were subdued. The whole campus was sad and quiet — exactly opposite to what would normally have been the buzzing start of a new year.

Arthur and June came back from town each evening looking drained and drawn. They kept to themselves.

John and I couldn't face even our friends. We taught our classes and performed our other duties in a daze. Whenever we weren't working, we sat around exhausted and stupefied. We barely ate or slept. Somehow, we stumbled on.

Townsend could not have been more helpful. Naturally he approved June's leave, but John and I could also take special leave for the week 'to whatever extent we needed'. The principal announced that the college day would close before lunch on Thursday afternoon for a memorial service, to be held at a small church just off the campus. A condolence telex arrived from headquarters, advising that the memorial service would be attended by a senior officer on behalf of the Secretary for Education. That was an unusual recognition of Gus's contribution, and no doubt also a tacit admission of guilt at the shabby treatment he had received.

We didn't take any special leave. Work took our minds off the situation, some of the time at least. But we felt hollow, as though the centre had dropped out of our world.

At lunchtime on Thursday, we joined the entire staff and student body to walk silently to the small open-air church. That was not really a building at all. A pandanus roof rested on poles. Only waist-high basketwork panels linked the roof poles. The congregation comprised many hundreds, far more than the church could hold. Somebody had developed lists for who would fill the pews, and everyone else had to stand outside in glaring sunshine.

Students had decorated the church with colourful wild flower garlands to create a visual feast. Several who had known Gus especially well acted as ushers. We were shown to our place in a front pew, next to June and Arthur. We had expected Father Luke, as Gus's friend, to lead a non-denominational service (Gus was a nominal Anglican but he had not been religious). But to our surprise two other clergymen also officiated, the three of them taking turns to lead the programme. For the college, deputy principal Isobel led one section of the programme and delivered a eulogy. The prayers and songs from hundreds of tuneful voices were truly beautiful. A recording of a boy soprano singing the Pie Jesu from Fauré's requiem — something Gus had sung himself as a young chorister and had always loved — charged the air with beauty and grief.

Fearful that the students might loudly display their emotions, John and I had intended to set an example of quiet and dignified grief. But as soon as the service started, we began crying copiously. We just couldn't stop! Fortunately, the students didn't follow our lead, while the officiating ministers carried on regardless.

As the service drew to a close, a huge bright blue butterfly fluttered in. We exchanged glances. Gus had often dressed in a vibrant shirt of the same blue hue, looking dignified and handsome. Without speaking, we shared the same thought — it was Gus! We stopped crying and smiled. The clergy lost our attention completely as the brilliant butterfly circled the altar and made several languid circuits right around the church. Others followed our eyes. Some had similar smiles. A few of the more religious people frowned at our obvious pagan thoughts.

After the service, we had a quiet lunch with June, Arthur and a few college staff. The students sent over beautifully presented snacks, along with colourful wreaths of tree and hedge flowers. We learned the reason for the multiple clergy. Father Luke had intended to officiate by himself. But the local Anglican minister, who had barely known Gus at all, had nonetheless claimed Gus as one of his flock and insisted on taking part. And not to be left out, the third minister from another Protestant denomination had insisted on a slot too (to be fair, we were using *his* church). June thanked Father Luke with a massive and beautiful hardwood table that Gus had carved by hand. It would make a fine altarpiece for his church.

We all felt that the memorial service had been a splendid tribute to Gus and that the college had done him proud. 'Wait a minute,' mused Mark. 'I didn't expect our new principal to attend, and Isobel did a fine job representing the college. But wasn't someone from headquarters meant to be there, to represent the Secretary for

Education? Did that happen?' Apparently not. Nobody had seen anyone from headquarters there.

Bohdan spoke up. 'Maybe not at the memorial service. But Ross Johnston — the curriculum head at Colleges Division — was here on campus at the same time, seeing Townsend at his house. Several students told me about that. They wondered why he drove in the back way and hadn't come to the service. Cowardly and disrespectful, I call it.'

Everyone drifted off home. We slept a bit better that night and survived a busy Friday at work. The weekend passed quietly, with condolence visits from staff and students to June and to us. By Monday morning, life had somehow restarted. June would take another week off and I would cover for her. Ray Curtis had reorganised biology classes until a replacement arrived for Gus. Otherwise, it was back to business as usual.

The beautiful funeral wreaths and decorations faded fast in the heat

We heard through the grapevine that our former inspector Simpson had 'extended his annual leave' and hadn't returned from overseas. We could guess why! With that satisfying knowledge and the diversion of work routines, our pain began to dull. June resumed her duties, which returned my workload to normal.

Aged and far away, Gus's parents had not been able to attend the memorial service. The news of his death had hit them without warning. John glumly wrote them a sad letter, extolling Gus's hard work and strong principles. He mentioned the professional victory Gus had achieved, without going into detail. 'I feel like a lieutenant writing back home from the trenches, after our captain's been killed leading us to victory.'

21. Battle Resumes (John)

TERM ONE ROLLED ON. We grieved intensely for Gus, not just for our personal loss but for the tragic waste of human capability his death represented. It seemed so unjust and unfair that he was gone, forever. Elisa spent some evenings at June's house, trying to fill the void and cheer her up.

Work occupied most of our time and we enjoyed it. Many students in our guidance classes, now in their second and final year, had become more like personal friends. We watched them mature personally and intellectually, and helped them whenever we could.

Two weeks after the memorial service, staff assembled for the routine weekly meeting. Townsend announced that a replacement for Gus would arrive next week and thanked those who were covering his duties until then. And with one of the previous year's representatives 'gone finish' and Gus deceased, the next staff meeting would need to elect two new staff representatives to the college's Governing Council — we should please think about that. Townsend continued through various administrative matters. In the drowsy heat, many of us were only half-listening.

Townsend reached the end of the agenda. 'Thank you, ladies and gentlemen. Before we close, I have one more announcement to make, and I expect a professional response please. Our first routine inspection visit of the year will be next month. The inspector will be Martin Simpson.'

Everyone sat up sharply. I jumped to my feet. Voices called out: 'What?' 'Are you serious?' 'You've got to be joking!'

Townsend called for order. Hubbub subsided. 'I expected that some of you would be unhappy about what I have just announced. It's not my decision. Headquarters have advised me that Mr Simpson will be our inspector. It's my duty to support that decision whether I personally like it or not. And that's true for all of us.'

I stayed standing and spoke. 'Mr Townsend, I'm astonished to hear what you just said, after everything that happened last year. And after Gus's death. As our principal, surely you have a professional duty to the staff and students here to tell headquarters that Simpson is *not* acceptable to this college.'

Townsend stared hard at me. 'Mr Mendzela, you are out of order. Don't *you* presume to tell *me* what my professional duties are.' He paused and looked around the room. 'As I've said before, this year is a fresh start. That will be all for today, ladies and gentlemen. Meeting closed.' He stalked out.

The bell rang. Staff hurried off singly and in small groups towards their classrooms. Many shook their heads or muttered.

I wasn't leaving it there. If the headquarters gang thought that Gus's death had cleared the way for them to carry on like before, then they were wrong. I owed it to Gus, and to our students, to stop them.

My first step was to insist Townsend read the report on inspection procedures that had been presented to the Secretary for Education, plus the purloined letter to Drysdale and the magazine article describing homosexual activities with students. He couldn't refuse — they clearly concerned the college, not just individuals. But he returned the papers to me a day later, refusing to comment or act on them. I spread the word about that and floated the idea that action by our to-be-elected staff representatives to the Governing Council would be essential.

The next weekly staff meeting elected our friend Mark (as a continuing staff member) and Gaius (both a new staff member and a national teacher) to the Governing Council. And much to Townsend's dismay, the staff immediately voted by a large majority to bring their concern about Simpson's inspection procedures to the Governing Council at its first meeting of the year. Mark quickly offered to also table my report to the Secretary for Education. And I announced that I would write privately to the Council, informing them of the later actions taken by the secretary to block our transfers and alter our inspection ratings.

Surely Keravat's Governing Council would overrule Townsend.

It didn't. Mark explained what went wrong. 'Townsend had the agenda and the meeting process jacked up with the chairman in advance. He buried the staff concern about inspection procedures in his report by describing it as a hangover from last year that he would deal with as part of his "fresh start". When I tried to table your report to the Secretary for Education under other business, Townsend moved a motion to block that. He claimed that inspection procedures were a professional matter for the Education Department, outside the scope of the Council's charter.

'You know what the other members are like — community worthies without much governance experience to guide them. Townsend persuaded them that the Governing Council was not the place to resolve conflicts between staff and the Education Department. The chairman deliberately closed discussion before anyone else could say much. Townsend's motion not to receive your report was carried, narrowly. Then I tried to table your letter to the Council, and the same thing happened. The Council won't meet again for months, so that avenue is blocked now.'

Mark looked upset but also determined. 'I'm not giving up.'

And he wasn't. Together, we drafted a letter to the Secretary for Education from 'the undersigned Keravat staff'. The letter informed the secretary of the new developments, expressing grave and urgent professional concern. 'It would be against the best interests of the college and its students for Mr Simpson to return to Keravat before all the allegations against him have been fully and properly dealt with.'

Then Mark waged a careful campaign for hearts and minds. He used key pieces of evidence — Gus's report and his unfair rating, the magazine article on body art, and staff minutes — to recall and demonstrate the previous year's events. The list of signatures began with his own and a few lower-profile names before those of the prior year's objectors were added. As Mark toured the campus over several days, the list grew longer. He quietly persuaded even newly arrived staff to take a stand. Finally, everyone had signed up except Townsend, Isobel and Elisa's department head Bill Tolley. Mark dispatched the letter directly to the Secretary for Education by air courier.

Townsend wasn't giving up either. Over drinks at the club, he sought sympathy for his plight. 'I'm being drawn into matters that don't concern me, and college morale is suffering. I can understand John and others being upset over Gus's death, but pursuing a vendetta against the inspector won't help anyone. Let's make a fresh start and get on with normal life.'

The national teachers took matters further. They were all liable to be inspected. Naturally they worried about that, and they certainly didn't want Simpson as their inspector. They proudly posted a notice that a delegation from their professional association would visit Keravat the next day to talk with staff about their concerns.

That delegation's visit was not a success. Townsend rejected requests to allow a staff meeting and refused to release anyone from their normal duties. All the delegation could do was meet with individuals who were not busy with students at the time and take away copies of our key documents. They promised to contact the Education Department and 'do what they could', but left us with the impression that wouldn't be very much.

Bohdan worried about inspection even more. His unsatisfactory rating from the year before automatically led to re-inspection this year, and now his contract renewal would be on the line. Always impulsive, Bohdan returned from a weekly trip to town with important news. 'I engaged a lawyer! He's a national not an expat, the same guy Christine and Gus used last year. He wants to write directly to the Secretary for Education about my case.'

'That might not be a good idea,' I mused. 'How competent is he in this field? Will he know what to say? Any legal action right now might just confuse matters.'

'Well, I don't care!' Bohdan retorted. 'I'm the one most at risk here, and I need to protect myself.'

Eventually we reached a compromise. We would engage the lawyer jointly and give him all our information, but we would keep the engagement confidential and refrain from any specific action for now.

Accompanied by Bohdan, I went to meet our new lawyer Mr Lapani. The meeting went well, better than I hoped. Lapani had studied the information package that we had given to the Secretary for Education. He seemed to know his stuff and to appreciate the delicacy of the situation. 'We need to give the secretary time to respond to the new letter from college staff and dismiss Simpson purely on administrative grounds. That way he can avoid any further publicity about sexual involvements with students. As it happens, I know the secretary personally. I can easily arrange to talk with him informally when I travel to Moresby. But as you suggest, let's wait a little while and see what happens.'

Ten days ticked slowly by. We heard a rumour that Simpson had 'returned from leave', and wondered what to do next.

We didn't wonder for long. Townsend opened the next staff meeting with an announcement. 'I had a telephone call from headquarters. It has been decided that Mr Simpson will not return to this college until all of the allegations against him — which he strenuously denies — have been fully resolved through proper process. Inspection visits will be rescheduled accordingly. So your letter has led to results, and you can all stop thinking about those issues now please.'

Good news for us. However disgruntled he might be by our success in challenging 'authority', Townsend tried to appear formal and neutral. In the same spirit, we refrained from celebrating our success in public.

22. Stresses and Strains (Elisa)

TOWNSEND'S announcement that Simpson was still under investigation reduced the emotional tension, not just for our group but for the staff as a whole. And June was back at work, stoically teaching more or less as normal.

We began to enjoy local culture and attractions again. On one trip to Rabaul, I stumbled upon a PNG art book in one of the 'we sell everything' stores. Its graphic black and white plates pictured stunning and sometimes fearsome examples of traditional woodcarvings. I was enraptured and decided to ask Isaac, our local carver, to create something resembling one of the photos.

What I wanted was a wooden basket hook. Once a precious hook hung from the roof inside a hut, villagers could entrust to it safe-keeping of their precious food stores. They could simply hang string bags full of taro and sweet potato from the hook, out of reach of rats and mice.

Isaac accepted our commission with enthusiasm. The particular basket hook I wanted was shaped like a human figure, balancing on an elegant horizontal half-moon with pointed ends. It would be easy to hang string bags full of produce from either end. I looked forward to when I would have this wonderfully artistic yet practical device hanging from our ceiling.

We resumed our personal routines of weekly trips to town and market and excursions with students to beaches and snorkelling spots. That helped heal our sense of loss and created pleasant diversions.

Staff social activities resumed too. 'Club night' at the nearby sports club was a regular event. Heavy drinking there sometimes had consequences. On one memorable occasion, we drove home past Kevin Maitland's 4WD utility lodged against a roadside tree, seriously crumpled. Clearly unhurt, our head of Social Studies and his passengers were laughing uproariously. We stopped to help, but Kevin waved us on.

Our new house wasn't working out as well as we had hoped. Yes, we had more room and better furniture, and the nightly chorus from stray canines in the forest around the campus was now too distant to bother us. But we suffered a new set of intrusive noises instead. We were too near the steady deep throb of the township's diesel generators to enjoy any real quietude. The 'aid post' just next door attracted many visitors during the day, plus occasional night arrivals for urgent treatment. Worst of all, their rooster would often strut under our slightly raised house at dawn to emit a piercing 'cock a doodle doo' right under our bed.

A death certificate for Gus arrived from the hospital. The recorded cause of death — 'hepatic failure' — was technically correct. Liver failure didn't just happen though. Apart from a reference to falciparum malaria as a 'contributory factor', its cause was unexplained.

Sure, malaria was endemic in the area, but it would rarely kill a healthy adult. Indeed, many college staff had bouts from time to time. Dengue fever was common too, causing flu-like symptoms and sometimes more serious problems, but it rarely killed anyone.

Gus's body had been sent to Port Moresby for cremation soon after the funeral. And we didn't want to intrude on June's grief by asking personal questions. All we could conclude was that Gus had underlying health problems that he hadn't taken seriously enough, and that the medical care he got was too little and too late.

Explaining that to students was not easy. Those continuing from the previous year knew there had been disputes between Gus and headquarters. Many came from environments where sorcery was still practised, and an enemy's mysterious death might be viewed as the outcome of poisoning or supernatural forces rather than disease. Despite our best efforts, rumours circulated.

Bohdan burst into our house one evening: 'The students say there are lights on in the laboratory where Gus worked, and you can hear someone walking around in there at night. Some think it's his ghost!' John went to investigate, only to find Gus's replacement diligently preparing the next day's work. We told that story to student leaders to help them challenge rumours of sorcery. As time moved on, those rumours gradually died out.

John was still mourning heavily though. The bottle of whiskey we kept in the refrigerator for an occasional evening drink with visitors started depleting even on nights without visitors. One Friday night John stayed up for hours, morosely drinking. Tired, I went to bed and left him to it.

Saturday began quietly enough. John was still sleeping heavily, no doubt seriously hung over. I was enjoying a quiet coffee — until I heard him scream!

Rushing to the bedroom, I found John writhing on the bed in a heavy sweat. He looked to be in agony. 'It's my stomach!' he gasped. 'Get help!'

I raced to the aid post next door and ran back with its two medical attendants. They looked in dismay at John, still gasping on the bed, and then at each other. The older man spoke. 'Madam, I am sorry. All public servants in this province are on official one-day strike today. Our aid post is closed. We have been instructed to respond only to emergencies.'

'Well this *is* an emergency!' I shouted. 'Get the ambulance and take him to hospital!'

Knowing that not long ago another expatriate staff member had mysteriously died, they were quick to oblige. With their help, John managed to stand up. He had slept naked under the sheets as usual, and I hastily wrapped a short sarong around his middle. The attendants helped John into the ambulance — really just a four-wheel-drive vehicle with a cot in the back — and drove off at high speed towards Rabaul Hospital.

I collected Bohdan for support and followed in our car. The hospital was at least 45 minutes away, and even with adrenaline kicking in I couldn't drive at the pace of the ambulance. I felt terrified. What would we find when we got there?

A complete anticlimax. John was sitting on a bench outside the hospital entrance under a large sign saying 'Closed Today'. Wearing only a sarong, he looked ridiculous but also absolutely healthy! Relief flooded into me.

As we sat dumbfounded in the car, John walked over. 'Yes, I'm fine now. I started feeling better soon after the ambulance set off. By the time we got here I felt perfectly okay. The aid post staff could see I was no longer an emergency case, so they started to worry about being seen to break the strike. In the end they just dumped me here. I did get in to see a doctor, who could find nothing wrong with me and told me to leave. So here I am — no money, no documents, in just my sarong. I'm glad to see you! Let's go home.'

Relief and annoyance battled within me all the way home. Annoyance turned to anger that afternoon when I found not just one but *two* whiskey bottles under the sink. John hadn't just finished the bottle in the refrigerator — he had drunk the entire spare bottle as well, all in one night! Hardly surprising that his stomach had played up, probably with a severe attack of colic.

We had a stern talk that evening. John had to agree that there was enough trouble around us without stupidity like that. Drinking heavily wouldn't bring Gus back or do anyone any good. There would be no repetition, I ordered. And for once I was obeyed.

But I continued to worry about John. More and more, he was making it his professional and personal mission to 'get Simpson out'. He didn't seem to realise how some might interpret that within the PNG cultural environment of 'payback'.

Meanwhile I was developing a mission of my own. Many good students in the previous year's graduating class had scored poorly in English on the external exams, especially compared with their other subjects. The internal results for the first-year students showed a similar pattern. But those poor results weren't evenly spread. Those students lucky enough to be in my class or June's had done well; the problems lay elsewhere. Some students quietly grumbled about being disadvantaged. Even Bill Tolley agreed that something needed to change, though he still failed to do any of the basics like adequately cover the curriculum or even mark student work.

Instead Tolley hatched a plan to 'even results out'. We would institute 'team teaching', whereby teachers would regularly be swapped between classes. Everyone else in the department opposed that idea, which we felt would just disrupt lessons and relationships. I pushed instead for more rigorous preparation of standardised teaching materials and lessons. I also volunteered to take an extra class again, to give others more prep time. My colleagues agreed. As the department's newly elected minuting secretary, I recorded our key discussion points and agreed actions.

At the next departmental meeting, Tolley refused to accept my minutes and commit to the collectively agreed actions. He declared that as department head, he and he alone would decide future teaching policies. Furious, we all walked out of the meeting. I went to see the principal. To my amazement, Townsend wasn't helpful or even interested. 'If you and Mr Tolley don't get on personally, then that's your problem. I can't intervene in teaching policy or department administration.'

The next English department meeting followed a similar sequence of events. Once more the entire department walked out on Tolley. But this time we *all* went as a group to see the principal, and followed up with memos from each of us to him as principal to document our individual professional concerns and our shared dissatisfaction with how the department was (not) being led. That was the end of Tolley's 'team teaching' notion. Townsend could no longer blame personalities. He asked us to continue our professional work to our best standard for now and take up our concerns with the new inspector who would visit the college next term. We agreed to do that.

23. Surprise! (John)

It was Tuesday, six weeks after Gus's memorial service. Term one would end soon. The college had become calm and business-like. All the new staff had settled in well, Simpson was being investigated and surely would not be returning, and the events of the year before had faded from most minds. Then came the surprise.

Townsend entered the staffroom at morning break and called for attention. Officiously, he read an announcement. 'A Committee of Inquiry into inspection procedures will arrive at the college this afternoon. The Committee of Inquiry is chaired by Mr Gai Luten, the First Assistant Secretary for Education. The other members are an inspector from outside Colleges Division and a representative of the Teaching Service Commission that has technical responsibility for certifying teachers. College staff are invited to individually and confidentially present evidence to this committee if they so wish. The Committee of Inquiry will consider all the evidence and report its findings to the Secretary for Education.'

Townsend looked around, then continued. 'The deputy principal's office will be made available to the Committee of Inquiry for the duration of their visit. If you wish to meet with the committee, make an appointment through my secretary. Please schedule meetings an hour apart and outside your student contact time.'

We certainly did wish to meet with the committee! Bohdan, always impetuous, grabbed the first slot. I was next and last for the day, while Elisa and others booked for the next morning.

But Bohdan wasn't with the committee for long. A few minutes after he went in, I spotted him outside the admin block, beckoning me frantically. I gave my class exercises to work on and hurried over.

'Look at this, John. Before I could say anything, they handed me this document and told me to go outside and read it, to "clarify the professional position before you give evidence". And now I see there's a copy of this paper in everyone's pigeonhole! What the hell is going on?'

I studied the document. It was an official Education Department circular, dated just two days earlier and signed by the First Assistant Secretary — the man chairing this Committee of Inquiry. The circular had, its introduction stated, been issued to 'clarify the inspection procedures that have always been in force and would continue to be applied in the future'. Then the circular proceeded to 'interpret' the long-standing secretary's instructions that had been the basis for my report on Simpson's irregularities. To my amazement, the circular's 'list of accepted procedures' specifically cited all the techniques used by Simpson and disputed by the staff.

'Bohdan, this is ridiculous! This Committee of Inquiry must be a farce, designed by the Education Department to exonerate Simpson. We'd be foolish to participate.'

'But John, if we don't participate, then they will say there is no evidence against him. Don't we have to get our evidence on the record?'

Bohdan was right. 'Okay, let's give evidence, but only under protest. And I will challenge the chairman to explain why this circular has mysteriously appeared now, just before the inquiry began. And ask to see his instructions.'

We agreed how we would individually register our protest before giving evidence. Bohdan returned to the committee's office. I returned to my class.

Forty minutes later, it was my turn. The committee members introduced themselves. We shook hands warily.

It was time to challenge. I held up the circular. 'Mr Luten, I've read this circular that has just been delivered to staff. Why has this circular appeared just now? Is it connected with the problems here last year? And may I see your instructions for this inquiry please?'

The chairman, a heavyset middle-aged national, leaned forward confidently and replied coolly. 'Mr Mendzela, *we*, not you, are the persons appointed to make enquiries here. Our terms of reference from the Secretary for Education are our affair, not yours. But since you ask, of course the circular is connected with the problems here last year. It explains the department's approved inspection procedures, to assist your understanding. If you no longer wish to give evidence to the committee, then you may withdraw.' It sounded like a prepared script.

My script was ready too. 'Mr Luten, issue of this circular is an improper attempt to bias the proceedings of this inquiry. And since you are the signatory of that circular, it is improper for you to chair this inquiry. I will give evidence, but only under protest. Please record my protest, and then I will proceed.' They all ostentatiously made a note.

A tense discussion began. I explained the main points of the objections to the previous year's inspection procedures and answered a few obvious questions. I showed them my inspection report with two stamps on it and asked them what that would look like to future employers. I concluded by giving each member a copy of my report to the secretary on Simpson's inspection procedures.

The chairman leaned forward again, more eagerly this time. 'Yes, we have that report. But we are also concerned with the other report the secretary received, the one that your colleague Mr Gale prepared alleging sexual relations between Education Department officers and students. Can you tell us more about that? Do you have any further evidence we could see?'

Their game was clear now. I wasn't playing. 'Mr Chairman, you have already demonstrated a lack of impartiality. I will not trust this committee with that information.'

Luten glared at me and closed the interview.

The committee of inquiry came and went for the next two days. Some staff who had intended to give evidence withdrew after seeing the chairman's circular. Who could blame them? Why make a futile gesture that would probably lead to payback from the Education Department later on?

Elisa, Mark and several other staff — including two department heads, Kevin Maitland and Ray Curtis — persevered. Each of them had only futile discussions similar to mine. Elisa and Luther raised the additional concern that — contrary to regulations — their department head Bill Tolley had not been inspected or rated. They were closed down on that. Meanwhile the committee took the initiative to request evidence from our principal Townsend, his deputy Isobel, my main department head Grant and Elisa's department head Bill Tolley. We wondered who was really being investigated...

And that wasn't all. Christine visited to tell us she had been requested to give evidence too, at her own workplace on Thursday.

As she excitedly explained that night, Christine had refused to give the committee any of her husband's letters, and 'told them nothing'. But they had still spent hours at her school, closeted with her principal Jim Boone. She explained further. 'I'm sure Boone's one of that gang too. He was appointed two years ago after some trouble at a school on the mainland, maybe even a court case. The national staff don't trust him. In fact, they got up a petition to protest when he first came. But nothing was done.'

And the grapevine informed us that senior officers from Colleges Division had been seen in Rabaul town 'on other business' throughout the committee's proceedings, staying at the same hotel and entertaining their local friends. A friend of ours who was a regular at the hotel summed it up: 'It's been like a gay bar in here this week!' The news that the Committee of Inquiry was a blatant cover-up spread around the college.

An hour had been set aside on Friday afternoon for the committee to meet with the full college staff and answer questions about its work. We were ready. So was Townsend, in the chair. Every member of staff who attempted to discuss the committee's terms of reference, the new circular, or the inappropriateness of Gai Luten as chairman after his production of the circular was ruled out of order. And no member of staff was interested in talking about anything else. The 'meeting' petered out into hostile silence after 15 minutes. The committee members left the campus to fly home.

With the farcical proceedings of the Education Department's 'Committee of Inquiry' concluded, Townsend and Tolley were riding high. And their confident body language showed that as we moved through a week's break and into term two.

. . .

Our group felt subdued and isolated. The only question now was how high the cover-up went. Perhaps the Secretary for Education was being deceived by his subordinates? We decided to give him the benefit of the doubt, for now at least.

I wrote privately and confidentially to the secretary. I politely protested about the inappropriateness of the new circular and the resulting unsuitability of the committee's chairman for that role. I also described the staff meeting with the committee and stated mildly that because of the chairman's circular the secretary's Committee of Inquiry did not 'appear to be fair'.

The secretary replied promptly, in an envelope labelled 'Confidential'. His letter did not respond to my objections, but merely 'noted them for attention'. 'The Committee of Inquiry will make its report to me in accordance with its Terms of Reference, and I will consider that report carefully. In the meantime, I will not entertain further correspondence or communications about these matters.'

My letter and the secretary's reply weren't as confidential as their envelopes suggested. Several days later, Townsend issued a written instruction that any correspondence by staff on matters related to the college must be sighted by him before being sent, and that any letters on official matters received by staff must be shown to him as principal. Chatting in the staffroom, I openly questioned his authority for such a circular. So did others. That got back to Townsend.

At the next staff meeting, Townsend angrily threw two bulky folders on the floor. He stated they were for staff information and contained excerpts from official sources that gave him authority for his instruction on viewing our correspondence. Bohdan quietly asked what Townsend would do if Bohdan wrote to his mother, in Czech, about the college. Townsend retorted that he would find someone to translate the letter for him. 'And I don't mind telling you all that I'm sick

and tired of these issues. To be frank, it's affecting my health.'
Townsend was losing his rag!

We had no way of knowing how long it would take the secretary to
make the next move, or what that move might be. But I could do
other things in the meantime. It was simple to obtain and hand
around to staff a short legal opinion from our lawyer Mr Lapani that
Townsend's instruction on staff correspondence violated the privacy
and freedom of staff members that PNG's constitution guaranteed.
No one — not even Townsend himself — paid any further attention
to his instruction after that.

And the Governing Council finally had its next meeting. It naturally
discussed the visit of the Committee of Inquiry into inspection
procedures. To fully inform the council about the previous year's
events, especially the secretary's remedial actions in relation to college
staff, Mark presented my report and letter again. This time
Townsend lost the vote and both items were tabled. But Townsend
did manage to have the report classified as 'an information paper
only' and have my letter read out without any discussion.

Mark smiled as he described the meeting. 'Actually, the council
members found your letter disappointing. Unofficially, they all know
the underlying issue is homosexual involvement with students, not
inspection procedures. But the students are too ashamed and too
frightened of the authorities to complain, and the council members
are too timid to start any discussion about what is really going on. So
officially, we all tiptoe around that topic and don't even mention it!'

24. Divisions and Diversions (Elisa)

AFTER THE COMMITTEE OF INQUIRY fiasco, staff unity began to fissure. John remained grimly determined to remember last year and see justice done, and our friends supported him. Townsend continued to run his line of a 'professional fresh start' and successfully befriended heads of department and a few of the new staff. Many other staff tried not to take sides. Professional cooperation continued, but the strained atmosphere made work much less fun.

An off-duty entertainment made the split worse. The annual 'talent night' at the sports club should have been a chance for everyone to have a good time. I did some unaccompanied singing, another staff member played the piano, an amateur magician took the stage, and someone even read poetry. But the highlight of the night was a surprise song-and-dance routine spoofing Gilbert & Sullivan's 'Three Little Maids from School Are We'. Mark had persuaded two male colleagues to join him in dresses and make-up, and mince about the stage to the strains of 'Three Little Poofs Gay Are We'. Mark's ingenious lyrics included rhyming gems like 'one chromosome less from infancy' and made unmistakeable references to individuals from headquarters chasing boys around town. The trio had our group and even the neutrals in stitches! Townsend glowered from the bar while those firmly in his camp fought to keep their faces straight.

My department head Bill Tolley was no longer just lazy but also frequently absent from work. Rumours began to circulate about 'a drinking problem'. Tolley's students grew more and more unhappy, and several asked him directly for a transfer to another class (which he of course refused). Bohdan and Luther also struggled with their work at times, but they were usually too defensive to admit that. June and I carried a heavy workload as we prepared materials for everyone's classes and informally tutored individual students from Tolley's classes.

The English department disintegrated as a professional team. Tolley refused to hold any staff meetings and hid his own class results from the rest of us. June and I operated as we saw best without consulting him. The other staff — Bohdan, Luther and a new national teacher Gaius — oscillated between working with us and retreating into a shell of their own. The troubles of the English department became common knowledge amongst the staff, and students who felt disadvantaged grew restive.

John and I quarrelled regularly over what I should do about Tolley's incompetence. I still hoped for some constructive outcome. I had always believed that demonstrating positivism and a helpful approach was the best way to solve most problems. I also knew that change rarely happens quickly. Working with June to provide support and teaching aids for the other teachers and their students was my preferred way forward. John believed only aggressive confrontation could change anything now. The arguments with John left me feeling cowardly and depressed.

· · ·

Matters came to a head over the annual curriculum development meeting for English department heads from all the colleges, to be chaired by Ross Johnston as head of curriculum for Colleges Division. By rotation, this year's meeting would be held in Rabaul. It was an established practice for our head of department to take along all of us — as English department staff from the nearest college — to contribute experience and ideas. But Bill Tolley wasn't having that. He alone would participate in the meeting. 'I can and will speak for all of us.' We didn't agree, but we couldn't invite ourselves there.

Internal exams for term one had finished weeks earlier, and students were keen to know the outcome. All other departments had released results and returned papers to students over a week before. After ignoring multiple requests from teachers and students for English department results, Bill had finally promised a deadline of today. So I was furious to discover that Bill had not just failed to distribute the result list and the marked exams as he had promised but had actually padlocked the list and papers in his office before he left for the curriculum meeting.

In the staffroom at morning break, several teachers complained about the missing results. I explained that the results were locked in Tolley's office. The new head of Expressive Arts department over-heard. 'If anyone needs to get into Bill's office to get anything, I can lend them bolt cutters.'

I decided to take up his offer. 'Thanks Evan, I'll collect them straight after break during my prep period.' Everyone in the staffroom heard our exchange; no one commented further.

Twenty minutes later I walked towards Bill Tolley's office with the bolt cutters, trying to look casual. That wasn't easy. A metre long and heavy, the bolt cutters had conspicuous bright-yellow handles. By good luck I was wearing a vivid yellow dress with large polka dots, so I could hope that as long as I kept the bolt cutters on the side away from the admin block, they wouldn't attract too much attention. I kept my eye on that admin block though — surely someone from the staffroom had tipped off the principal.

Either no one had, or Townsend wasn't around. I reached the door of Tolley's office and set about breaking in. The huge heavy steel padlock defied my attempts to quietly chew away at the shackle. Sweating in the humid air, I abandoned my intent of silence and mustered all my strength to squeeze together the handles of the bolt cutters. With a sharp snap, I was through. The padlock clanged loudly onto the floor. I quickly grabbed the broken lock, entered the office and secured the results list and exam papers. Looking as calm as I could manage, I strolled back to my own office. If anyone had been watching, they stayed mute and hidden.

I immediately distributed the results list and marked papers to my colleagues for onward dissemination to students. Then I returned the bolt cutters to Evan and lodged the dismembered padlock in Tolley's pigeonhole. I added a polite note that explained how I had felt it important to help him deliver on his promise to distribute the department's papers today, despite him 'forgetting' to leave a key to his office. I hid the note and the lock under other papers already there.

I told John my story over lunch. He chortled and promised to watch the admin block from his nearby classroom until Tolley returned. Over dinner, John described what he had seen. 'Tolley came bounding out of his car, head high and looking pleased with himself. He trotted up the steps into the mailroom. Then he emptied his pigeonhole. I saw him hold up the lock and read the note. His grin vanished, his shoulders slumped, and he shuffled out.' I felt well satisfied with that outcome.

The next evening, John drove us into town for our weekly shopping trip. Bohdan, Luther and Christine joined us for dinner. Bohdan boisterously suggested we visit the hotel where most official visitors stayed and have drinks there first. 'The head of curriculum might still be around. We could say hello!'

We stationed ourselves at a table in the crowded bar, just outside the restaurant exit. And sure enough, when we peered in, we spotted Superintendent Johnston in there eating dinner. I waved to him nicely. He pretended not to see me. The last thing he would want to do is talk to us.

We had Johnston trapped! 'Let's take our time here,' I suggested. Johnston dawdled over his dinner. We dawdled longer over our drinks. Suddenly the restaurant door banged open loudly. Heads turned all along the bar. Johnston raced past us at a furious pace, looking straight ahead and almost running as he barged through the bar to the outdoors area. There he skidded forward and rapidly braked, teetering dangerously at the edge of the swimming pool. Recovering his balance, and now the centre of everyone's amazed attention, Johnston scurried down the corridor to his room.

We didn't stop there. June wrote a short letter to Johnston to regret that she had not seen him at Gus's memorial service and then hadn't been able to catch up with him at the curriculum meeting. John wrote him a letter too, to express his personal concern that some staff had interpreted Johnston's absence from the memorial service as a deliberate snub, which was 'of course quite untrue and unfair. It would be good to have an explanation to counter those damaging perceptions.' The letters came back a week later under a note from Johnston saying that he 'would not accept or respond to such correspondence'.

To help forget our professional problems, John kept up our adventurous drives. One Saturday we set out for a mountain village renowned for its beautiful setting. We had been told the village was reachable by road in a four-wheel-drive vehicle — sometimes. I insisted we take companions to give them a break from the norm and to make the journey more interesting (and safer). Several male staff came along, including our national colleague Garemo who could speak the local language of the village. We set out early to make sure we could return before the torrential rain that descended on the mountains most afternoons.

The road proved even tougher than expected — just a narrow dirt track, never straight for long. Deep mud made John's driving hard work. At one point the track disappeared under a landslide, forcing a long off-road detour. We felt a sense of relief and achievement when we crested the last hill and saw a picturesque village far below. A steep but obvious dirt track would take us there. Ignoring the several old and unattended vehicles scattered around at the top of the hill (and my worried question about them), John drove us down and parked at the edge of the village.

The villagers welcomed us warmly and invited us to tour their community. Houses were entirely traditional. A school and a church had been beautifully constructed from bush materials and decorated with colourful flowers and handicrafts. We had brought food and cigarettes to share, and Garemo helped move conversation along whenever our stumbling pidgin let us down.

With clouds gathering for the usual afternoon downpour, it was time to leave. We piled into our vehicle and set off, waving goodbye. But after a few metres, the car floundered and then stuck fast. We got out and saw with dismay that our wheels were no longer even visible. Instead, each wheel had become a massive ball of wet clay. On this terrain, we had no hope of even reaching the steep slope back to the road, let alone climbing it.

A depressing conversation in pidgin with our hosts ensued. No, they confirmed, it was not possible to drive any normal vehicle up or down the steep track. Everyone knew that, because of the wet clay, only a bulldozer could do that. That was why everyone parked at the top and walked down. To have come down here we must have a special vehicle, right?

Wrong. After a few futile recriminations — mainly directed at John — we formulated a plan. We would scrape the wheels clean, gather wood and stones, and build a short causeway over the clay. That would give the car some initial traction. One person would drive while everyone else pushed. If we could create a flying start and the driver gunned the engine in lowest gear, the vehicle might just make it to the track and climb to the top. And we would have to work fast to beat the rain!

John was decisive. 'Elisa, you're the lightest. You'll have to drive.' I started to object, then didn't. In truth, we had no other option. Everyone toiled furiously to complete the causeway. I climbed in and took the wheel. The rest of our expedition and a dozen local helpers stationed themselves behind the car.

I engaged the lowest gear and floored the accelerator. Shedding pushers as they fell behind or fell over, I reached the uphill track. Recalling my instructions — gun forward hard, no matter what — I kept the accelerator floored and the engine howling. My steering had only sporadic effect as the vehicle meandered upward. Halfway up the slope, the car turned and headed towards the sheer 100-metre drop on my left. Terrified, I kept the engine going full blast and twisted the steering wheel hard right. Somehow the vehicle turned away just before going over and slithered upwards again.

After what seemed like an eternity, I reached the summit. Shaking with tension, I stopped the vehicle but kept the diesel engine running in neutral. The rain started a few minutes later: a few drops at first, then a torrential downpour.

I was still shaking when the others finally breasted the top of the slope on foot. Weary and wet as drowned rats they were, but triumphant too. I was the hero of the day!

Still in shock, I was in no mood for celebration. Ignoring everyone's congratulations, I began recriminations. I had just — by great good luck — survived the consequences of a poorly researched trip. And I let fly at John about that.

After a few embarrassed minutes, John took over — 'Let's leave it there for now, shall we?' — and inched us safely home through mud and rain. That night he apologised and described in vivid terms the horror they had all felt when I was sliding to the edge of the abyss and their elation when I somehow miraculously righted the vehicle.

Our tale of adventure, stupidity and heroism made the rounds of the campus and even reached Rabaul town. We hadn't been the first to go down that hill — naive visitors did that from time to time. But we *were* the first to get back up under our own steam, without hiring a bulldozer!

Townsend had a different holiday diversion. He had naturally taken possession of the principal's comfortable residence. Screened by trees from the campus and with its own access track, Townsend had more privacy than most. But not much went unobserved in our small world. It soon became common knowledge that he entertained a male student guest from another part of PNG for most of the week. At the social club, Townsend explained that the young man was an orphan who had recently graduated from a high school where Townsend as principal had befriended him. His supporters gave him the benefit of the doubt. The rest of us wondered.

25. Many Meetings (John)

TERM TWO CHUGGED ALONG. Questions at staff meetings about the Committee of Inquiry outcome elicited no response from Townsend except that 'the report and its recommendations are confidential'. Headquarters was stalling. That wasn't likely to be good news for us.

I kept digging for more evidence. Liaison with Aiyura College unearthed fresh conflict there. One departing staff member had publicised his letter of resignation, which complimented students and staff but expressed shock 'to see such a vast, entrenched, wasteful bureaucracy at the very top of the education hierarchy'. And *their* Governing Council formally resolved to reject any attempt by Simpson to return as inspector, because of the dissatisfaction with his inspection procedures there last year. Luten, the Committee of Inquiry's chair, had been not merely informed but directly involved in all those matters. So had Tavitai, the nominal head of Colleges Division. Yet no Aiyura staff had been interviewed by the so-called 'Committee of Inquiry'. In fact, no one at Aiyura had even known about the committee. All very suspicious.

Our national teaching staff had a fresh idea. Why not tell the *Minister* for Education what was going on? The Minister was a politician, not a bureaucrat like the secretary. As Minister for Education, it was his job to oversee the Education Department on behalf of citizens and voters. Their professional association would be happy to contact the Minister 'unofficially'. We passed on all the evidence given to the Secretary for Education the year before and to the Committee of Inquiry this year. Nothing official came back, just an assurance that the Minister had 'looked into the matter' and that 'something' would happen soon.

And something did. Two weeks later, Townsend read out part of a letter from headquarters to a routine staff meeting. It stated that the Committee of Inquiry had made its report to the secretary, with 11 recommendations. Townsend folded the letter away and continued less formally. 'Only one recommendation has been released so far. It concerns our inspection arrangements. Mr Simpson will not be inspecting Keravat College this year. Instead, we will be inspected by Mr Miller, an inspector based in Lae.'

Good news at last! But not as good as it first sounded. Fielding questions, Townsend revealed that Miller would also inspect Aiyura, the other college that had complained about Simpson. However, Simpson would continue to inspect the remaining two colleges, plus two high schools formerly inspected by Miller. And that was all we would be told. 'The other recommendations of the Committee of Inquiry, and its full report, remain confidential.'

Townsend's announcement satisfied most of the staff. Public discussion lapsed.

I was far from satisfied. At best, we had won a compromise — Simpson had been sidelined and Keravat had a breathing space.

Miller might be okay. More likely not — he had been part of the Ratings Conference that issued our 'Unsatisfactory' ratings a year earlier. And what were the other 10 recommendations about? Was the Secretary for Education acting gradually, or just stalling? As things stood now, Simpson would be free to continue his unprofessional activities elsewhere.

Once again, Bohdan acted impulsively. He returned from town one evening looking smug. 'I've laid a complaint about my unchanged rating with the Ombudsman Commission!'

I exploded. 'Why the hell didn't you talk to me first? And what on earth is the Ombudsman Commission?'

Bohdan gave me an information leaflet that explained the commission's role and a copy of its latest annual report. 'Look here. The Ombudsman Commission protects people against improper administrative actions, *and* it reports directly to Parliament. I heard about them in town and went straight there. Their Rabaul officer said that while the commission looks into my complaint, the Education Department should take no action based on my "Unsatisfactory" rating!'

I read the leaflet and calmed down. The Ombudsman Commission was a constitutional and statutory body that did indeed have the role Bohdan claimed — on paper at least. But their annual report wasn't encouraging. The commission seemed to have a huge and growing number of cases, few successes, and inadequate resources. And it was only an advisory body, with no power to overturn improper administrative actions or enforce its own recommendations.

Our wrangle resumed. 'Your complaint is probably buried under a massive pile. And even if it isn't, making life more complicated for the secretary could be counterproductive. We still need to give him the benefit of the doubt, until we know more.'

Bohdan didn't repent. 'That's easy for you to say. I'm the one at greatest risk. My contract runs out at the end of the year, and if the new inspector doesn't change that rating, I won't get renewed.'

He had a point. Anyway, it was too late to argue. Bohdan's complaint had been filed. We agreed to wait a while and see what happened next before doing anything further, on any front. A phone call to our lawyer Lapani confirmed that thinking.

We didn't need to wait long. At Monday morning announcements, Townsend surprised us again. 'Inspector Miller will arrive tomorrow for his first inspection visit of the year. He will work with me on administrative matters first, and then on Wednesday he will visit all staff due for inspection. The inspector will attend Thursday's regular staff meeting to take questions and leave immediately after that.'

Mark informally sounded out the staff. He reported that the general mood was to give Miller a chance and see what happened. Bohdan, after calling our lawyer Lapani for advice, agreed to cooperate fully with Miller to demonstrate good faith and protect his position. The staff meeting on Thursday would be our chance to ask questions and gauge Miller's attitude.

But that meeting shed little light on anything. Miller refused to share any overall impressions of the college — it was only his first inspection visit. And he could not comment on his visits to individual staff or his discussions with department heads — those matters were personal to the staff concerned. He also refused to discuss inspection procedures, events at the Ratings Conference, or the changed ratings that had followed it. Those issues all fell within the scope of the Committee of Inquiry and so they now rested with the Secretary for Education. Soothingly, he described the secretary as 'the system's final check and balance. What occurred here last year has not been forgotten or ignored. Several matters are still under action and can't be discussed yet. As your new inspector, I'm just following my orders and doing my job.'

Miller's smooth brush-off of every question couldn't be faulted. Unable to hide a satisfied grin, Townsend closed the discussion.

Elisa glumly described how Miller had performed just as smoothly when he met with the English department. Yes, Miller had read department meeting minutes and the memos of concern that English staff had given to Tolley and to the principal. Yes, the term-one student assessments had been inadequate. And, yes, Bill Tolley as someone 'first year in country' should have been inspected last year. But Bill was now committed to making major improvements in all key areas, including support for our two national teachers Luther and Gaius. So, we should all please pull together again as a team in the best interests of our students.

And now that he was aware of all those issues, Miller, as our inspector, had promised he would take personal responsibility for monitoring the department's progress. The English department could expect a lot more time and attention during his next visit. In the meantime, the principal would attend department meetings on his behalf.

Elisa sighed. 'It all *sounded* fine. But it *felt* phoney. I watched Tolley nod and smile the whole time, like someone in on a secret. Anyway, all we can reasonably do is to go along with the inspector's approach.'

Bohdan reported that his personal inspection visit had been brief and formal, with no issues arising. Miller had told him that he would 'restart the process, independently of last year'.

So *officially* the Secretary for Education was still progressing his response to the Committee of Inquiry's report, while our new inspector was saying and doing all the right things. But we suspected that something more sinister might be going on behind the scenes. Could we do something *unofficially* to check?

Yes. We could bring Lapani's offer into play. On our routine Friday afternoon trip to town, Bohdan and I visited his office. We reported events since our last discussion and instructed Lapani to seek the informal meeting with the secretary that he had previously suggested. Perhaps he could find out what was really happening. 'Of course,' Lapani agreed. 'I can meet the secretary on Tuesday when I'm in Moresby on other business. I'll update you as soon as I get back.'

Tuesday rolled into Wednesday. On Wednesday afternoon, we called Lapani's office. 'I'm sorry, he has not returned yet,' his secretary told us. 'He may not be back for a few days. But you could try calling him. He gave me a phone number where he can be reached this evening if I need to speak with him.'

At 7 p.m. Bohdan and I huddled around his home phone. I dialled the number Lapani's secretary had given us. An unfamiliar voice answered: 'Hello, this is the Manu residence.' Bohdan and I looked at one another in surprise — we had apparently called the Secretary for Education's home! Unsure what to say next, I stalled. 'Excuse me, but I was given this number to contact Mr Lapani this evening.'

'Oh, you want Mr Lapani? He is here now, in a meeting. Would you like to speak with him?'

I didn't, or at least not right now. 'No thank you, please don't disturb him,' I dodged. 'I will call him at his office tomorrow.'

The speaker continued, all too helpfully. 'Is there any message? Shall I say who called?'

I quickly disengaged. 'No thank you, that's fine. Good evening.'

Elated, we enjoyed a cool beer. In fact, several cool beers. Next morning, Lapani's secretary called Bohdan to say Lapani would return from Moresby that evening. We arranged to see him on Friday afternoon.

Lapani didn't look happy to see us. Even before we shook hands, he began putting us off. 'I'm very, *very* busy today with many urgent matters. Unfortunately, I haven't been able to do anything more for you since we last met. I wasn't able to see Mr Manu in Moresby. He wasn't at all receptive to meeting with me. I could not even get through to him on the telephone.'

Our faces must have showed shock. 'I know this is disappointing for you. I'm very sorry,' Lapani continued. 'But my advice is that we should take no further action for now. Perhaps you could come to see me again in a few weeks when you know more.'

To my great relief, Bohdan kept quiet for once. Thinking quickly, I recovered myself. 'Okay we understand. Thank you for trying. We'll get in touch again when you're less busy.'

We left his office quickly and waved goodbye to the secretary. I wondered: had she told Lapani about giving us the phone number? Better not enquire.

We drove back to the campus in silence, in our own thoughts. Conferring with Elisa and Mark, our group reached a clear consensus. Something *must* be going on behind the scenes, and it wasn't likely to be good for our cause. And there was no way we could trust a lawyer who lied to us, his clients.

'There's something else you should know,' Mark advised. 'Townsend had a lot to drink at the club last night. He held forth at the bar with a few pals, and I overheard some of their conversation. Apparently, Townsend agreed to become principal only on the understanding that all the troublemakers would be transferred out first. When you got those transfers cancelled, he didn't want the job. But headquarters finally persuaded him that "things would be sorted out another way". That's why he turned up late at the start of the year.'

Mark paused, then continued. 'And since everyone else is talking out of turn, I'll tell you something that, strictly speaking, I shouldn't. At my first meeting as staff rep on the Governing Council, the minutes from last year's final meeting were routinely circulated. The council had been advised to expect a different appointee for Townsend's job, a long-serving high school principal who was a family man and well-qualified. That guy had apparently even accepted the post. Then suddenly and with no explanation, Townsend — a man with no family and weak qualifications — was being appointed instead.'

Mark paused again. 'I've followed that up unofficially with a couple of council members. The impression they got at the time, off the record of course, was that the other guy was "unacceptable to Colleges Division" for some reason. Now we know why: they wanted their own man in here.'

We concluded that either the Secretary for Education was running with the headquarters gang, or he was unwilling to act against them. Probably the same story with the Minister for Education. And that gang would certainly act against *us*. We couldn't rely on anyone in the Education Department, or even on our so-called legal adviser. Going to the media would be unprofessional while we remained in our current roles and probably wouldn't do any good. *We*, not the headquarters gang, were in trouble now.

I played a wild card and phoned Brother David. He was guarded. No, he didn't know any more than we did about what was — or wasn't — going on. And David was not keen to make enquiries. 'John, I'll be frank with you. Some of the people you're challenging have strong support from nationals who are pillars of our church. I can't easily go up against them if the secretary won't. Let's just wait and see what happens.' Our conversation petered out.

Lapani's fee account for 'services to date' arrived a few days later. It wasn't high. We decided to pay it and avoid any further contact with him.

The only option left was to take on the whole system. I decided to prepare a comprehensive complaint to the Ombudsman Commission, citing not just the individuals we knew were guilty of unprofessional and improper behaviour but also the entire Education Department for covering that up.

The break after term two gave me time to do that. I first obtained June's written authority to act on behalf of Gus and use his files as I saw fit. Next, I prepared an overview letter for the Ombudsman Commission. It explained how our group had discovered administrative and professional abuses and tried to bring them to the attention of the proper authorities. But after the Secretary for Education had resolved some immediate concerns, the system had closed ranks. Only after further pressure from the Keravat staff was a departmental Committee of Inquiry appointed. And the behaviour of that committee led staff to believe that it had no intention of dealing fairly with the matters it was supposed to look into.

Now the failure of the secretary to release the committee's report or recommendations confirmed our impression that the department's 'inquiry' had been a ruse to placate Keravat staff. Simpson had merely been transferred away from two colleges for the time being, with no action taken against him. Abuses of the type already perpetrated by Simpson and his supporters were likely to continue elsewhere.

And, I concluded, 'since all normal administrative channels have been exhausted, I am presenting these matters of concern as a formal complaint to the Ombudsman Commission'.

My full complaint began with a narrative that recorded, dated and explained all the relevant events at Keravat over the previous 18 months. It continued with the evidence I had given to the Committee of Inquiry. The analysis then proceeded over six distinct topics:

1. Irregularities in inspection programmes and procedures in colleges, especially Keravat
2. Involvement of Drysdale, Simpson and others in improper activities with students
3. Improper procedures within the Education Department in relation to inspection ratings
4. Attempted deceitful transfers of Keravat staff at the end of the previous year
5. The unfair proceedings and unsatisfactory result of the 'Committee of Inquiry'
6. Recent irregularities concerning the new Keravat Principal, Steven Townsend

I attached numerous appendices. The complaint and its supporting documents made an impressive pile.

Mark took the whole package away for review. He came back the next day smiling. 'Great job, John! I especially like the way you've even nailed Townsend. Apart from his foolish instruction on correspondence, he would probably claim to be 'just following orders'. How did you find out that Townsend instructed our college registrar to issue a Keravat student concession card to his boy visitor, and pay overtime wages to a driver to take him to the airport? How did you get the documentation supporting that?'

'Through the national staff,' I replied. 'They dislike corruption as much as we do, but it's too dangerous for them to take a stand directly. I asked Garemo to do a little digging amongst the college support staff for anything on Townsend, and this turned up. When proving maladministration, small things matter. After all, Al Capone was finally jailed for tax evasion.'

Mark gazed at me quizzically. 'But John, do you really think this Ombudsman Commission process will go anywhere? The corrupt guys are well entrenched, and they run in packs. No one seems able to touch them. If Gus couldn't succeed, how will you? Are you just making more trouble for yourself?'

I shrugged. 'I hear what you're saying, Mark. But I won't give up. Wise or foolish, I'm 100 percent committed.'

I took my package to the Ombudsman Commission office and lodged my complaint.

26. The End is Nigh? (Elisa)

THE COLLEGE YEAR ROLLED ON. I tried to keep our struggle with the Education Department in the background and focus on our students. But teaching wasn't much fun anymore. Miller's promise that the English department would improve proved hollow. Tolley continued to be lazy, often absented himself from work and became downright obnoxious to me. Sometimes he smelled of alcohol.

We had stopped playing bridge with Tolley and his wife some time ago. They found other partners. One of them — a visitor from town — vividly described his last bridge evening at Tolley's house. 'Bill was well gone before we even started. He bid and played stupidly. His wife — playing as his partner — kept making sarcastic remarks about that. Bill had trouble even sitting up straight. Finally, he slid off his chair, dragging the tablecloth and all the cards onto the floor. We made excuses and left. We won't be going again!'

Tolley's escapades came to a head early one weekday morning. A group of students found him unconscious in a ditch beside the playing field, smelling of alcohol. They struggled to lift him out and carry him back home and told the duty teacher what had happened.

Tolley failed to appear for classes that day. He sent in a note that he had been working too hard and had fainted on his way to classes.

Even Townsend couldn't ignore that exploit. He had a private interview with Tolley. Tolley's personal behaviour improved a little, but his professional incompetence and idleness continued. His cover story became 'I'm on heart medication that has occasional side effects'.

Department heads distributed half-year assessments — an important signpost for students — to guidance teachers. I studied the results for my guidance class carefully and compared them with the test papers that had been handed back to students. I found several mistakes in the English results. I asked my English department colleagues to check results for their classes — the same pattern of multiple errors emerged. We immediately raised the issue at a departmental meeting chaired by the principal. Tolley, with Townsend's support, undertook to check the results again. Next day he issued a memo to guidance teachers to say that the results that had been distributed were merely 'draft' and 'provisional'. 'Final' results would be issued shortly.

I'd had enough of Bill's lies and cover-ups. At my initiative, the rest of the English department issued a counter memo. 'The English results given to guidance teachers were not draft or provisional. Mr Tolley had one week to complete his grades after receiving marks. The numerous errors in those grades were only discovered because of the vigilance of guidance teachers and other English staff.' Much to the dismay of Tolley and Townsend, the dysfunctionality of the English department had now been officially communicated to all staff. And it was painfully obvious to our students too, especially those in Tolley's classes.

As he lost respect elsewhere, Tolley became more of a sycophant to Townsend and soon earned the nickname 'Toady'. One night a few of us indulged in a lusty chorus of 'What shall we do with a drunken toady?' with the rousing refrain 'Put him in a classroom until he's sober!'

Dysfunctionality wasn't limited to my department. Weekly staff meetings became ritual conflicts as John persistently asked questions that Townsend couldn't or wouldn't answer. Townsend's line of 'forget about the past' became more credible as memories of Gus's death and the previous year's events faded, and he gradually won over many of the staff. John's group of sympathisers eroded to a hard core of Mark, Bohdan and me, plus private support from Gabriel and the national staff. (We tried hard not to involve June in issues beyond the English department. She was still mourning and didn't need ugly reminders of the past.)

Personal life became unpleasant too. John was often on edge, speculating about what the Ombudsman Commission would do, what was really going on at headquarters and what might happen next. Even our friends found John poor company.

PNG, especially Port Moresby, had a nasty reputation for violent crime. Much of that crime was random, but planned payback could occur too. We felt lucky to be living outside the capital and well away from headquarters. Our surroundings in Keravat had always felt safe. But John grew worried. 'You never know what the headquarters gang might organise. Maybe even violence from local criminals or cronies.'

The growing tension told on me too. I slept badly and grew cranky. One day I lashed out at Aipat. Our small teaspoons kept mysteriously disappearing — we guessed he was taking them and didn't really mind. But then soupspoons went missing too. I blew my top and sent him back to his 'boi-haus' (the small concrete block building behind our house) in disgrace. That evening, I opened a rarely used drawer — and found most of the missing spoons!

During the night I awoke to hear muttering outside. It was Aipat, tending a small fire and moaning to himself. 'Missus' had been cruel to him. 'Mi no bai stilman, me bai gutpela man. Mi no kisim pinis nating.' (I'm a good man, not a thief. I didn't take anything.) I felt guilty. I knew there was a large measure of humbug in this carefully staged performance. But for once, he really was a wronged innocent. I humbly apologised the next morning — 'mi bai sori tru, Aipat' — and domestic work returned to a positive footing.

The break between terms two and three came as a welcome respite from the daily hassles on campus. Bohdan rushed in late one afternoon to offer us a unique opportunity. A mountain village inhabited by the Bainings people, a minority local tribe, was about to conduct an initiation ceremony for its young men for the first time in years. Normally such ceremonies were private. But this time teachers at the village primary school had — as an unusual honour — been invited to attend. One of those teachers was a drinking chum of Bohdan's, and he had invited us to tag along.

Initiation ceremony starts with tribal elders in the background

An hour later, after a hectic drive over dangerous trails, we sat on the ground amid a crowd of silent villagers. Rhythmic drumming gradually grew louder as night fell. Then a large bonfire blazed up in the clearing ahead of us. A dozen young men emerged from the darkness, arrayed in 'garments' made from local plants. Enormous bark masks suggestive of strange Disneyland animals topped off their costumes and hid their faces. The drumming swelled to a climax, then stopped.

In dramatic silence, other costumed figures materialised from the darkness. Hidden behind barkcloth screens painted with serpentine shapes, they didn't seem young. Strong firelight shone through the screens to reveal that several of these figures carried live serpents. We guessed these were the tribe's elders, here to initiate the young men.

A series of individual challenges followed. Each young man in turn approached the elders standing behind the barkcloth screens and answered a series of questions chanted in the local language. Those

An initiate confidently strides towards the fire

proceedings concluded, the elders with their screens and serpents vanished into the darkness.

Fierce drumming recommenced. One of the young men danced quickly through the bonfire. He retraced his steps and stayed in the fire longer. Other initiates did likewise, competing to demonstrate their courage and indifference to pain. One by one, the young men reached their individual limits and disappeared into the darkness. Drumming stopped as the last initiate left.

We had watched a stunning spectacle. Keen to acquire one of the initiation masks, John asked our companion from the primary school how to do that. 'Not possible,' he was told. 'All the costumes must be destroyed, so that those who have been initiated put their boy status behind them. They have become men!' We left deeply grateful for the experience, with only our memories and a few distant photos as precious souvenirs.

Isaac the carver still visited us from time to time. But each time we asked when our promised basket hook would be ready, he seemed evasive — 'mi wokim yet' (I'm still working on it). Frustrated, we decided to take advantage of the term break to visit him at his village. To our amazement, he proudly displayed not the portable basket hook carving we had expected, but a man-sized statue perched on a crescent moon base, all carved from a single tree trunk.

The oversized 1.2 metre "basket hook" Isaac carved

The picture we had shown him as a model had no scale, so Isaac had applied his own judgement. No wonder it had taken him so long to finish. We now had a stunning sculpture, as tall as me, to take home one day.

Townsend enjoyed the term break too. College support staff informed us that he had once again arranged for a young male visitor to stay with him. A different boy this time, who was kept discreetly away from the main campus.

I thought a change of routine would be good for us. We deliberately stayed away from the local club during the holiday week and skipped the Saturday night social that normally brought our small community together. Bohdan stayed away too.

Mark called over on Sunday afternoon. 'There's something you should know. Townsend got tanked up at the club last night. He started feeling sorry for himself, saying all this crap hanging over from last year was making the college an unhappy place. It was damaging his reputation, and even his health. His exact words were — and I quote — "It's giving me the shits!"'

We all laughed. 'Oh, such a shame!' John observed sarcastically. 'If he had handled things differently everything would be sorted out by now.'

'But that's not the important part,' Mark continued. 'Later, I overheard him talking privately with your department heads: Grant Riddell and Bill Tolley. I was cleaning up in the back, and they couldn't see me. First, he swore them to confidentiality, saying he shouldn't tell them anything yet. I couldn't hear all they said after that, but the gist of it was that you two and Bohdan would "get what you deserve". You wouldn't be around much longer, so they needed to plan for that.'

John wasn't fazed. 'That's just talk. I'm not afraid of them. Sure, they could terminate our contracts. But that would cost them money and be highly public. They wouldn't dare!'

Mark wasn't so sure. Neither was I. We agreed not to tell anybody else what Mark had overheard. Not even Bohdan, because he would be sure to talk about it.

Term three began busily on Monday, and we soon forgot Mark's warning. But on Tuesday evening, Bohdan brought more bad news. 'Christine's been sacked from her teaching post on the formal recommendation of an inspector. She has 28 days' notice to leave PNG. Here's a copy of the paperwork!'

John studied the documents, checking them back and forth. Then he looked up grimly. 'I don't think Christine can fight this. She only has a probationary contract. She's not professionally qualified as a teacher. And her work permit is tied to that particular job. What does she plan to do?'

'Nothing,' Bohdan said. 'She told me she's sick of PNG and wants to leave anyway. She's gone to stay with a friend in town.'

Bohdan looked haggard. 'I think I'm next. The inspector is coming back in a few weeks. I'm still stuck with that "Unsatisfactory" rating, and he'll screw me. Just like that other guy did with Christine.'

John wouldn't accept that. 'It's not the same situation. You have a formal contract, and you can't be given another "Unsatisfactory" rating until the end of the year. Your contract runs out then anyway.' He paused, then resumed. 'Let's face it, Bohdan — none of us will get our contracts renewed. We have no legal right to renewal, and they don't have to give reasons for not renewing. Elisa and I have the right to work in PNG, here or somewhere else, for one more year. You have the right to work in PNG only until the end of the year. That's all. You should probably search for a job somewhere else to line that up *before* the new rating comes out.'

Glumly, Bohdan left to start his research. John and I discussed what we should do. There was no point approaching our department heads about Townsend's confidential 'briefing' to them — they would just deny everything. John concluded that we should just carry on as usual and see what happened. 'Don't worry, Elisa. Like I told Mark, they won't dare sack us. Townsend's probably talking nonsense — wishful thinking on his part.'

'Well, maybe they have something else in mind,' I persisted. 'I think we should take action, not just wait. The English department is a disaster. I'm going after Tolley before he comes after me.'

The next morning, I approached June. 'Miller's coming back in two weeks. I think it's time we documented Tolley's incompetence in a formal report to the inspector. What do you say?'

June sighed. 'Personally, I'm past caring. I'm going home at the end of my contract regardless, and I'd like a quiet life until I do. But if you write something up for the inspector, I'll sign it.'

Over the next few days, I prepared a confidential report on Tolley's poor performance as English department head. I pulled no punches. I cited the falsification of class averages the year before as an early warning and itemised his many missed deadlines and unfulfilled commitments since then. I documented the lack of staff meetings, Tolley's failure to give professional support to his other staff, and the excessive workload June and I carried to compensate. I cited specific instances of how his performance had not changed since Miller's visit and described how the English department had lost all credibility with other staff and the student body. And in a tone more of sorrow than anger, I also outlined symptoms of Tolley's apparent drink problem. I concluded that he could not and would not deliver the professional conduct and leadership the English department needed.

June was impressed. 'Well done! No inspector could ignore that. Where do I sign?' I dispatched the report to Inspector Miller, marked 'Private and Confidential'.

College life rumbled on, apparently as usual. Kapti Day came around again, to everyone's great enjoyment. But we noticed changes in our colleagues. Conversations on professional matters grew brief, not chatty. Apart from Mark, Bohdan and June, no one would sit near John or me in the staffroom. The tense atmosphere suggested a storm about to break, with everyone holding their breath. Gossip about Townsend's promise that we would 'get what we deserve' was sure to have spread, and we couldn't blame people for disassociating themselves from potential trouble. But personally, it hurt!

The annual college sports day was a welcome diversion. Maybe even a chance for staff to work as a team again. John's creative suggestion that staff should be able to enter events and compete against students was eagerly adopted. Deputy Isobel chaired a staff meeting to develop a list of individual responsibilities. Looking up at the end, she spoke brightly. 'I think we have most events covered now. Oh sorry, I forgot one thing. Who's for the high jump?'

Bill Tolley immediately volunteered. 'That's me!' I saw June stifle a smile. After my report to the inspector, I felt sure Tolley really would be 'for the high jump'!

Sports day was great fun. John and I entered the 1500 metres and performed respectably. We didn't even mind one of the new teachers losing track of the lap count and making us run an extra 400 metres. In fact, John improved from fourth place to a bronze medal as other contestants ran out of stamina. Everyone enjoyed the prizegiving and socialising that followed the events. Some refreshing unity and fun before the inspector's visit of the next week.

27. Yes, They Would Dare (John)

IT WAS Tuesday after sports day.

The night before, Mark had reported from the latest Governing Council meeting. 'There's no new information to share, I'm afraid. Townsend repeats what he's already told the staff and blocks any questions about the Committee of Inquiry outcome. We spent the meeting time on trivia instead.'

We told Mark about Elisa's report to the inspector on Bill Tolley. Mark agreed that something must happen now. 'It's just eight weeks to final exams. No inspector can ignore an incompetent wrecking a key department. If Miller won't act, then I'll take Elisa's report directly to the Governing Council myself.'

Elisa came home deeply upset. 'Look at this!' 'This' was a handwritten memo from Townsend, informing her that she would no longer be guidance teacher of class 12E — the students she had personally cared for and grown attached to. Deputy Principal Isobel would take over that role. 'They can't do that, can they?' I assured her they could.

We talked through what might be behind this move. Why not remove my guidance role at the same time?

I summed up our conclusions: 'So we think they've done this to stop you checking results for your guidance class and showing up Tolley. Nasty bit of payback, with no care for the students at all. The next guidance classes aren't until next Monday, so let's think for a day or two before reacting. You will still teach English to 12E in the meantime.'

Wednesday morning break had just started when a secretary came through the staffroom door. It wasn't usual to see secretaries in the staffroom. Chatter died down as we all looked at her. She made a strained announcement: 'Mr Townsend wants to see Mr and Mrs Mendzela and Mr Doubek in his office immediately please.' Then she turned around and left, almost at a run.

We knew this was it — whatever 'it' would be. I stood up slowly and calmly. Elisa and Bohdan followed suit. We said nothing to each other or to anyone else. We could feel all eyes on us as we walked the short distance to the admin block. I led the way. Ahead, the secretary held open Townsend's office door.

Then I spotted Townsend on the roadway off to the left, walking *away* from the admin block. 'You want to see me I believe, Mr Townsend?' I called loudly after him. 'Where are you going?' He ignored me and hurried around the corner. We continued walking calmly towards his office. I spoke cheerfully and loudly to the secretary, pretending not to understand the situation. 'Excuse me, Narita, I am confused. How can we see Mr Townsend in his office if he has just left?' She ushered us in and silently closed the door behind us.

Inside, five chairs crowded around a small table. Behind two of the chairs stood national men. One was short, slight and formally dressed in a safari suit; the other was a tall burly individual, dressed casually. Both were strangers to us.

'Please sit down,' said the man in the safari suit. 'My name is Oveo Koi. I am an Assistant Secretary for Education. I have letters for you.' His manner was smooth and rehearsed.

We said nothing. Everyone sat down. Koi handed each of us a large envelope. 'Please read the letter and check the supporting documents. Then if you have any questions, I will try to answer them.'

We opened the envelopes and studied our letters in silence. The letterhead on mine read 'Public Service Commission'. The letter was individually addressed to me and signed in ink by the chairman. Its text was brief.

'The Public Service Commission has determined that it would be in the best interests of Papua New Guinea to terminate your employment contract. Consequently, this letter notifies you that your contract has been terminated, without notice, in accordance with clause 11.1. The remuneration and benefits payable to you under the contract in those circumstances have been calculated and paid into your bank account.'

The other documents in the envelope comprised a sheet of monetary calculations that ultimately arrived at a sizable total and a payroll slip that documented payment of that amount into our bank account. The calculations, based on a total of six months' pay plus gratuity and repatriation allowances, seemed correct.

I looked up and spoke coolly. 'Mr Koi, before I say anything, I would like to check the letters of my colleagues. Then I can speak for all of us.'

He shrugged. 'As you wish.'

The other letters were identical. Elisa's calculation and payment were precisely the same as mine. Bohdan had received a lesser payment reflecting his contract expiry in about four months.

I looked at Elisa and Bohdan. Both gave me the nod. Choosing my words carefully, I surprised myself by speaking with quiet conviction. 'Mr Koi, we do not accept the situation presented in these letters, or your authority to deliver these letters to us in this way. Before responding, we will seek legal advice. Therefore, I have no questions for you at this time.'

While I spoke, Elisa and Bohdan both began taking notes. Koi looked flustered. Our calmness clearly disconcerted him. 'As you wish. But you should know that I have instructed the principal that your duties here at the college are ended, and that as you are no longer Education Department employees you should leave the college premises immediately.'

I replied icily. 'Certainly, Mr Koi. I'm sure we can do that, pending legal action of course.' I looked at Elisa and Bohdan.

Elisa spoke first. 'I have a question first, Mr Koi. What about our students? Or doesn't the Education Department care about them?'

Koi was ready for that one. 'The Education Department and the college will make all the necessary arrangements for your students. They are no longer your concern.'

Pen in hand, Bohdan addressed Koi's silent partner. 'And who are you? Why are you here?'

The man looked embarrassed. 'I'm Mr Koi's driver.'

Bohdan persisted. 'And what is your name please?' The driver looked at Koi, who nodded. The driver gave his name and painstakingly spelled it for Bohdan to write down.

In silence, the three of us picked up our paperwork and left the office. We huddled a short distance away. The bell had rung while we were with Koi, so staff and students were already back in their classrooms. But we knew there were many eyes on us.

I spoke first. 'I think we should leave the campus and talk at our house. I have a class now. What about you two?'

Elisa replied for both of them. 'The whole English department has a non-teaching hour now. We don't have any specific commitments.'

'Good. You two go to our house. Take our car. I'll quickly tell my class what has happened, then I'll walk back and join you there.'

Bohdan demurred. 'John, I think they brought the driver along because they were expecting trouble. We did the right thing to stay cool and put them on the defensive. So maybe we should *all* leave right now, to avoid confusion.'

'You're probably right, Bohdan. But this class is my guidance class, and I want them to hear the truth. From me personally.'

Elisa and Bohdan hurried off. I walked the short distance to my classroom and climbed the stairs. I half-expected another staff member to be there or the class to have gone elsewhere, but everything seemed just as normal. The students looked at me uncertainly, sensing something wrong.

I began in a calm tone. 'I am sorry to say that I will not be your teacher anymore. The Education Department has terminated my contract, with immediate effect. Mrs Mendzela and Mr Doubek have also had their contracts terminated. We have been ordered to cease all duties and leave the college immediately.'

The students looked at me and at one another in dismay but said nothing. Seeing their shocked faces, my calm tone began disintegrating. 'I have been informed that the principal will make arrangements for you from here.' My lip quivered as I struggled to finish. 'It has been a pleasure to know you and teach you. I wish you all the best for the future.' Blinking back tears, I began walking to the door. 'Please conduct yourself well in this difficult situation. Goodbye.'

Still nothing was said. I walked quickly down the stairs. Feeling crushed, but keeping my head high, I marched away from the classrooms and towards our house. Distantly, I heard bangs and shouts from my classroom. I didn't look back.

Elisa and Bohdan were waiting for me. We soon agreed next steps — drive to town and engage a lawyer, an expatriate this time. We wouldn't take the money and run. We would fight.

```
PUBLIC EMPLOYMENT (NON-CITIZENS) ACT 1978

NOTICE OF TERMINATION UNDER CLAUSE 10.1.2


TO:  MRS. E.L. MENDZELA


TAKE NOTICE that upon the recommendation of the Secretary of the
Department of Education, my Commission has considered the said
recommendation and was of the opinion that your employment be
terminated in accordance with Clause 10.1.2 of the Employment
Agreement dated 27/11/79 between yourself and the Independent
State of Papua New Guinea.

AND TAKE FURTHER NOTICE that by virtue of Clause 10.1.4 of the
Agreement, I hereby, give you three (3) months Notice of your
termination as from the date of service of this Notice.  This
notice period will be paid money in lieu.

AND TAKE FURTHER NOTICE that I direct you to cease duty close of
business 26/8/81, and you will be paid all your entitlements in
accordance with Clauses 10.1.4, 10.5 and 10.6.
```

Sacked under clause 10.1.2: "best interests of Papua New Guinea"

28. Opportunity Knocks Again (Elisa)

THIS TIME, I wasn't letting go. 'Well, they did dare, John. You were wrong! Admit it.'

The two of us were sitting in the hotel bar at sunset after a frustrating afternoon. Peter Robinson, the expatriate lawyer we wanted to engage, had not been able to see us for several hours. When we finally got in, for just 15 minutes, conversation focused on engagement conditions and fee budgets while his secretaries photocopied our documents. And Peter hadn't been optimistic: 'You know what this country is like. Any legal process involves a lot of time and money, and powerful people find ways to slow it down. I'll study your documentation and get back to you in a few days.' We left Peter's office depressed, feeling there was no justice in the world. Adjournment to the bar seemed the only thing to do.

John replied quietly: 'I do admit it. I was wrong.' He looked worn and defeated for a moment. Then he perked up. 'But didn't we give them a shock! Instead of being afraid, we took the battle to them. They're not used to that. Gus would have been proud. Let's drink to him.'

I wasn't keen on another round of drinks. We'd had several already.

Before I could say any more, Bohdan returned to the table elated. 'They let me use the hotel phone. Luther is coming to join us, and Christine. If we can't do anything else today, let's at least enjoy some dinner and a bloody good party!'

An hour later, the five of us were ready to order dinner. Luther — my national colleague from the English department — told us what had transpired at the college after we left the campus. 'First there was a lot of noise from John's classroom, and then during the rest of the day more and more students went off by themselves instead of attending classes. Then Tolley cancelled all English classes anyway. Mark and some others went to Townsend and demanded a staff meeting, and we had that at the end of the day.'

Bohdan was eager to hear more. 'What happened at the meeting, Luther?'

'Townsend introduced Oveo Koi, Assistant Secretary for Education. Koi was quiet at first. All he would say was that a decision had been made at the highest levels to terminate the contracts of people who were opposing the Education Department and disrupting the college. The details of that decision "were not open for discussion".'

Luther paused, then continued. 'At first, Koi got lots of questions, even from new staff — about the termination, about the Committee of Inquiry, about contracts, about Simpson and so on. But he just repeated that same line. Then he got aggressive. I remember his exact words: "Listen. Be clear about this. The contracts of those three have been terminated, for good reason. And the same thing can happen to anyone else who opposes the Department or disrupts this college."'

'The meeting quieted then. Mark said that the Governing Council would naturally have concerns and started to develop that theme.

Townsend shut him down, saying that was a matter to be considered in due course. In the end everyone went home.'

After a silence, Christine spoke. 'Luther, you PNG nationals are out of date. In your heads, you are still under colonialism. Your people in high positions are just puppets for those expat bastards. No national stands up to them. So now, let's drink to all those good people from overseas who have had their contracts terminated — including me.'

Luther glowered and didn't reply. I changed the subject to the menu, and soon we were all busy eating and drinking. In fact, we weren't the only ones doing that. The restaurant, normally quiet on week-nights, was crowded. I commented on that.

'Oh, that will be the conference,' Luther informed us. 'The NBC — National Broadcasting Corporation — is holding a conference here, so there are a lot more people around.' He pointed to a rotund and balding national man heading for the toilets. 'Look, there's Rodney Sinclair. He's chairman of the NBC.'

Luther brightened. 'Why don't you talk to him? Maybe he could help.'

John snarled. 'Why bother? Fuck him. Christine's right. We're on our own. No one's going to help us!'

Bohdan stood up. '*I* will talk to Rodney Sinclair.' He strode toward the toilets, unsteady but determined.

As I watched Bohdan wobble out, a familiar face caught my eye. 'Look!' I cried. 'It's our new friend the Assistant Secretary for Education. Maybe we should talk to *him*?'

And, indeed, it was Oveo Koi. He had entered the restaurant alone and slipped onto the bench seat of a reserved table nearby. Koi studiously ignored our pointed stares and quietly ordered dinner.

'Fuck him too!' John muttered. 'Just another puppet!' he said more loudly. John had definitely drunk too much by now! How would I keep him in order?

Bohdan returned, now fast and steady. 'John, I talked with Rodney Sinclair. He has two reporters who want to see us in their hotel room. Right away.' He pointed to the far end of the restaurant, where two young national men stood near the door. They beckoned to us.

John snapped back into focus. 'Great work, Bohdan! We'll go with them now. Elisa, Luther, Christine — keep that little bastard Koi pinned here. Don't let him telephone anyone.'

John and Bohdan hurried over to the two waiting men and exited. Koi watched them leave and looked anxious. I gave Christine and Luther the eye, and we all moved over to Koi's table just as his dinner arrived. 'Hello, Mr Koi!' I began. 'What have you ordered?'

Koi's eyes darted from side to side. He looked desperate to get away. But with me ensconced on one side of his bench seat and the statuesque and shapely Christine on the other, the small man had no easy escape. We both pressed close to keep him trapped. Koi shrank inwards as he gobbled his dinner and rose to leave. But then Luther, seated opposite, wondered whether he and Koi had distant relatives in common. PNG politeness required a long conversation about that. To our amazement, the normally quiet and self-effacing Luther gave an Oscar-winning performance. His enquiry into family connections and ancestors persisted for over an hour. Koi was securely pinned down, like a butterfly on a collector's board. Finally, after about 90 minutes, I saw John and Bohdan returning. We ended Koi's confinement, excused ourselves and returned to our original table (still laden with our long-cold dinners).

'You've been gone ages John! What happened?'

John could hardly contain himself. 'It was terrific! Those young reporters studied at colleges themselves, and they saw some of what went on there. They already knew all about people in the Education Department getting involved with students. But just like us, they couldn't speak out in public before. Now that we've been sacked, they can ask us why, and the NBC can broadcast whatever we say as public information.' He paused for breath. 'They interviewed us and taped everything for the radio. Our story will be on radio news at 11 a.m. tomorrow!'

'But the real credit goes to Bohdan. Tell them what you did.'

Bohdan smirked. 'It was nothing. I just followed Sinclair into the toilets, and there he was — pissing into the urinal. All I said in a loud voice was — "Are you Rodney Sinclair, chairman of the National Broadcasting Corporation?" He lost it for a moment and nearly fell in!' We laughed uproariously. 'Then he stopped pissing and turned around. "Yes, I am. What do you want?"'

'I told him "I was a teacher at Keravat College, and I have just had my contract terminated for opposing homosexual expats who are screwing your PNG students."'

'He zipped up and said, "Come with me!" Before I knew it, we were with those two reporters doing the interview.'

Watching our animation from his table nearby, Koi's eyes widened. He scurried out of the restaurant. Christine and I waved cheerfully at him. Then we gleefully ordered more drinks. I moved onto soda water though — someone would have to drive everybody home!

29. Raising the Game (John)

I WOKE WITH A HANGOVER. I was home in bed, but how did I get here? My mind was blank for a moment. Was it the weekend? Then memory returned vividly: the sacking letter, our coolness under fire, saying goodbye to my students, the long afternoon in town, the lawyer's depressing advice — and finally the miraculous triumph of the radio interviews in the hotel room.

The priority now was to get students listening to the radio news. I had to get onto the campus, even though we had been ordered to leave it.

Elisa and I decided that I would visit the campus to clear personal property from our offices, hand in keys and tidy up any other administrative formalities. And I wouldn't go alone. I'd take an external party as witness, so that we couldn't be accused of stealing college property or any other impropriety. Meanwhile Elisa would hold the fort at home.

I drove the short distance to Father Luke's house. I found him outraged by the sackings. I told him we were taking legal action, but I didn't mention the radio bulletin. I explained my official reason for visiting the campus, and Luke readily agreed to be my witness.

I hadn't explained my unofficial intentions. I drove us into the campus and then around a long circuit past the playing field, dormitories and classrooms. I had chosen my time carefully— morning break. Students milled about in small groups. Some ran to the road, eager to talk. I waved and stopped the car several times but would only say, 'Listen to the 11 o'clock news on the radio!' We could see that message spreading as students rushed to tell their friends.

As I hoped, an unspoken message was spreading too. Sitting in the front seat, and as a tall man highly visible, the much-respected Father Luke was obviously on our side. Luke was certainly embarrassed, and possibly annoyed by my subterfuge, but he just sat still and quiet.

It didn't take long for me to visit our offices, take out the few personal possessions there under Father Luke's gaze, and take our keys to the admin block. Townsend, doubtless warned of my arrival, stayed in his office with the door shut. Isobel met us on the steps. We declined her invitation to come into her office and stood on the veranda instead.

I could see silhouettes inside the wire screen of the staffroom. Many students were no doubt watching too from around the mess hall or somewhere else. Our little drama was being played for a large invisible audience.

Obviously acting under instructions, Isobel took custody of the keys and ran through a checklist of other matters. Shamefaced, she suggested we didn't come to the campus again. 'It's Education Department property, and Mr Townsend is in charge as its caretaker. You can continue to live in your staff house for the time being. The secretaries will deliver any official or personal correspondence to you there.' Father Luke listened carefully.

'Oh, don't worry, Miss Barnes,' I replied with a sarcastic smile. 'We won't come here. People can come and see us if they want. In fact, Elisa and I still have some teaching materials that we were working on at home. Please send our department heads to collect them. They can clarify any teaching issues at the same time.'

I said nothing more and just stared steadily at Isobel. She started to say something, then just smiled weakly and retreated into her office.

Father Luke fumed. 'Not even a word of goodbye, never mind thanks. Disgusting!' I drove slowly around the long way again. This time Luke sat tall, waving and greeting the students we passed.

It was almost 11. I took Father Luke back home and asked him to go and see Bohdan, get him to clear his office and return his keys, and accompany Bohdan as his witness. 'And please do that in a quiet time.'

Father Luke nodded. 'Yes, I will. But wait a minute — what's this about the radio news?'

'Just listen to it first, and then Bohdan will explain. I've got to rush.'

I arrived home just in time for the 11 o'clock news bulletin. Elisa and I listened eagerly. We didn't expect our sacking to be the lead item, so we were not surprised when the announcer first read out international news items and stories about national politics.

But then he ended the bulletin. We weren't on the news at all! Disheartened, we turned off the radio and speculated on what had gone wrong. Somehow the story had been blocked. What could we do now?

Glumly, we started to organise our teaching materials for collection. We were finishing that task at 12.30 when Bohdan burst in excitedly. He looked with dismay at our gloomy faces. 'What's wrong?' he demanded. 'Didn't you like the story on the radio?'

'What story on the radio?' I asked. 'We weren't on the news. The reporters didn't deliver.'

'You're dead wrong!' he grinned. 'It wasn't on the 11 o'clock bulletin, but it was on at noon. PNG time, remember? I taped the 12 o'clock news — here's the tape.'

We listened eagerly. The *lead* story dramatically announced the sacking of three teachers at Keravat College without notice. The newsreader explained that the teachers alleged homosexual abuse of students and administrative cover-ups at Keravat and other colleges, and that they would be taking legal action. It was the type of story everyone hears on the news all the time without paying too much attention. But this story was about *us*, and we felt giddy to finally hear the truth stated in public.

Mark was next to arrive. 'Congratulations! I don't know how you did it, but that story on the news has certainly energised the students. Most of them were in classes and missed the 12 o'clock bulletin, but by now everyone's heard a tape. Several staff have demanded another meeting. The whole campus is buzzing. I don't think much will get done at work parade today!'

I punched the air. 'Great! We won't stop here. *They* sacked *us*. We're no longer professional employees required to be discreet. We're free to tell the whole truth, anywhere we like. I'll call the newspaper and try to get stories running there too. Better yet, I'll go to town this afternoon and see the *Post-Courier* reporter personally.'

I did that, with great success. By Friday morning, radio news had dropped our story from their hourly bulletin as stale. But the *Post-Courier*, PNG's leading and most reputable newspaper, would run it on Monday under the bold headline 'Sacked for Scandal Probe'. The *Post-Courier*'s Rabaul reporter Simon knew some of the students and took a personal interest. The front page was reserved for the outcome of a political conference being held in Rabaul over the weekend, but he assured us that our story would feature prominently on page 3. Simon promised to keep the story running after that with fresh details.

'Sacked for scandal probe'

Three Rabaul teachers claim to have been sacked because of their probing into an alleged moral scandal and abuse of power in high Government posts.

The teachers were issued with termination notices last Wednesday at Keravat National High School, East New Britain. They are Mr John Menzela, his wife Elizabeth, and ▓▓▓▓▓▓▓

Mr Menzela said they were given letters of termination at 11 am and told to stop their work at 1pm the same day.

He said the letters, signed by the PSC chairman, ▓▓▓▓▓▓ gave no reasons other than that the sackings were considered "in the best interests of Papua New Guinea".

Mr Menzela said a teacher, from Tanzania also had been dismissed for similar reasons.

I have been involved in going to the Education Department

and other official bodies with information on corrupt practices within the Education Department, he said.

Mr Menzela said the corruption alleged concerned personal morals and administrative abuses.

He said he was concerned at abuse of position regarding teachers and students.

Mr Menzela said he had compiled reports on his investigations, one for a commission of inquiry set up by the Education Secretary, and one for the Ombudsman Commission.

After the radio news bulletins, PNG's main daily picks up the story (Post-Courier)

Mark came and went, bringing us news of the latest developments on campus. Townsend ordered the students not to hold meetings or discuss our termination, and he threatened disciplinary action if they did. He also refused to hold a staff meeting to discuss 'media speculation'. Angry staff members retaliated by talking directly with students about the background to the sackings. Students started getting angry too, especially boys who felt insulted and furious at being publicly linked to homosexuality. Classes became poorly attended and desultory.

Saturday brought fresh good news. By telephone from Rabaul, Christine gleefully related how she had boldly gone to the political conference and (through national friends) personally met the Prime Minister and Deputy Prime Minister to discuss her case. What had concretely emerged was that she would see a representative from the Prime Minister's office on Monday, while we as the sacked teachers were invited to see that person on Tuesday.

Sunday was even better. 'A thunderhead is building,' Mark explained. Students met on the sports field after church. They now demanded an official explanation for our dismissal and would boycott classes until they got one. Emotions ran high. Unpopular with the students and unwilling to answer their questions, Townsend wouldn't be able to handle the situation.

'Anything could happen now!' Mark concluded.

It wasn't all good news though. Radio news bulletins over the weekend repeatedly featured statements from the Education Department. 'The three teachers were sacked after a formal Committee of Inquiry, set up to look into complaints against them, recommended that action. Their claims of improper activities by the Department or any of its employees have no foundation.' We were astonished. It wasn't complaints against *us* that the Committee of

Inquiry had been set up to investigate! But, of course, most listeners wouldn't know that. The Education Department was playing dirty.

Sunday evening was conference time. Our group agreed that legal action and publicity were progressing well. The students, now advised by vocal supporters amongst the staff, would put public pressure on the Education Department. We three sacked teachers would avoid contact with students, so we could not be credibly accused of stirring up trouble. Our house was well away from the campus, so that was fine. Bohdan's house was on the campus, but on a dead-end track away from routine activity. He agreed to stay inside and come and go only by car. Mark and June would keep everyone informed.

Monday brought a blur of activity. I drove into town with Bohdan while Elisa again held the fort at home.

First stop was the *Post-Courier* office to update our sympathetic reporter, Simon. He took lengthy notes and sketched the next day's front-page headlines: 'School Out on "Probe" Sackings'. Next, we visited the Ombudsman Commission office to ask that the commission now urgently investigate both our original complaint and our subsequent contract terminations. The Rabaul officer assured us that he had heard the news bulletins and had already contacted head office.

Then we made ourselves visible around town, saying hello to as many people as possible. We lunched at the hotel before visiting our lawyer, Peter Robinson.

Peter had heard the news bulletins. He now showed strong interest in our case. We brought him up to date on events. After listening to a tape of the Education Department statements that had been broadcast on the radio news, Peter drummed his fingers for a few minutes.

Reaching a decision, he spoke in a tone of authority. 'I'll make a phone call now. You can listen — but don't make a sound.'

Peter dialled a number from memory. When the other party answered, he spoke smoothly but with urgency. 'Hello, this is Peter Robinson. Please put me through to the chairman. He knows who I am. I need to speak to him urgently on client business.'

Bohdan and I looked at one another in surprise. Another stroke of luck.

After a short delay, a brief conversation ensued. Peter summarised the outcome briskly. 'Let's be clear Rodney. The National Broadcasting Corporation has repeatedly broadcast bulletins that completely misrepresent the situation. It is not my clients who were subject to a Committee of Inquiry. That makes your bulletins defamatory and professionally damaging. It's irrelevant what the Education Department told you — we both know that legally the Broadcasting Corporation as publisher is the liable party. You can do what you like about it, but I will speak to my clients tomorrow about a defamation suit. Thank you and goodbye.'

He turned to us. 'That will close down any more Education Department statements on the radio, for a while at least. You carry on quietly doing what you're doing now, and we'll see what happens next. Just make sure you don't do anything that could be construed as you personally stirring up the students.' We drove home happy.

Our group met that evening to report progress and plan next steps. An official boycott of classes was now operating. The students had declared to the principal, with dignity and through the proper channel of their male and female captains, that they would not return to classes unless the Secretary for Education visited the college and explained his actions to them. Shocked into a response, Townsend had promised to communicate with the Education

Department. He ordered staff to stay away from the students; they should instead perform administrative duties or prepare teaching materials. Isobel and some heads of department were complying with Townsend's orders, but most staff now openly defied him. They were either talking with student leaders about the crisis or helping individual students with their studies.

Tuesday would be another busy day in town for Bohdan and me, while Elisa would again have to hold the fort at home. The most important activity would be our confidential meeting with the Prime Minister's representative. Our group would reconvene in the evening at our house. That way Elisa, Bohdan and I would stay off campus, while Mark and June could not be accused of neglecting their duties.

PNG "Post-Courier" Tuesday, 1/9/81

School out on 'probe' sackings

Most of Kerevat National High School's 440 students boycotted classes yesterday amid controversy over the sacking of three teachers.

Only a handful of students in each class attended lessons.

But the protest was peaceful and free of trouble, students and staff at the school in East New Britain Province said.

The three sacked teachers have alleged victimisation for their role in probing and complaining of administrative abuses within the Education Department.

One of the teachers, Mr John Menzels, said they were given termination notices at 11am last Wednesday and told to stop work at 1pm the same day.

Homosexuality claim

The letters, signed by PSC chairman Mr ████████ said only that the sackings were considered "in the best interests of Papua New Guinea," he said.

The Rabaul representative of the Ombudsman Commission has visited the school after complaints and a written report from the teachers.

It is believed previous complaints last year and early this year involved allegations of homosexuality in reports that were "hushed up".

On Saturday night, students at the school mess were warned by senior staff not to create any trouble or the school could be closed down and staff dispersed to provincial high schools.

Later, a radio report quoted the Secretary for Education, ████████ as saying students should not listen to people no longer on the teaching staff.

He said the sacked teachers had been careful not to advise students on action concerning the dispute.

The teachers had cautioned students against doing anything that could harm their exam prospects, ██████ reportedly said.

A spokesman for the sacked teachers said yesterday legal advice was being sought on "certain statements".

And the students were told yesterday to expect senior Education Department officers to visit the school to answer their questions.

In reply, the students demanded "this should be done soon".

Students demand answers, and will boycott classes until they get them (Post-Courier)

30. Personal Exchanges (Elisa)

TUESDAY STARTED BADLY. Grant Riddell, John's head of Maths Department, knocked on the door early. John was still getting dressed, so I opened the door and invited Grant to take a seat.

Before Grant could sit down, John emerged from the bedroom. Grant started to say hello, but John interrupted curtly. 'This is my home, and I didn't invite you. Just say why you're here and what you want.'

Grant's smile disappeared. He remained standing. 'All right, let's stick to professional matters. Isobel told me that you and Elisa still had some teaching materials from the college. I've come to collect them.'

'Fine,' John said. He brought over one of the two piles of books and papers we had gathered up and handed it to Grant. 'Take this. Tell your corrupt bosses that's everything for maths. And when is your good friend and professional colleague Mr Tolley coming for English department property? Or is he too gutless?'

Grant bristled. 'There's no need for that tone. We've always been professional and civil with one another, and I don't see why that has to change. But if you want to be aggressive, maybe you can explain why your class rioted immediately after you went to see them, before you even left the campus. How professional was it to stir students up like that?'

John was unrepentant. 'Rioted? Don't talk rubbish! I know exactly what happened there. Mark was teaching next door and he heard every word I said. I told them I couldn't be their teacher anymore because my contract had been terminated, and I asked them to conduct themselves well. Then I said goodbye and left. Naturally they were upset and probably turned over some of the desks before leaving the room. That's all. Is that explanation good enough for you? Or do you want to make an issue of it?'

'No, I'll leave it at that,' Grant said icily. 'And I confirm that I have your keys and that your office is clear and tidy.'

'Well, that's everything then.' John turned away.

Grant didn't. 'There's one more thing. Bill Tolley felt he might not be welcome here, so he asked me to collect the English department materials for him.'

John brought over the second pile and dropped it on the floor at Grant's feet. 'Tolley's right. He's not welcome here. And neither are you. This house welcomes only competent and ethical staff who care about the welfare of their students. That rules you out once, and him twice.'

John stood close to Grant with folded arms and spoke angrily. 'There's the rest of what you came for. Pick it up, then piss off and don't come here again!' Grant coloured up. Without another word, he bent down, picked up the second pile of papers, left without closing the door, and drove off.

I was furious. 'Did you have to do that, John?' I challenged. 'We want people on our side. Grant may not be a friend, but you don't need to make him an enemy. So why do that?'

John glared. 'Because I wanted to. I'm sick of timeservers like him who talk about professionalism but don't show any when the pressure comes on. They can all piss off!'

The strain of our situation was affecting John harder than he realised. I knew Aipat was listening from the backyard. He might not understand what was said, but he would certainly know if John and I quarrelled. We needed to maintain a united front, so I didn't press the point any further.

John left for town grumpy. But he returned in the evening elated.

'Just as promised, Bohdan and I had a confidential discussion with a guy from the Prime Minister's office. He's not just some minor bureaucrat. He's a sort of regional operative in the Security Intelligence Service, which reports to the Prime Minister. We met at the hotel and he took us away to an unmarked office that was very secure and very well-equipped. He listened carefully, asked good questions, and took notes and names.

'At the end he told us that even though homosexuality is illegal, the government doesn't like to prosecute people for it. But they won't put up with people using their official positions to abuse citizens. Especially expats abusing young nationals. They already knew about that sort of thing going on through the Education Department, but they had no evidence. Now, after talking with Christine and us, they have. He will compile a report for his superiors and they will act quietly behind the scenes.'

I wasn't convinced. '*Another* report? How long will it take to "act quietly behind the scenes"?'

John looked rueful and strained again. 'Okay, I know how you feel. But right now, I've had it. I know it's early, but I'm exhausted. I asked Bohdan to update Mark and June. I don't want to see anybody or talk about anything. I just want to get some sleep.'

A car drove up outside, followed by a quiet knock at the door. I answered. It was Father Luke.

'Hi there!' he said cheerily. 'I hope everything's okay?' He sat down, and I went to the kitchen to make us all a hot drink.

John growled. 'Yes, everything's okay — if you call getting sacked for doing the right thing okay.'

Father Luke put on his best pastoral manner. 'Can I do anything to help?' I knew he was sincere, but in our current circumstances he did sound trite and false.

John blew up. 'Yes, you bloody well can! We're in the firing line, not you. Instead of being mealy-mouthed, why don't you take a public stand and write a letter to the newspaper?'

Father Luke jumped up, offended and furious. 'Mealy-mouthed, am I? Well, I bloody well will write a letter to the paper. Good night to you!' He stalked out, banging the door as he left. Father Luke had never to my knowledge sworn before — so I knew how upset he must be.

I was upset too. 'Well done, John! How to lose friends and antagonise everyone. And fancy swearing at a priest. What an idiot you can be!'

We wrangled for a time. Then, out of energy, I went to bed. John hit the whiskey bottle.

I couldn't sleep, and I didn't want John drinking all night. I was about to creep out and attempt a reconciliation when I heard a car drive up, followed by a loud knocking on the door. From the bedroom door, I watched John answer. It was Father Luke again.

He stood in the doorway holding up a piece of paper. 'Will this letter do?' he asked with arched eyebrows.

I quickly took over the situation and ushered the priest in.

John silently sat down with the letter and read it carefully. Then he smiled. 'This letter will do just fine, Father. Thank you very much.' He began to chuckle. 'Would you like a whiskey? You've certainly earned one, and I owe you an apology for being so rude before.'

The tension broke. Father Luke read out his letter. It was a strong public statement supporting the sacked teachers and their claims. As a minister of the church, he could testify from his own personal knowledge that 'the sacked teachers are being victimised for probing the wrongful behaviour of senior officers in the Education Department'. John congratulated him on a great letter, and soon we were all laughing together. John apologised several more times for his behaviour. 'Sorry, Father, but I'm afraid things are getting to me these days.'

Father Luke brushed away the apology. He was feeling proud of himself. 'I'm glad you like the letter. I'll take it to the newspaper office first thing tomorrow.' He looked doubtful for a moment. 'Of course, the bishop may not approve, but I'll worry about that later. I'm not asking his permission.' A rueful smile crossed his face. 'Regardless, I'll have to do penance for losing my temper, and for swearing.' He took his leave.

We went to bed. John fell asleep straightaway. But I tossed and turned for a long time as I wondered what the next day might bring.

31. War of Attrition (John)

THE NEXT FEW days were quieter, for us at least.

Colleagues brought us messages and news from the campus. Individual students, small groups and even complete classes sent us emotional letters and touching personal gifts. But we also heard that some students had more mixed views. A rumour circulated that we had been paid vastly exaggerated sums of public money. And some male students who had endured catcalls of 'homo' when visiting town were furious with us and the media about that.

The student boycott of classes was completely solid, fuelled by a single simple demand that Mr Manu, Secretary for Education, visit Keravat in person to explain matters to them. Townsend hid in his office — all he would say was that he had informed headquarters of the situation. And most staff backed the students, not Townsend. We decided we could relax our 'no contact with students' policy. We would still stay away from the campus, but individual students could visit our house in their normal free time. Several groups from our guidance classes did that, and it was great to chat and laugh with them again.

Media coverage of what had become known as 'the Keravat affair' continued. On Wednesday morning radio news read out a brief statement from the Secretary for Education. He had 'not authorised the accusations about the sacked teachers that had been broadcast over the weekend'. Well done, Peter! And to our great delight, on Thursday and Friday radio news bulletins included fresh facts about the sacked Keravat teachers: the attempts to bribe us with promotions, the attempted transfers to remote places, our changed inspection ratings and the involvement of a fourth teacher who had suddenly and tragically died. The reporters at the Broadcasting Corporation were using the documents we gave them to keep the story bubbling.

PM's man probes school

P.N.G. "Post Courier" Wednesday. 21.9.83.

An officer from the Prime Minister's Department is investigating complaints from teachers about alleged irregularities in the East New Britain Education Department.

The officer, based in Rabaul, is believed to be looking into the Keravat National High School controversy and related matters, after teachers saw the Prime Minister, Sir Julius Chan, and the Deputy Prime Minister, Mr Okuk, in Rabaul last week.

Teachers had complained about the conduct of education department staff at Keravat over the past two years and the treatment of teachers who had disputed decisions.

The officer has interviewed teachers who were at Keravat before being transferred.

Meanwhile, students at Keravat decided yesterday to boycott classes until they see senior staff from the Education Department headquarters at Waigani.

The boys' school captain, ████, said students and their leaders had decided to boycott classes today, tomorrow and next Monday.

He said senior officers had been expected at the school Tuesday this week, but were now scheduled to arrive next Monday.

He said students were upset at claims of sexual contact between teachers and students.

"There is no truth in such claims," he said. "It may have happened in the past but there is nothing like that now and we are concerned about this for the current students and those coming here in the future."

Expat query

Meanwhile a teacher has claimed that expatriates without proper qualifications or training were holding senior positions in the Education Department.

"The termination of three teachers (at Keravat National High School) highlights a widespread problem within the Education Department," a spokesman for the sacked teachers said yesterday.

● Sir JULIUS . . . probe into East New Britain education "irregularities."

Our secret meeting with the Prime Minister's security service is leaked (Post-Courier)

Meanwhile the *Post-Courier* ran daily stories about the sackings, our claims about the Education Department, and the growing student unrest at Keravat. A small story, 'PM's Man Probes College', appeared, based on information from Christine. Father Luke's letter was published on Thursday, under the bold headline 'Chaplain Backs Sacked Teachers'. A dramatic interview with the female college captain ran under the headline 'Students Ready to Battle — Keravat Sackings Spark Fight Mood'. Not to look out of touch, *Niugini Nius* — the other national newspaper — began running copycat stories.

Not everything went our way though. We were dismayed to see the headline 'PM Denies Keravat Investigation'. The Prime Minister's office officially denied that any investigation by them into the Keravat affair was under way or would occur. We found out that Christine had talked up her meeting with the Prime Minister not just to the newspaper but all over town, and unsurprisingly he had backed off from direct involvement. One battlefront closed down — bloody annoying!

Chan denies school investigation

The Prime Minister, Sir Julius Chan, told Parliament last week he had been misrepresented by the Post-Courier in a report of alleged irregularities in the East New Britain Education Department. Thursday's report said a Rabaul-based officer of the Prime Minister's Department was investigating the Keravat National High School controversy, after teachers had met Sir Julius and the Deputy Prime Minister, Mr Okuk, in Rabaul. Sir Julius told Parliament neither he nor Mr Okuk had met Keravat teachers in Rabaul to discuss the issue.

Sir Julius also denied any knowledge of an investigation by an officer of his department.

He had given no instruction for an investigation, he said.

He said the Post-Courier report was an attempt to have him "personally involved" in the matter.

Confidentiality destroyed, the PM (officially) ends investigation #3 (Post-Courier)

My mood wasn't improved by a phone conversation at June's house. Her message that *Niugini Nius* wanted to talk to me sounded encouraging. But their reporter interrupted my attempt to tell him our story. 'Okay, I've heard about that. But all that administration and contract stuff is boring. If you want us to splash a story, we need to know more about these homosexuals and what they do. That's the kind of detail our readers want: Who's screwing who?' I told him that wasn't the sort of reporting we wanted to encourage. We couldn't agree, and he hung up. That quenched *Niugini Nius*'s interest; after Friday they printed nothing more for a long time.

Elisa and I made our usual Friday afternoon trip into town to buy groceries and dine at the hotel. But we first followed our new 'shopping' routine — call in at the *Post-Courier* office to see Simon, visit the officer at the Ombudsman Commission (who was in regular contact with his head office in Moresby), and drop in on our lawyer Peter.

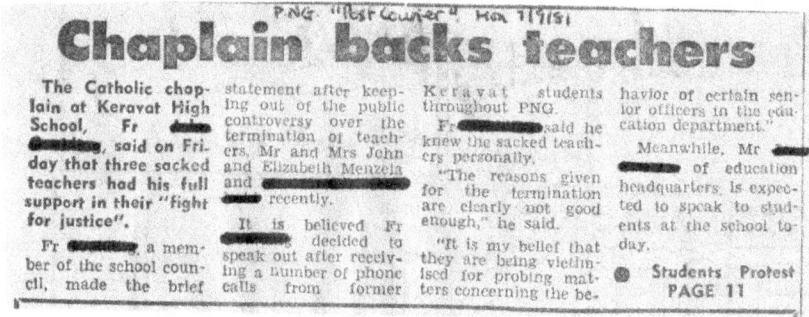

Chaplain backs teachers

The Catholic chaplain at Keravat High School, Fr ██████████, said on Friday that three sacked teachers had his full support in their "fight for justice".

Fr ██████████, a member of the school council, made the brief statement after keeping out of the public controversy over the termination of teachers, Mr and Mrs John and Elizabeth Menzela and ██████ recently.

It is believed Fr ██████████ decided to speak out after receiving a number of phone calls from former Keravat students throughout PNG.

Fr ██████████ said he knew the sacked teachers personally.

"The reasons given for the termination are clearly not good enough," he said.

"It is my belief that they are being victimised for probing matters concerning the behaviour of certain senior officers in the education department."

Meanwhile, Mr ██████ ██████ of education headquarters is expected to speak to students at the school today.

● Students Protest PAGE 11

Father Luke charges in (Post-Courier)

We felt perky. I observed to Peter that the battle was going well, and we now seemed to have a chance of winning. He looked at me with surprise. 'You came in here and asked me to take up your case, knowing that would cost you money. I presumed you wanted to fight and win. Why else would you ask me to take up the case?'

'Because we wanted to do what was right and embarrass those who were doing wrong. We were happy to spend money just to achieve that. We didn't expect to win.'

Peter just shook his head and rolled his eyes.

P.N.G. "Post Courier" Mon 7/9/81

STUDENTS READY TO BATTLE

Keravat sackings

spark fight mood

Students claiming to represent the majority of Keravat National High School students say they will "fight for what is right".

███████████ and ████████ said last week that Keravat students weer shocked over the sacking of three teachers on August 26.

"If everything had been normal, the three teachers would have been given three months notice. Instead, they were given three months pay for nothing and notice at 11am to leave at 1pm the same day." Ms ██████ nd Ms █████ loi said.

"Our main concern is the reasons behind these sackings and why the hurry to get them out so quickly."

They said Keravat student leaders were now supporting the views of the bulk of the students, although one or two student leaders still voiced "the administration's views".

Ms ██████ and Ms ██████ said: "The people concerned did not consider our education —especially the grade 12—as our exams are only eight weeks away.

"It's our country and we are the leaders of the future. We care for what goes on. Keep the good and fight the bad. We will go on fighting for what we believe is right."

The students will "fight for what is right". (Post-Courier)

At the hotel afterwards, that conversation with Peter stayed in my head. 'No wonder we seemed a bit strange to him,' I observed to Elisa and Bohdan. 'We were being naïve then. It's not enough to be right. Let's toast — from now on we're fighting to win!'

That evening Mark came round with exciting news. 'Well, folks, we are progressing! Townsend announced today that a different Assistant Secretary for Education — Tavitai, the one heading Colleges Division — is flying over from Moresby. He will speak to the students on Monday.'

'Oh him!' I said scornfully. 'Elisa and I met Tavitai over dinner when we first arrived. In fact, that's the only time we saw him. He may be in charge of Colleges Division on paper, but we saw then how Simpson treated him as just a figurehead. There's no value there!'

'I'm not sure about that,' Mark mused. 'The students are organising their meeting with Tavitai directly, not via Townsend or the staff. They don't want any expats around. In fact, they won't allow any staff to attend — so we'll have a quiet morning. Tavitai will meet with the staff separately in the afternoon.' Mark grinned. 'Townsend's not looking happy!'

'Oh, the poor man. Perhaps he's got the shits again,' Bohdan suggested. We guffawed and had another beer.

Gaining in confidence, we spent a pleasant Saturday receiving a steady stream of student and staff visitors. I realised we hadn't had a real day off, away from our troubles, for ages. I suggested to Elisa that we spend Sunday afternoon at the beach and then dine in town. Bohdan and a couple of the national staff would join us.

A relaxed Sunday ended with dinner and wine at the usual hotel. Our party wandered into the bar for a nightcap before driving home,

Bohdan in the lead. He stopped abruptly in the doorway. 'Look who's at the bar. It's Assistant Secretary Tavitai! Why don't we go up and talk to him?'

Elisa objected. 'That's a bad idea. It can't do us any good. Let's just go home!'

Bohdan wasn't dissuaded. He led the way up to the bar. 'Good evening, Mr Tavitai,' he said loudly. 'What a surprise to see you here! Don't you remember us? We used to work for you at Keravat College before your Education Department sacked us.'

Other patrons stared as Tavitai turned around. He looked nervous but stood his ground. 'Yes of course I remember you. But I am here on official business, and I do not want to talk to you, especially in a public place.'

A thought flitted across my mind: might a private discussion with him achieve something positive? But I boiled over uncontrollably instead. 'And why would *we* want to talk to *you*, Mr Tavitai? You are not really Assistant Secretary for Education. You are just a puppet for the expatriates who tell you what to do. Why should anyone want to talk to a puppet? Especially a corrupt puppet?'

We now enjoyed rapt attention from everyone in the bar. Tavitai recoiled a little, but he stayed calm. 'Would you care to repeat that remark? In writing, perhaps?'

Elisa quickly pulled us away. 'This is crazy. Let's get out of here — now!' She was right of course. We needed to withdraw. I took a deep breath before speaking again. 'Enjoy your day at Keravat tomorrow, Mr Tavitai.' I stalked out. The others followed.

32. Temperature Rising (Elisa)

MONDAY DAWNED HOT AND BRIGHT. We stayed off campus and out of sight. Staff visitors kept us in touch with events.

As Mark predicted, staff passed a quiet morning. The entire student body decamped to the secluded sports field behind the boys' dorms, where a tense Assistant Secretary Tavitai joined them. That meeting lasted several hours, and the students remained there to talk privately long after Tavitai had walked back down to the admin block, looking gloomy.

The day of meetings continued. The students resumed their private discussions after lunch, while staff met with Townsend and Tavitai in the staffroom for two hours. And then Tavitai met with a deputation of student leaders who waited for him outside the admin block, before returning to the principal's office for a closing discussion with Townsend.

After an early dinner, our core group convened at our house — me, John, Bohdan, Mark, Father Luke and June. Mark informally took the chair. 'Right, let's first confirm the current position and how we got there. Then I have a surprise for you.' He described the frustrations of the staff meeting. 'Tavitai had promised to brief us. But he refused to say anything about his meeting with the students, except that he had answered their questions and strongly advised them to end their boycott and resume their education.'

June interrupted Mark's narrative. 'And then the storm broke. I've never seen the staff so angry. Just about everybody had questions for Tavitai, and they weren't polite about it. Townsend had all he could do to keep the meeting in order!'

Mark consulted his detailed notes of the meeting and resumed. 'It took a long time to sort all the issues out. But here is what we were told, or not told:

- The Education Department acknowledges that Mr Drysdale had behaved improperly with students, both privately and in the course of his duties. Since he has left PNG and his current whereabouts are unknown, no further action will be taken, and no further discussion should occur. Former principal Mr Beckham behaved properly in that matter.
- Several Keravat staff made allegations of similar behaviour by Inspector Simpson and other Education Department officers and brought those allegations to the attention of the Secretary for Education. The secretary established a Committee of Inquiry. After thorough investigation, the committee found no substantial evidence of wrongdoing by any of those officers, who will all continue in their current roles.
- Four Keravat staff who were inspected by Mr Simpson last year attached objections about his inspection procedures to their personal reports. The Secretary for Education reviewed those objections and changed the ratings on two

of the individual reports. He also recognised the need for greater clarity about inspection procedures. Accordingly, a circular was issued immediately before the Committee of Inquiry visited Keravat to clarify the official position in those matters.

- The Committee of Inquiry gave the secretary a confidential report. One recommendation was to terminate the contracts of three teachers. That has been done.
- In response to staff concerns, the committee also recommended new inspection arrangements for colleges for this year. Those arrangements are proceeding. Colleges Division will determine inspection arrangements for next year at the appropriate time.
- The terminated teachers have made misleading public comments that have unfortunately been reported in the media. In response, the Education Department has stated its official position and is now considering appropriate legal remedies.
- Keravat students have naturally been affected by this series of unhappy events, and some have reacted inappropriately. The Department has thus far been tolerant. That tolerance will now end. Any students who do not return to classes tomorrow morning and properly attend future classes will be disciplined and if necessary expelled.
- Keravat staff are required to perform their duties under the authority of the principal and must refrain from discussing these matters any further.'

There was silence for a time as we digested Mark's summary. 'And how did the staff take all that?' I asked.

Mark beamed. 'Well, we had the usual crew toeing the Department's line — Deputy Isobel, Toady Tolley and Grant

Riddell from maths department. A few of the new staff were quiet too. But there was plenty of challenge. Gabriel, the national staff and two of the new guys — Glen and Tim — led the charge. Why was the Department more concerned with its own power and administration than with student welfare? Why did it ignore good professional practice for inspections, and invent new rules to justify Simpson's behaviour? What right did the Education Department have to gag staff and prevent discussion of professional matters, in a democratic country? What was the department doing to meet its responsibilities for welfare of minors under Section 38 of PNG's constitution? And so on. Tavitai stuck firmly to his script — what I just outlined.

'Townsend came in for stick too. What did he consider *his* responsibilities to be? Why was he siding with headquarters against his own staff and students? Townsend wouldn't answer.

'And, of course, all the time there was an untouchable topic — Gus. Tavitai avoided mentioning him directly, and no one else wanted to out of consideration for June.

'Finally, everyone got tired of going round in circles, and Townsend was about to end the meeting. Then June threw in a grenade.'

June looked pleased with herself. 'All I did was ask Tavitai to explain why no one from the Education Department attended Gus's funeral. Tavitai looked blank for a moment and then said, "That is incorrect. Superintendent Johnston from my division attended, to represent the secretary. He told me so himself, the next day at headquarters."'

Mark beamed again. 'Four or five people spoke up at once, saying Johnston *didn't* attend the funeral. Tavitai looked around the room and couldn't argue. He turned to Townsend, who explained that Mr Johnston arrived too late due to a misunderstanding. But he had presented official condolences to the college.'

'You could have heard a pin drop for a few seconds. June spoke up again. "I don't recall you telling me that before, Mr Townsend."

'Then she looked straight at Tavitai. "And what else don't you know, Mr Tavitai? Perhaps you've got other things wrong too?"'

Mark chuckled. 'Neither of them replied. They just mouthed like stranded fish for a few moments. Then Townsend quickly thanked Tavitai and closed the meeting. Tavitai left the campus without another word to — or from — any of the staff.'

John asked what we all wanted to know: 'What happens from here?'

Mark replied thoughtfully. 'The students, not the staff or the principal, have decided that. My class captain came to me to explain. The students will return to classes tomorrow and continue to attend on Wednesday. But they told Tavitai that unless the Secretary for Education comes personally to the college by Wednesday afternoon, the boycott will resume. And it will continue indefinitely after that, until he does come. They gave Townsend the same message, neatly written up in a letter signed by all the class captains.'

Father Luke looked worried. 'I don't think Manu will come. He'd lose too much face. And he knows the students really value their education. He'll just call their bluff, and hope everything dies down.'

Mark took a cassette tape out of his pocket. 'Here's my surprise. I don't think the students are bluffing. One of my students gave me this. It's a tape of their meeting with Tavitai. Listen.'

Mark played the tape. It was double-sided, almost two hours long. Recording quality wasn't great, but we could hear and understand the various speakers. Proceedings began with a confident speech from Tavitai. He acknowledged student concerns about losing their teachers and about the media reports. He explained how the Education Department had behaved properly in all matters. So they should stop listening to troublemakers, return to classes, and resume their education. Now he would answer any questions they still had.

The students responded impressively. A number had questions ready. They pressed Tavitai hard on one topic after another. The students were specific and well-informed, even about technical matters like inspection procedures. Tavitai dodged some of the detail, but he sounded increasingly lame. Some students began muttering while he spoke. A few shouted at him.

Then a male student who had not spoken before gave a superb speech that comprehensively challenged Tavitai's interpretation of events. He concluded by saying, 'Mr Tavitai, I think we students accept that you came here to speak to us in good faith. But you are wrong to say that the Education Department has behaved properly. You have been the victim of a conspiracy by your senior officers. We want the truth, and we are entitled to that. Please return to head-quarters and tell your boss — Mr Manu, the Secretary for Education — that he must come here and give us that truth. We will return to our classes tomorrow only on that condition.'

Tavitai's subdued answer could barely be heard above the static on the tape. 'Alright. I have explained the situation to you, to the best of my knowledge and ability. I will take your request to the secretary. But please, I ask you to think of your education and your future. Return to your studies and avoid rash actions.' A little scattered applause followed as he left.

John was delighted. 'No wonder Tavitai looked downcast when he left that meeting. And he got no joy from the staff either. He's going back with nothing to show for his visit here.'

Father Luke looked worried. 'I agree the students aren't bluffing. But things could easily run out of control from here. Let's pray for a good outcome!'

33. The Cavalry Rides In? (John)

LUNCHTIME VISITORS TOLD us that Tuesday was quiet and orderly on campus. Students and staff alike seemed relieved to be back in classes as normal. Student leaders met quietly and privately in their free time. They didn't confide in the staff, but as far as anyone could tell their position — and their Wednesday deadline — had not changed.

The media reported on the latest events: Tavitai's visit to the campus, the interim return to classes, and the renewed student demand that the Secretary for Education personally come and speak to them. The Education Department issued a terse public statement that declared the secretary would 'not respond to any ultimatum' and urged the students to resume their education. Who would blink first? What was going on behind the scenes?

Restless, I decided to drive into town in the afternoon. Bohdan, ever hopeful that the Ombudsman Commission would act on our complaints, left before me to visit their office. I would check in with Simon at the *Post-Courier* and our lawyer Peter and then meet Bohdan at the hotel.

But halfway to town, everything changed. Bohdan was driving back *towards* me at top speed, flashing his lights and sounding his horn. I pulled over. So did Bohdan.

'John, great news! I went to the Ombudsman Commission office and met two guys from the Public Service Commission there. They came in from Moresby on the early plane, and they're here to urgently investigate our case. The Chief Ombudsman himself requested this! It's all still highly confidential. They're a few minutes behind me in a rental car. They want to meet with us privately first — right now — and then officially visit the college tomorrow.'

Tired and cynical, I didn't feel impressed. 'Well, I'm not sure I want to meet with them. It was the Public Service Commission that terminated our contracts, remember? How do we know this new so-called investigation isn't just another cover-up?' Bohdan's face fell. I held up my hand. 'All right, let's do it.'

Another car pulled up next to us a few minutes later. Two professionally dressed young national men got out. They introduced themselves and presented business cards from the Public Service Commission. And they felt trustworthy. I agreed we would keep their involvement confidential, for the time being at least, and arranged a rendezvous at our house. That would be out of sight of the campus, and no one from the college or the village knew them.

My first positive impression wasn't wrong. Back at home, we chatted over coffee before getting down to business. In their normal roles at the Public Service Commission, Bernard was a lawyer who dealt with legal disputes while Ovea was a regional manager. They had been assigned to act as a two-man team and make a special investigation of our case. Both came across as capable, experienced and well-intentioned.

Bernard began the meeting. 'We understand your employment contracts have been terminated. Let's start there. Please tell us how that happened.'

I looked at him, bemused. 'You must know more about that than us.' I brought my files to the table. 'Here's the letter the Education Department delivered to me — from *your* Chairman of the Public Service Commission.'

Bernard explained that the Public Service Commission — the PSC — was indeed our ultimate employer, in fact the legal employer of every public servant. But within that legal relationship, the PSC naturally relied on the various government agencies to recruit and assess their own national and expatriate staff. A contract might be terminated under the 'in the best interests' clause in various circumstances. For example, an expatriate might unluckily kill someone in a road accident and need to leave PNG urgently for his own safety.

Ovea continued their explanation. 'In this case it was the Education Department that requested early termination of your contracts. They quoted a supporting recommendation from a departmental Committee of Inquiry. Naturally, the Public Service Commission issued the standard letter with the "in the best interests" clause that we use in such circumstances and sent those letters on to the Education Department for action. But yesterday our chairman received an urgent request from the Chief Ombudsman to look further into your case, and he seconded us to this investigation. That's all we know. Please tell us your story.'

I did, in detail and with full supporting documentation. Bohdan and Elisa chipped in with further information from time to time. Bernard asked many questions, focused on documentation and specific facts. Ovea mostly stayed quiet and observed us. It was several hours before they got up to go, taking with them Bohdan's personal copies of all our documentation.

Ovea closed the meeting positively. 'Of course, we need to check all this and prepare a formal report for our chairman. But I can tell you now that you have nothing to worry about. We'll fix this and ensure the wrongdoers in the Education Department are properly dealt with. It's terrible that students have had to suffer. I admire your willingness to do the right things on their behalf.'

Bernard was even more complimentary. 'I've been involved in many complicated disputes, but I've never seen such comprehensive documentation. Congratulations on a superb job. Maybe after our report I can use these papers to do a PhD thesis,' he joked.

We were buzzing! But Ovea cautioned us. 'Remember, this discussion must stay confidential to the three of you for now. We'll visit the college tomorrow, and interview other people there. I will speak to the students and make sure they don't resume their boycott. And then we will have to return to Moresby, do more checking within our own organisation and at the Education Department, and prepare a report. All that will take at least a week, so please be patient. Just live quietly here in your house. Stay off the campus as much as possible and keep a low profile.'

We surely would. But we couldn't help wondering what Townsend and the Education Department might be planning for tomorrow, when the student ultimatum would expire.

34. Invasion! (Elisa)

WEDNESDAY — the last day for Secretary for Education Manu to turn up, or the student boycott would resume — dawned bright and clear. We rose early, optimistic that the PSC investigators would now drive events to a just conclusion. Bohdan, John and I had all agreed to leave the college vicinity for the day, until news of the PSC investigation spread from other sources.

From our house in the village, we saw Bohdan leave early for town in his minivan. Next the various staff who lived off campus drove up the main access road to the campus at their usual time. And with great satisfaction we watched the rental car carrying Ovea and Bernard proceed up the same road half an hour later. It would be a good day.

John and I left for town, driving past the familiar landmarks and with the usual cheerful waves to villagers. Halfway there we noticed activity at the large police barracks that housed the provincial riot squad but thought nothing of it.

We enjoyed spending an afternoon in town like normal people. We shopped for groceries and then relaxed over a long lunch. Keen to reach home before darkness fell, we left Rabaul in the late afternoon. Halfway back, activity at the police barracks seemed more substantial. Several extra vehicles were drawn up in a line. Armed police walked around. We looked apprehensively at one another. John sped up.

PSC officers arrive at campus to start investigation #4 (Post-Courier)

With the working day over, we decided to drive straight to June's house on campus. But an improvised barrier of branches and old tyres on the access road halted us. Students were manning barricades! They recognised us, moved the blockage aside, and waved us through. We felt alarmed. What had happened today?

At June's house, the front door stood open. A student was using her telephone. Mark sat slumped in a chair nearby. Reluctant to interrupt, we stood in the doorway bewildered. Mark spotted us and came outside.

'What's going on?' I asked.

'It's been just unbelievable,' he said slowly, shaking his head. 'I'll start with the good news.'

Mark's story unfolded, haltingly at times. We sat down on the steps and listened in amazement.

'The day started normally. Classes were fully attended and students were keen. I looked after John's former classes next door as well as my own.

'In the staffroom at morning break, we found two strangers. They introduced themselves as officers of the Public Service Commission, here to conduct an independent investigation into the sacking of the three teachers. They would want to speak to some of us individually about that tomorrow. In the meantime, when classes ended at one o'clock, we should ensure that all students went to the mess hall for lunch. They would introduce themselves there and ask the students to cancel their boycott and continue attending classes while their investigation proceeded. Staff should say nothing to students about the investigation until then.'

Mark glowered. 'Townsend was there too, looking tense and pale. He didn't say a word. The sneaky bastard!'

Mark was a former priest. I had never before heard him swear.

'You can imagine our delight! I walked to my next class whistling, which made the students laugh. Then about 12.30, everything changed. We heard vehicles driving into the campus from the back road. They were those police Land Cruisers with barred windows so you can't easily see who's inside. Everyone watched through the class-room windows with amazement as six of those vehicles drove up to the admin block. About 50 riot police got out and formed a line between the classrooms and the admin block. They cut off the mess hall too. The police were armed with shotguns, tear gas and semi-automatic rifles — I couldn't believe it. Townsend came out onto the veranda, looking smug, and shook hands with their leader.'

We listened open-mouthed as Mark continued. 'The sight of armed police enraged the students. At first, they just shouted angrily from the classrooms, calling the police and the principal all sorts of names. Then some of the male students started advancing down the stairs, shouting abuse at the top of their voices. Anything could have happened.

'I was close to the admin block and headed there, towards the police line. So did Tim, Glen and Luther. I sent Tim back to mobilise other staff to send students back to their dorms, away from the police. That worked well. Within about 10 minutes, most of the students were out of sight.'

Mark paused for recollection. 'Meanwhile our group wasn't allowed to go to the admin block. The police line halted us, politely enough but firmly. They were "under orders not to let any staff or students into the administration block or the mess hall".

'Next, Ovea and Bernard emerged from the mess hall where they had been waiting to meet with the students. Somehow, they talked their way through the police line to the admin block. They ignored Townsend and spoke to the police leader for several minutes. His manner soon changed! He waved our little group forward and we were able to challenge Townsend.'

Mark explained the origin of the police invasion. Townsend had called the police the previous day and asked them to be ready to come to the college if required. And in force, in case students turned violent or started damaging property. So overnight, the riot police were alerted. Then, *after* he had heard why Ovea and Bernard had come to the college, Townsend called the police again. He asked them to arrive on campus before one o'clock to protect Education

Department property. The police leader confirmed the details of both calls.

Mark grimaced. 'Of course, Townsend's real motive was to stop Ovea and Bernard meeting the students. But those two guys were terrific!'

Mark outlined how Ovea and Bernard had taken charge of the situation. They had impressively explained their role to the police leader (who turned out to be the Provincial Police Commander no less). Then they negotiated an agreement. The students would come to the mess hall to meet with the investigators at 2 p.m., one hour later than originally scheduled. The police would withdraw from campus in the meantime. 'The Police Commander told Townsend and us that his "force" would retire to the small police station in Keravat township and wait there for further information. The police re-embarked and their convoy pulled out, followed by jeers and taunts from some of the students. Luckily the police didn't react to that — in fact their discipline was remarkable in the circumstances.

'But before the meeting in the mess hall could start, a small group of boys started throwing rocks. They were really worked up and wouldn't listen to anyone. Nothing serious at that stage though — just small stones banging onto the iron roofs. Most of the students went to the mess hall in a disciplined manner, and the meeting there got started.

'Staff weren't invited to the meeting. Some went home for lunch, and some tried to calm down the rock-throwers. I stayed at the admin block with a few others to keep an eye on Townsend. He went into his office, making phone calls to headquarters I suppose.'

Mark shook his head. 'That's when the real trouble began. The meeting in the mess hall had barely started when Townsend came back out and told us to leave the admin block. "I've told the police to come back. They will take over now. You can all go home."

'I was furious. So were the other staff there. Glen started pushing Townsend, shouting. "Who do you think you are? Do you want to get someone killed?" I had to hold him back.'

Mark smiled at that recollection, then resumed his story. 'Five minutes later the convoy returned. The police had a new plan. They parked at the admin block again and then surrounded the mess hall full of students, with their weapons ready. That incensed the students. Some of those inside went berserk, yelling and smashing up the wall panels. Other students outside the cordon started doing damage elsewhere. It was chaotic and noisy. Townsend looked pleased at first, then panicky as he could see things getting out of hand. Finally, he went pale and collapsed onto the floor — fainted, I guess. The Police Commander had him taken away in a police vehicle, and told us that he was in charge now, not the principal and not the staff. He just ignored anything we had to say.

A staff member confronts police outside the damaged mess hall
(Post-Courier)

'After their initial reaction, and seeing Townsend taken away, the students calmed down. The Police Commander got a megaphone from his car. He went to the mess hall, with me and a few other staff trailing behind. Through the broken fibreboard panels, we could see inside. Bernard and Ovea were standing on a table, with the students clustered around them.

'Using his megaphone, the Commander stood at the entrance and read from a message. "I am informing all students that this college is now under police control, at the direct request of Mr Manu the Secretary for Education. He has ordered that a compulsory referendum will take place immediately. Each student must vote either to return to class or to leave the college. Any student who refuses to vote will be expelled. I will give you one hour to organise and hold the referendum. Do not attempt to leave this building or challenge my officers." Then he went back to the admin block.'

Mark wearily shook his head again. 'There were eight or ten staff around by then. No deputy principal though, and only one department head. Our staff group went into the mess hall to talk with Ovea and Bernard — no one stopped us that time. The students milled around, talking to us, to the investigators and to their leaders. They were scared all right, but angry and defiant too. No way would they submit! One student got a chant started — "No Police, No Vote."

A truce plan is developed under police guard (Post-Courier)

'Somehow, we developed a practical proposal. Our main goal was to persuade the police to leave the campus. Three of us — Ovea, Glen and me — went to see the Police Commander. We tried to convince him that the students were too agitated to hold a referendum now. That could be done tomorrow instead. We pointed out that if the situation got out of hand and students got hurt, he could be held to blame. And that many of these students had influential parents. It would be in the best interests of everyone to let the situation cool down.'

Mark brightened up. 'Eventually the Commander saw sense and backed down. "My force will retire to the police post in the village until morning. But the campus remains under police orders. None of the students can leave. At the first sign of trouble or damage we will return."

'So that's how the day ended. The police packed up and left. So did Ovea and Bernard — they're heading back to Moresby to tell their boss about their findings so far. On the surface everything has calmed down, but of course the students are still really upset. Staff have been talking to them and I think things will be okay overnight. But some of the boys say they are ready to fight the police. They've set up barricades on both roads into the campus.'

John spoke up, quietly for once. 'What do we do now?'

That didn't need a long discussion. We could be sure of just two things. Yes, the PSC investigation would finally blow the whistle on the Education Department. But that would take days. Meanwhile, any attempt to impose a referendum on the students or force them to attend class might lead to serious violence. It would also distract attention away from the PSC investigation — which was probably just what the Education Department wanted.

We decided that John, Bohdan and I needed to keep a low profile and avoid becoming involved. Mark and Father Luke would use their church network to reach senior politicians in Moresby who might bring the Education Department under control. Mark would report back as soon as he could.

John and I drove the short distance home, recrossing the student barricade with a cheery wave. I made a quick dinner. Bohdan returned from town and we briefed him on the drama of the day. No one felt much like talking afterwards, but we couldn't go to bed without hearing from Mark. Time dragged. It was almost midnight when Mark arrived, haggard but happy.

'Well, we got a result. It took a while. After that earlier publicity from talking with Christine, neither the Prime Minister nor his deputy would talk to us. We eventually got through to the Minister of Education at home. Luckily, he had seen the magazine article about Drysdale and all the reports given to Manu and the Committee of Inquiry — remember when our national staff sent that documentation directly to him? And he'd heard the media reports about the sackings. So, as the minister, he was sympathetic. But also reluctant to intervene. "Why not just let the PSC investigation take its course?" he suggested.

'We explained the risks to the students if the police returned to the campus or other forceful actions occurred. But of course, he's really a politician, and thinks like one. Risks to the students didn't concern him much. What *did* persuade him was when we suggested how bad he would look in public if serious trouble broke out and he had done nothing to stop it. Finally, he agreed to call the Secretary for Education first thing in the morning and instruct him to cancel the referendum and send the police away.

'The students wanted to attend classes tomorrow anyway, now that they know about the PSC investigation. I'm sure they will retract, or at least defer, their ultimatum to the secretary. Then the college can continue as normal while the PSC investigation proceeds.'

'Congratulations Mark. A great day's work!' I enthused.

'Thanks,' he said wearily. 'And by the way, I also got the chairman of our Governing Council to call an emergency meeting for Friday. Townsend will have to explain himself there. Anyway, it's late now. We can meet at June's house tomorrow. Be sure to come in via the bottom road to avoid meeting any students or staff.'

Mark departed for home. So did Bohdan. We went to bed, exhausted but relieved.

35. 'The Nazis Are Back!' (John)

WE WOKE LATER than usual and enjoyed a quiet breakfast. I wanted to sort my files — especially our growing collection of newspaper stories — and make a quick trip to town to update Peter about the PSC investigation. Elisa felt restless, so she set off to walk the short distance to June's house.

Twenty minutes later I got into our car to drive to town. As usual, I carried all my files with me for security. By now that meant lugging a large box.

I pulled out onto the road, set off through Keravat towards Rabaul— and stopped dead. In the front yard of the police post, a large body of armed police was mustered in parade order. They were listening to instructions from an officer who was standing on the veranda with a megaphone. Tension was visible in their body language. Whatever they were being instructed about, the riot squad certainly wasn't going home. What could I do?

I turned off the road and rattled over the bumpy dirt track to Father Luke's house. I held down the horn as I roared into his yard and jumped out, shouting. Luke rushed out to see me, another priest in tow.

'Father, you must get to the campus immediately. The police are invading again!'

'John, you must be mistaken.' Father Luke was calm. 'We sorted all that out last night. And Father Gunther has come a long way to see me this morning. I can't leave right now.'

I was anything but calm. 'Whatever you and Mark sorted out last night fell over. I don't know what's happening, but you *must* get over there and do something.'

Another car horn, loud and repeated, interrupted us. Bohdan rattled into the yard in his minivan. He jumped out, shouting in a strong Czech accent. 'Father, the Nazis are back!'

'Who's back? What are you all talking about?' Father Luke asked, becoming agitated. His visitor looked back and forth at us, utterly bewildered.

Bohdan shouted again. 'The Nazis are back, Father! They're leaving the police station in a big convoy, headed for the campus. I just drove past them and came straight here. Someone will get killed if you don't stop them. Jump in and I'll drive you part way up the back road —you can cut through to the campus on foot from there.'

'Bohdan's right. Go with him Father, now'! I urged. 'I'll go in the bottom road and head for June's house.'

Father Luke jumped into Bohdan's van. Our vehicles roared along the dusty dirt track, Bohdan in the lead. In my rear-view mirror, I saw the visiting priest standing forlorn in a cloud of dust.

The police post seemed deserted as we drove by. Bohdan turned off up the back road; I carried on to the main campus entrance. The barricade there had been scattered into the bushes. No one was visible round about. I drove on cautiously to June's place and parked behind the house, out of sight of the road. As I ran up the back stairs, Elisa opened the door, her eyes wide. 'Just come quietly to the front windows. Don't let anyone see you.'

A scary sight awaited. Most of the student body — several hundred at least — were tightly assembled at the bottom end of the sports field, about 80 metres away. A cordon of armed police encircled them. Their commander stood a little apart from the cordon, visibly arguing with Mark and Glen. Father Luke was running towards them from the far side of the sports field. Some other staff could be seen at various places. A few stray students who had escaped the round-up hid behind trees outside the road that circled the sports field, watching nervously.

June explained what had happened. 'We had a confused situation on campus this morning. Staff tried to hold classes as usual. Some students came to class, some stayed in their dorms, and some tried to organise a meeting at the mess hall. There was a bit of banging about, mostly just stones on the roof. I was working in my office near the admin block so I could see everything that happened there.

'First one of the students went in. You know Amos Taimo? Not the brightest, but hard-working and always keen to please. He went to see Isobel, who a few minutes later took him to see Townsend, who was back in his office after his fainting fit yesterday. Ten minutes after that, the police commander drove in and joined them. He left a few minutes later, in a hurry.

'I assumed the commander had been told about withdrawal of the Education Department's demand for a so-called referendum. But just as morning break started, I could hear vehicles growling up the back road to the top of the campus. A few minutes later, a long line of police began walking down, weapons at the ready. They looked menacing! Their line extended right across the campus, so students had no way to escape without running into the bush.'

June paused for breath. 'After some initial shouting, the students went really quiet. They wanted to stand their ground, but they were afraid to make contact. They kept retreating as the police line rolled down. Then some of the police showed up *behind* the students — they had probably walked up the bottom road. The students ended up surrounded, and the police tightened the cordon to what you see now. They won't let staff inside it.'

June had witnessed another drama at the admin block when the four national teachers arrived there as an angry and determined group. Townsend stayed inside his office with the door locked, even when they banged on it. Isobel came out and tried to calm them down. June heard some of the discussion. Isobel claimed that Amos Taimo had told her about a student plan to take over the campus and brought her a list of their leaders. So, Townsend had called the police again, and their commander had taken over from there.

June smiled brightly for a moment. 'Well, that *really* enraged the nationals. They almost broke down Townsend's door, shouting: 'You and all your fucking queers leave our country or we'll kill you. Get the police out of this college, now!' Townsend wouldn't come out, so they turned away and went to the sports field. Then the police commander arrived again and met Townsend on the veranda. I heard Townsend say his life had been threatened, and he wanted police protection. A few minutes later a police car drove him away. Then I walked down here.'

She paused for breath again. 'And one more thing. I spotted Miller, our new inspector, peering out of Townsend's office. He must have turned up last night to take charge behind the scenes. Miller's probably in contact with headquarters right now.'

We returned our attention to the drama on the sports field. The commander ended his discussion with Father Luke and the staff. Standing on one of the police vehicles, he addressed the students through his megaphone. They listened, defiantly. So did we, anxiously.

'I have spoken to your principal. He has asked me to protect college property from further damage. I have here a list of the leaders of these troubles.' He read out 11 names. 'I want those students to report to me here for questioning, right now. Otherwise, I will arrest you all.'

There was no reaction from the students. After a minute or so, the commander spoke again. 'I will allow you one hour. If the students on this list have not reported to me by then, I will arrest you all. In the meantime, none of you will leave here. And you will have no contact with college staff or anyone else.'

The commander retreated inside his vehicle. When Father Luke and staff members tried to approach him, police turned them away. Townsend was nowhere to be seen. Nor was deputy Isobel.

The police cordon pulled back a little but stayed intact. We could hear voices rise and fall as the students talked urgently amongst themselves. Time was racing by. What would happen?

I knew we had to stay out of sight. But we could still do something. 'June, start calling people. Everyone you can think of — PNG media, our embassies, BBC World Service, ABC News in Australia. Tell them lives are at stake. Get as much publicity as you can. That's the best way to protect the students.' June got busy on the phone with vivid eyewitness accounts of the situation.

The allotted hour expired. The students fell silent as the police commander climbed on his vehicle and resumed his megaphone. He spoke confidently. 'The leaders I named must report to me now please. Then my officers will release the rest of you.'

The students didn't move and didn't speak. The police commander, looking surprised, waited a few moments. Then he tried once more. 'This is your last chance to avoid arrest. Anyone who points out those leaders to me will be free to go.'

The students remained still and silent. Thwarted, the commander issued orders we couldn't hear. The police opened one side of their ring, nearest the main access road, and converted their elliptical cordon into something more like a long rectangle. Within minutes, over 300 students, flanked by police, were walking in column down the access road towards the highway. Father Luke and some staff walked along too, outside the guards. The procession passed within 20 metres of us as we kept out of sight. All the police vehicles drove away down the back road a few minutes later. What had been a crowded sports field was now deserted.

We received second-hand news for the rest of the day as others came and went. First the students were marched to the Keravat police post and kept cordoned off while staff argued for their release. Then police vehicles took them 'for questioning' to the main provincial police station, a 40-minute drive away in Rabaul. Staff stubbornly followed in private cars. The student mood remained stubborn too, and there were too few police escorts to prevent quiet conversations amongst them.

At Rabaul police station, normal facilities were overwhelmed. The students were channelled into an earthen compound surrounded by a barbed wire fence. There they had a few toilets and could walk around. But no food or water was made available, despite the intense heat and humidity. College staff protested but were kept away from the students.

Their job done, the riot police handed custody of the students over to the town police and departed. The town commander proved amenable to staff pleas that the students were minors under their pastoral care. First, he made water available. Then interrogations began, but with staff sitting in. Individual students were selected at random and questioned about their activities at the college over recent days. Those first questioned explained — truthfully or not — that they had attended classes normally and certainly had not been involved in any rioting or damage. Released without charge, from outside the fence they spread the word about how to gain release to the students who were still inside.

With no success from their early interrogations, the police changed tactics. They charged the remaining 200-plus students with unlawful assembly and wilful damage. With no facilities to detain the students overnight, the police released them on verbal bail guaranteed by college staff.

As nightfall loomed, staff had organised the two college trucks into a shuttle service to return the students to campus. Some students arrived in high spirits, singing loudly from the trucks. Others seemed chastened or almost in shock. Staff organised a late dinner at the mess hall. Class captains resumed their duties, happy to support the staff who had supported them. By the time 'lights out' arrived everyone was ready to turn in after an exhausting day. The student dormitories were soon shrouded in darkness and silence.

Our group gathered at Mark's house for a debrief and a much-needed nightcap. We were now more numerous. Glen, Tim, Gabriel, the four national staff and several others who had backed the students and rejected Townsend's authority joined us. Initially the mood was uncertain. Should we celebrate the fact that the Public Service

Commission investigation was now under way, led by honest and capable officers who had witnessed first-hand the treacherous police invasion? Or should we mourn the fact that the education of our students had been seriously disrupted, with many no doubt traumatised by arrests and criminal charges?

Gaius, one of the two new national staff at Keravat this year, was normally a quiet and religious teetotaller. Many, me included, had privately considered him timid and conformist. But Gaius had stuck by the students all day and personally 'threatened Townsend's life'. Now he spoke up loudly and raised a beer bottle. 'We Papua New Guineans finally stood up for ourselves. Our students can feel proud. Let's drink to them!'

We all raised glasses.

'To the students!'

'It's all right for you, Gaius,' complained Tim. 'But Townsend won't dare return to the college after your threat to kill him.' He pretended to sob. 'Now I've got no principal to look up to for professional leadership.' Everyone chortled. More stories and jokes about the day's events flowed.

Even Father Luke, by nature a worrier not a warrior, joined the levity. 'I'm glad John and Bohdan made me come to the campus. But calling the police Nazis was going a bit far, Bohdan. Father Gunther is from Germany and very conscious of history. He probably felt quite upset!' Suddenly he stood up. 'That reminds me. I haven't been home yet. I wonder what he's been doing all day. I must go!'

Father Luke's departure reminded everyone else of the late hour. The party broke up.

36. Our Home No Longer?
(Elisa)

THE NEXT FEW days were exhilarating. Dramatic reports of the police action at Keravat dominated local radio news and the *Post-Courier*'s front page: 'Riot Bid — College Raid' followed next day by 'New Swoop by Riot Cops'. For half a day mass arrests of college students featured in the hourly BBC World Service bulletin. Australian papers and TV news carried the story too. Queues developed for every telephone around the campus, as worried calls from concerned relatives of students (and staff) flooded in while reassuring calls went out.

The drama of the police invasion and student arrests naturally took centre stage, but the visit of PSC investigators to the campus became public knowledge too. The *Post-Courier* carried photos of the investigators taken during the first day's events. (Simon had come along that morning to interview students and instead had witnessed the police invasion.)

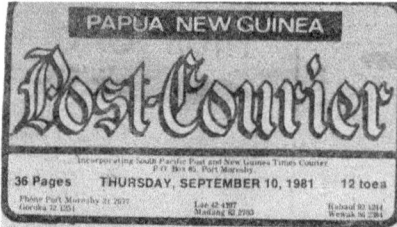

The first police invasion makes the Keravat affair front page news (Post-Courier)

Secretary for Education Manu publicly defended his department's actions, saying that the sackings were 'fair' and the students had been misled. He also threatened legal action against Father Luke for his public statement in the *Post-Courier*. But scandal could no longer be stifled. Father Luke counter-attacked vividly with another letter: 'If I end up in court it is in a good cause. If I end up in jail, I do not care because it is worth it to get something done. If two expatriate people wish to live together that is their business. But when men pick up and abuse my students and parishioners it becomes my business because I am opposed to sexual exploitation.'

We heard how college routine gradually returned to normal over Friday, as staff resumed teaching duties and students trickled back to classes. At the end of the day, Isobel announced to a sullen staff meeting that 'Mr Townsend has left Keravat, permanently'. She said nothing about inspector Miller, who was apparently no longer around either.

Without much conviction, Isobel had explained how the list of 'ring-leaders' had appeared and what Townsend had done (which of course she 'had not personally agreed with'). She said she had sent their informant Amos Taimo home on sick leave, to protect him from payback.

The second invasion and mass arrest of students shocks the nation (Post-Courier)

Isobel had received no instructions from headquarters. She didn't know what would happen to the college, or who would take responsibility. After some discussion staff resolved that, in the best interests of the students, they should operate the college as normally as possible pending further information.

'POLICE SHOULD NOT BE INVOLVED'

● LEFT: Some of the Kerovat students in the Rabaul police station yard last Thursday afternoon.

Students under arrest in Rabaul before being charged (Post-Courier)

The emergency meeting of the Governing Council began as planned on Friday afternoon. It didn't last long. Mark and Gaius came over to our house to explain.

'Isobel came in with a letter from the Secretary for Education, hand-delivered an hour earlier from town. It quoted some section of the Education Act that referred to "extraordinary circumstances", under which he supposedly had the right to halt the meeting. No one was sure what the law said, and Isobel apparently couldn't find a copy of the Education Act. The chairman was furious and resigned on the spot. So did several other members, and we no longer had a quorum. That's it then for our Governing Council. Another story for the papers!'

We went over to June's house to use the phone. I called Ovea at the Public Service Commission. He had been following events in the media and wasn't surprised by anything that had happened. 'Those guys are desperate to keep the lid on. I promise you they won't succeed. Our report is nearly ready. Bernard is checking the legal detail to make sure our recommendations will be 100 percent effective. You can expect to hear from us next week.'

Reassured, we enjoyed a quiet Friday night and spent Saturday afternoon relaxing at the beach.

Sunday morning brought a surprise. John answered a knock at the door as I prepared breakfast in the kitchen. He wasn't there long and returned as I was making coffee. 'Who was that? What did they want?' I asked cheerfully.

'That,' John replied slowly, 'was the police. A whole carload of them in the yard. Armed too. An officer wearing a sidearm came to the door to give me this. It's an eviction notice!'

We read the letter together. It was on Education Department notepaper from Colleges Division. It stated that our contracts had been terminated several weeks ago and gave us 24 hours' notice to vacate our house — the property of the department — or face eviction.

'Can they do that?' I wondered aloud. 'Don't they have to behave reasonably? I'm no lawyer, but 24 hours' notice doesn't sound reasonable to me.'

John — who was a keen amateur lawyer by now — spoke with assurance. 'I doubt they can evict us at 24 hours' notice. Probably not at all, if we object. Anyway, there's nothing we can do on Sunday, so let's not worry about it. First thing tomorrow, I'll go see Peter and check out the legalities.'

Bohdan drove up a few minutes later. 'Hi Bohdan!' I said cheerfully. 'Want some coffee? Any news or special deliveries?'

He wasn't cheerful. 'I found this under my front door when I came back from church.' He held up a letter like ours. 'Did you get one too? They can't just throw us out on the street, can they?'

John repeated his assurance and intentions for tomorrow. Over coffee we agreed that they would both go to see Peter first thing tomorrow, while I stayed home. Bohdan would ask one of the national teachers to 'sit in' at his house and keep others out while he was away.

John and Bohdan departed for town the next morning. Aipat turned up for domestic duties as usual, and I kept us both busy with cleaning chores. Just before noon, I heard a noisy vehicle drive into the yard. Aipat went to see who it was, then hurried back. 'Missus, polis kamap!'

Sure enough, I could see a large, uniformed man standing outside the screen door. He knocked loudly. I opened the door. Judging by his stripes and prominent sidearm, he was a senior officer. 'Are you Mrs Men-de-ze-la?' he asked, struggling with the pronunciation.

I could see several police with rifles sitting in a large four-wheel-drive vehicle. My heart missed a beat, but I kept my expression calm. 'Yes, I am. What brings you here, officer?'

'I was ordered to personally deliver this document. It is addressed to Mr and Mrs Men-de-ze-la.' He handed me a sealed envelope and walked away.

I hastily opened the envelope. The letter inside, from the Foreign Ministry, was addressed to us both. 'You are hereby advised that following the termination of your employment contracts with the Education Department, you have no lawful reason to remain in

Papua New Guinea. The Foreign Ministry consequently requires you to leave the country within 14 days of this advice.'

I checked the date on the letter. It was 9 September, five days earlier. Did we now have only nine days left?

The officer was climbing into the front seat of his vehicle when I called after him. 'Excuse me, officer, please come back. This document is not correct.' He glared at me for a moment and then walked slowly back towards the house. I met him halfway. 'Look here, this is not today's date.' I pointed to the date on the letter and spoke slowly and firmly. 'I want you to write the date of delivery and your name on this letter please.'

He looked at me stiffly, unsure what to do. His men watched silently. I knew Aipat would be watching from the house — unless he had run away. Then the officer relaxed and nodded. He took the letter back to the car, wrote on it, returned and handed me the letter. 'As you have requested, madam.'

I checked the details. Yes, he had written today's date as 'date of delivery' with his name, rank and signature under it. 'Thank you very much, officer.' He nodded again, and we both retreated.

Safely back in the house, I studied the letter. It seemed properly signed, by the Foreign Minister himself. My thoughts whirled around. Could they really deport us, just like that? How could we pack up and leave within two weeks?

By the time John returned in the late afternoon with Bohdan, I was feeling low. I showed them the letter and explained how it had arrived.

John wasn't concerned. 'Peter told me they have no right to evict us from this house without giving proper notice. If necessary, he will take out an injunction to stop them. Here's a letter from him to the college stating that. I'm sure the same legal concepts apply to a deportation order too. And every time the authorities do something like this, they make themselves look worse to the media and the public. I already gave a copy of our eviction letter to Simon at the *Post-Courier*. But just to be sure, I'll go into town and see Peter again tomorrow.'

We decided that one of us would always stay at home from now on just in case something more happened. John left to take Bohdan home, deliver Peter's letter to the college office, and update our friends while I made dinner. For some reason, the 'date of delivery' the police officer had written down nibbled at my mind. What was special about 14 September?

Then it clicked. Today was indeed a special day for us. I prepared a few tasty snacks, opened a bottle of wine, lit candles on the table and turned out the lights.

John returned a little later. He stopped outside the door in surprise. 'Is the power off here? It's on everywhere else.'

'The power's fine. But I thought you might like a candlelight dinner on our wedding anniversary!'

I started chuckling. After a moment, John joined in. Soon we were both giggling. 'It's not every wedding anniversary that you get served a deportation order!' Our laughter became hysterical for a while, before we quieted and sat down to enjoy our 'anniversary dinner'.

Over the last of the wine, we mused on how strange the past two years had been. We'd found adventure in PNG alright. Conflicts, conspiracies, reports, legal proceedings and media briefings had become a way of life that took up most of our time. We wrestled with our old and cantankerous typewriter in intense heat and humidity and sneaked into the library at night to use the only photocopier for miles around. We drove at speed back and forth to town on a corrugated dirt road almost daily, to arrive stiff with dust and with sweat trickling down our backs. Now, within a fortnight, we had been sacked, threatened with eviction and notified of deportation — for doing the right thing by our students.

Whatever happened from here, we would never be the same again.

OFFICE OF THE SECRETARY

DEPARTMENT OF FOREIGN AFFAIRS AND TRADE
POST OFFICE WARDS STRIP

9th September, 1981

Mr and Mrs John Mendzella
Keravat National High School
Private Mail Bag
RABAUL
EAST NEW BRITAIN PROVINCE

Dear Mr and Mrs Mendzella,

I have recently been informed by the Secretary of the Department
of Education that your services with the Department have been
terminated and that any entitlements due to you as stipulated
in your contracts of engagements have been finalised and
settled with you.

In these circumstances I see no basis whatever for your
continuing to reside in Papua New Guinea. You are therefore
requested to make plans to depart Papua New Guinea within two (2)
weeks from the date of receipt of this letter.

NOTICE SERVED TO PERSONS OVER LEAVE
14.9.81 BY S/I ROBERT YEN

TOMARINGA MOBILE DEPOT
RABAUL.

Deportation notice served to Elisa – on our wedding anniversary!

37. The Lid Stays On (John)

BOHDAN and I enjoyed a successful Tuesday in town. Our lawyer Peter followed up our deportation letters immediately (Bohdan had received one too). He called the Foreign Ministry to explain that our contract termination was being legally disputed, and that he could, if necessary, apply to the court for a stay of proceedings on our deportation. He suggested that the media would probably want to report that as yet *another* dramatic development in the Keravat affair. The other end of the conversation claimed it was just standard procedure to issue such letters after contract terminations and soon agreed that those letters to us could be ignored for now. Peter formally confirmed that position and hung up.

We knew that the Foreign Ministry's suspiciously prompt letter was far from standard. The Education Department was pulling every lever it could lay hands on.

Post-Courier reporter Simon eagerly received copies of the deportation letters. He added them to a bulging file with the prominent label 'Keravat affair'. 'Here's today's paper,' he said proudly. We read several relevant items with interest, not least the headline 'Secretary's

Ruling Stops College Talks' over a story that explained the demise of Keravat College's Governing Council. And 'Minister Orders Probe' belatedly reported how the Education Department had failed to rescind its ultimatum as the Minister had instructed and sent the police in again instead.

All we needed now was that PSC investigation report. I resisted the temptation to hint about that to Simon — the story would break soon enough. Instead, we just expressed quiet confidence that some authority somewhere would surely put things right.

At our final stop, the Ombudsman Commission officer beamed. He made copies of all the new correspondence to fax to headquarters immediately. He was delighted to hear how his chief's request to the PSC had generated the investigation into our case by Ovea and Bernard.

Soon after I arrived home, June came around with the latest news. 'Well, everything's been announced. Isobel becomes acting principal. All classes end today. All students will be sent home, as quickly as possible. The Grade 12s will lose out on more weeks of tuition just before their exams. The staff stay here and continue on duty. What a farce!'

Newspaper stories kept coming on Wednesday and Thursday. '14 Days to Pack and Go' outlined the attempt to deport us. Several published letters blamed the Education Department for the events at Keravat. One warned ominously that 'The Secretary for Education must understand he is dealing with the children of many national leaders.' A *Post-Courier* editorial thundered: 'This row continues to lurch from one crisis to another. The situation will not be resolved until the whole truth is told.'

Provincial politicians joined the clamour. The premier worried that 'Keravat's good name has been misrepresented by the ungodly practices of a few teachers, students and education officials.' His deputy openly attacked the Education Department: 'The secretary should be ashamed of having ordered police onto the Keravat campus.' Questions were tabled in the national parliament too. The Keravat affair was going political.

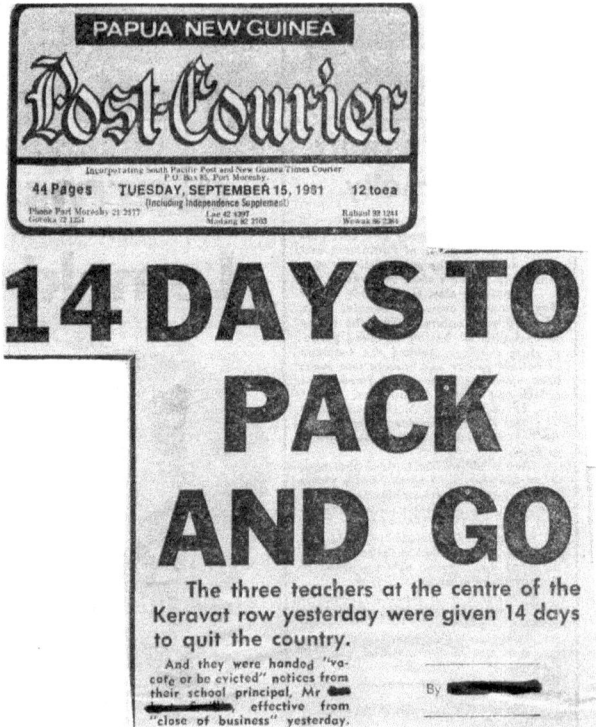

The Department's tactics backfire again, on the front page
(Post-Courier)

I walked to June's house late on Thursday afternoon, to update Ovea by telephone and find out when the PSC investigation's report would be ready. Ovea said hello quietly and then listened to my news. I urged that it would be in the best interests of everyone, but especially the students, for his report to be issued quickly and publicly.

Ovea was silent for some seconds. Then he spoke formally, in a subdued tone. 'I have just returned from a second meeting with the Chairman of the Public Service Commission. I regret to inform you that, on his direct instructions, our investigation has been closed. We have been instructed to make no recommendations. There will be no public report.' His tone grew more personal. 'John, I assure you that I have protested vigorously. I am very, *very* unhappy with this decision. So is Bernard. But there is nothing more we can do. I'm truly sorry.'

I sat back stunned. 'Ovea, this is unbelievable. Surely, you're not going to let those corrupt bastards in the Education Department win? There must be something you can do!'

I could hear great upset in Ovea's voice. 'John, Bernard is even now exploring every administrative channel open to us. But we are officers under the authority of our Commission, and we have received direct orders about this. Your contract termination may be wrongful, but it won't be reversed. I can't see any official way forward for us. Maybe I will try to do something as a private individual if I can. But you will have to keep fighting some other way. Or give up and leave.'

Numbly, I thanked Ovea for trying. I relayed the bad news to June, who had heard only my side of the conversation. I walked on to Bohdan's house, and then to Mark's. And then slowly home.

Elisa was waiting eagerly for news. But before I could say anything, my face told the story. Hers fell. A full briefing didn't take long. Where to from here, we wondered?

38. Fifth Time Lucky? (Elisa)

WE SUFFERED through a depressing Friday and weekend. The campus quieted as students began to understand the mounting damage to their education outcomes. Whatever happened from here, they had already missed numerous classes during the upheaval. Being sent home now meant they would miss many more and take their final exams at a serious disadvantage.

We exhaustively reviewed our situation. We had fought the good fight, hard and well. We still had adequate personal funds, even after paying our legal costs. But we would soon need to start earning an income again. To fight a long legal battle against an entrenched government bureaucracy would take time and money that we just didn't have, with no certainty of winning. We had got the truth out into the open. Now it was up to Papua New Guineans, not just us, to take action. With no practical way forward, it was time to leave.

On Monday morning we drove to town to arrange our departure. Flights out of PNG were available the following week, and we booked them. The travel agent gave us information about onward travel that would take us to England to see our families for the first time in four years.

While we lunched at the hotel, the day's newspapers arrived. And gave us unexpected cause for celebration. The Chief Ombudsman had publicly announced that *his* Commission would immediately begin its own major and urgent investigation into events at Keravat *and* more widely into Education Department administration. In accordance with the national constitution, he would report directly to parliament on the outcome. Consequently, he demanded that all administrative actions affecting the three terminated teachers be frozen. The battle wasn't over after all!

We returned triumphantly to campus. The college was a busy place. Our colleagues explained that Isobel seemed to be under urgent orders to fly all the students out before the end of the week. Expensive charter flights would be needed. Of course, the Education Department publicly denied any suggestion that impending investigations had sparked their panicked evacuation.

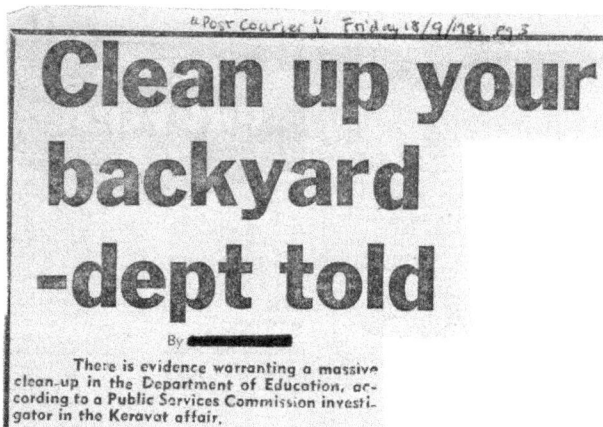

Blocked by his bosses, the PSC investigator bravely goes public.
"Why are staff who speak up given the sack?" (Post-Courier)

Tuesday was even better. The *Post-Courier* ran a bold headline: 'Clean Up Your Backyard — Dept Told'. True to his word, Ovea 'speaking as a private individual' made a public statement that the Education Department's Committee of Inquiry was a cover-up that was one-sided to protect a certain officer. 'The evidence warrants a massive clean-up in the Department of Education,' his statement continued. Ovea's photo, with a caption expressing concern for the safety of his nephew studying at another college, added a human-interest touch.

The college week rumbled on, punctuated by sad and noisy farewells as trucks busily shuffled students to the airport. Many came to see us personally, and we now felt free to be seen around campus. Our friends were gleeful; our opponents were glum. We cheerfully revised our departure plans and moved our flight bookings out several weeks.

The media week rumbled on too. The Secretary for Education declared Ovea's public statement out of order and threatened legal action against the Public Service Commission. Ovea retorted that he had spoken out as a concerned guardian of a young relative, not an official investigator. The PSC refused to comment.

Every day brought a new angle:

- Criticism of the cost of the Department's student evacuation: 'Fly-Out Bill Climbs High'.
- A stirring letter from Gabriel and the national staff: 'Deep-seated corruption headed by a clique of homosexuals whose only interest in PNG seems to be sexual exploitation of gullible youths.... No cover-up will succeed. The truth will triumph!'
- A warning letter from 42 Keravat students to the Education Department, under the headline 'Students Want Answers': 'We know what you're playing at, just a matter of time and

the kids will forget. But it is not going to be that way now. Please quickly tell us what you propose to do about the whole crisis and the demands we presented.'

- The weekly pidgin paper chimed in with dramatic photos of students behind barbed wire and translations of key stories from the *Post-Courier*.

The provincial premier spoke out again: 'Provincial Government May Take Over College'. The Provincial Assembly passed a resolution to condemn the actions taken by the Education Department at Keravat and call for the reinstatement of the sacked teachers. We became local heroes. People we barely knew, even people we didn't know at all, would come up to us in town to shake hands. Driving through villages provoked not just the usual friendly waves but sometimes cheering and even a few attempts at a salute.

One local political leader was brutally outspoken: 'Unless local governments and all responsible village leaders stand together to combat these immoral practices, the practice of homosexuality will badly affect our natural social life. If anyone, expatriate or national, is found guilty of homosexuality with any of our people, he should be charged and deported without delay, or sent to jail for not less than five years with hard labour.'

Discredited and overrun, the Education Department gave up the media battle and ran for cover. The secretary pledged that the Department would not comment again until the Ombudsman Commission completed its investigation.

Townsend never returned to his office. He did sneak back one afternoon to collect personal belongings from his house. Some passing students spotted him and jeered, and he exited the campus at speed.

John made a discreet telephone call to Ovea to thank him for his courageous actions. And found out there was more to that story than had appeared in the newspapers. Bernard's diligent checking had revealed that our termination letters had indeed been signed by the Chairman of the Public Service Commission, but they had *not* been confirmed by a quorate meeting of the full Commission in accordance with required legal processes. As a result, the legal validity of our termination was contestable. Ovea then persuaded his bosses that it would be prudent to get the PSC out of the line of fire by asking the Chief Ombudsman to make a fuller and wider investigation of the background to the terminations. Ovea's individual statement to the media had been a separate personal decision though, and he had already been formally reprimanded for speaking out.

On Thursday the Ombudsman Commission called us officially through the college office. With great satisfaction, we walked into the administration building to take the call. The secretarial staff were pleased to see us once more (Isobel wasn't). A three-man team from the Ombudsman Commission would arrive in Rabaul the next day to begin investigations. Would John come to their office for an interview with the investigation's leader on Monday, on behalf of us both? He readily agreed.

On Friday, Bohdan, Mark and several other staff received similar calls from the Ombudsman Commission and made appointments for Monday afternoon and Tuesday.

The last students left Friday afternoon, and the campus took on a bleak and empty air. Staff had long ago finished any residual work, and after weeks of upset and stress a lot of noisy socialising went on instead. We celebrated with those who had supported us and snubbed those who hadn't.

39. Secrets Revealed (John)

I ARRIVED at the Ombudsman Commission office in good time for my 11 o'clock appointment. Desks and tables in the outer office were piled high with documents being processed by their Rabaul officer and two new people. They ushered me into the inner office to meet the head of the investigation team. Vince Sollitt was a youthful and slim American expat. He introduced himself as the Commission's in-house legal expert and invited me to sit down. He seemed sincere and energetic.

Vince explained the investigation's protocols. 'I am interviewing you as an officer of the Ombudsman Commission. Under the constitutional and legal authority of that body, you cannot refuse to be interviewed. If you answer my questions untruthfully or refuse to answer any of them, that will be reflected in the Commission's findings and recommendations. Do you have any questions before we start?'

I didn't. Vince began in a firm tone.

'I've read all the written material you submitted to our Commission. It's clear and thorough. I may ask about a few specific details later.

But first I'd like to focus on the Education Department's internal Committee of Inquiry, and how that inquiry felt able not just to exonerate the inspector but also to recommend termination of your contract. Please tell me that part of the story.'

I explained how everything had seemed fine early in the year. The Secretary for Education had acted properly to overturn the retaliation of his officers in rating us 'Unsatisfactory' when we demonstrably weren't. Then we had at our own initiative blocked the attempts of those same officers to transfer us to remote postings outside the college system. We were expecting the secretary to take quiet internal action to remove Simpson and discipline the cronies who had lied and bent rules to protect him. So, despite Gus's tragic death, the college year began optimistically. Everyone was willing to forget the past and make a fresh start under a new principal.

But soon after Gus died, everything changed. Townsend's announcement that Simpson would return as inspector, and his willingness to accept that, had naturally angered staff. A professional protest to the secretary from almost all the staff had followed. So the staff, including Elisa and me, had initially welcomed the secretary's establishment of a Committee of Inquiry as an appropriate response.

'And that's when everything went wrong,' I continued. 'You've seen the paperwork. The circular on inspection procedures, issued by the Chairman of the Committee of Inquiry, demonstrated that we wouldn't get a fair hearing on concerns about professional administration. We faced a kangaroo court operating under terms of reference we weren't even allowed to see. A number of staff who would have given evidence saw the writing on the wall and backed away. And those who didn't back away found that the committee was not there to investigate the inspector. Instead, it was trying to gather and discredit the evidence of sexual relations with students. Townsend wouldn't let staff question the committee's role. The whole exercise became a farce.'

I paused. Vince had been taking notes and nodding from time to time. 'Tell me what you know about the Committee of Inquiry's report.'

'Only what Townsend told the staff. For a long time, we heard nothing. Then we were told just one recommendation — that someone else would perform inspections at Keravat and one of the other colleges this year. That was fine as far as it went. But it seemed like just a holding action, and we grew more and more suspicious about the rest of the report. The Education Department was clearly working towards a cover-up. With nowhere else to turn, I complained to your Commission.

'Nothing more about the report was officially disclosed. We could guess from the behaviour of Townsend and those who supported him that whatever was in there was bad news for us. And then the Education Department delivered our termination letters.'

Vince continued to take notes. 'How would you describe your behaviour during the time between Gus's death and the arrival of the committee?' he asked quietly.

'I'm not sure what you mean, Vince. Personally, Elisa and I were devastated by Gus's death — he was our best friend. Professionally, it was a tragedy for the college. Everyone felt that. But life continued, and we all started to come to terms with the fact that Gus was dead. It was the Education Department that behaved badly over that time, not us. First, no one from headquarters came to the funeral, and then came the announcement that Simpson was coming back as our inspector after all. That announcement generated the staff protest that led to the Committee of Inquiry.'

Vince put down his pen and picked up a bulky document. He checked some reference in it and then looked straight at me. 'During that time, did you threaten anyone?'

I was puzzled. 'What do you mean, "threaten anyone"?'

Vince continued to look straight at me. 'Did you act violently at any stage?'

'Of course not. Why would I?'

Vince stared intently. 'Did you promise to take personal revenge on the inspector for Gus's death?'

I was getting upset. 'What do you mean, "take personal revenge"? I was determined, for the professional reasons you know about, to get Simpson sacked. And I did what I could to achieve that. So did others — almost every staff member, even the new arrivals, literally signed up to that goal. I acted and behaved professionally to do the right thing despite the Education Department's obstruction.'

Vince put down his document and busily took notes for a minute or so. I felt angry now. I had thought the Ombudsman Commission was investigating our complaint, not investigating *us*. What on earth were these questions about? Was yet another cover-up under way? I decided that if it was, I wouldn't cooperate any further. I folded my arms and prepared to say that.

Vince glanced at his watch. He was silent and thoughtful for what seemed like many seconds. 'Look,' he said slowly, 'it's almost lunchtime. Let me ask you one more question now, and then we can continue after lunch. Do you have a gun in your possession?'

That startled me. What game was he playing? I decided to answer. 'Yes, I do,' I said stiffly. 'It's just a .22 rifle that I used to hunt rabbits back in New Zealand. It arrived with the rest of our personal effects when we moved here. The rifle's been properly licensed by the police.

The previous principal knew all about it and agreed I could keep it in my house. What's the problem with that?'

Vince looked thoughtful again for some moments. Then he seemed to come to a decision.

'As you probably guessed, I've been referring to the Committee of Inquiry's report. You've never been allowed to see that, and under our investigation protocols I'm not free to show it to you.' Vince looked intently at me. 'I'll take my team to lunch now. We'll be away about an hour. You and I will continue our interview when I return at one o'clock sharp, to finish by 2 p.m.

He rose to leave. 'I'll take my notes with me, but I will have to leave all my other papers here. Our Rabaul officer will lock the front door for the lunch break and stay in the reception area. You can go out to lunch yourself or stay here and relax if you prefer. There's water and coffee in the outer office, and here's today's newspaper.'

I tried to keep my face blank and my tone casual. 'That's fine, Vince. I'm not hungry, so I'll stay here where it's cool thanks.' I picked up the newspaper.

I heard voices in the outer office as Vince and his team left. I heard the front door lock. Then everything went quiet. I knew the officer in the outer office couldn't see me clearly.

Vince had been precise about his time of return. But to make sure, I forced myself to read the newspaper, or at least look like I was reading it, for a full five minutes. The second hand on my watch crawled.

After five minutes had passed, I reached across the desk and pulled over the Committee of Inquiry report, carefully memorising its original position. A quiet frenzy began as I read the report and scribbled notes on my pad.

The bulky report began with several prefaces. First came a letter from Secretary for Education Manu to First Assistant Secretary Luten that instructed him to chair the inquiry and appointed the other members. Then Terms of Reference were set out in four numbered headings. They required the Committee of Inquiry to develop findings and recommendations in relation to college inspection procedures, improper behaviour by department staff, any other relevant administrative matters, and potential improvements regarding all those matters. Last, there was a letter of response from Luten to Manu to state that the committee had completed its report which was hereby submitted etc. No surprises in any of that — I just noted each preface as a bullet point.

I turned the page. Here were the secret contents, at last. The report began with a list of the committee's recommendations — 11 in all, under the headings 'Immediate Action' and 'Normal Action'. I eagerly jotted them down, in full.

Recommendations: Immediate Action
1) Immediate transfer of M. Simpson to provincial
inspectorate
2) Immediate confiscation of .22 rifle in possession of J.
Mendzela
3) Immediate termination of present contracts of J. Mendzela,
E. Mendzela, and B. Doubek
4) Colleges Division to play a more effective management role
5) Secretary for Education to write to all concerned, informing
them of recommendations
Recommendations: Normal Action
6) Rewrite and re-stamp J. Mendzela's inspection report, and
destroy old copies with two stamps
7) Review and reissue policy guidelines and inspection
procedures

*8) Future college staff to be recruited from provincial high
school staff
9) Re-examine recruitment procedures with a view to ensuring
that criteria are such that only top-quality personnel are
recruited
10) Close watch to be kept on all expatriate teachers, and repatriation for those who display damaging attitudes and influences detrimental to the system
11) Legal action to be taken against G. Drysdale for damaging
PNG's image overseas*

Now I understood where Vince's question about my rifle had come from!

I checked the accuracy of my notes and looked at my watch. Time was moving fast — to stop at 12.50, I had less than 40 minutes left. I leafed through the rest of the report to understand its structure. A 'General Background' section came first, then detailed comments for each recommendation and finally a number of attachments.

'General Background' comprised eight pages of selective travesty. It began by stating that Simpson's inspection procedures were 'perfectly normal and acceptable, and in line with established procedures'. No mention was made of either the Secretary's Instruction on inspection procedures that I had relied on or the chairman's circular purporting to supersede that instruction. In fact, nothing specific at all was said about Simpson's inspection procedures at Keravat. 'Well, that was conclusive,' I thought sarcastically.

Next came quotations from Keravat's female captain, Helen, to the effect that she was invited to dinner at Gus's house and asked to write a statement. Initially. she was afraid to do so and refused, but Gus had demanded she write a statement. Finally. she did, fearful that otherwise Gus would stop her getting a university scholarship. And she had told the committee that the statement made by the deputy female captain Felicity was obtained in the same manner. What a pack of lies! 'Discredit our evidence and libel Gus at the same time — clever!' I reflected.

Finally, 'General Background' explained how the complaints about Simpson's inspection procedures were part of a personal attack on the inspector. Yes, the committee accepted the validity of Drysdale's letter that implicated Simpson in homosexual activities but decided that concerned the inspector's private life only. He was entitled to have that not looked into under the section of the Constitution that conferred the right to reasonable privacy. No mention of the constitutional exceptions such as criminal activities when that right to privacy did not apply. No mention of the fact that the young man referred to in the letter was a college student. No comments on professional ethics or morals.

I stopped for a moment and checked the time. 'Inspector now totally exonerated from criminal and unprofessional activities,' I mused. But race on — just 25 minutes left to gather as much info as possible!

I skimmed the supporting comments for each recommendation, scribbling down key points. My mind divided in a curious way. One part worked automatically to speed-read and speed-write. Another part developed an ironic commentary. My watch ticked on!

Recommendations: Immediate Action
1) Immediate transfer of M. Simpson to provincial inspectorate; Simpson to be replaced from a list of three inspectors (Miller was first on that list)

Mr Simpson had not behaved improperly, but nevertheless *'his presence could create tension'*. His personality *'led to conflict on occasion'*.

Well, well. A minor criticism of Simpson, probably the only one in the entire report! And this recommendation hadn't even been acted on, except partially and as an interim measure.

2) Immediate confiscation of .22 rifle in possession of J Mendzela
Needless to mention names, the committee had been told that Mendzela had publicly stated to an audience of four staff members that he intended to take vengeance at all costs on the inspector. It could only be suspected that he was not in best mental state.

I sat back amazed. This secret report labelled me crazy, without any evidence. Of course no one could be named, because I never said any such thing. No wonder Vince decided to circumvent his investigation protocols to let me see the report.

My pen faltered. I felt not just angry but nauseous. I took a deep breath and muttered to myself. 'No time! Snap out of it and get through the rest.'

3) Immediate termination of present contracts of J. Mendzela, E. Mendzela, and B. Doubek
These terminations were recommended on the absolute knowledge of the damaging influences these officers are capable of embedding in Papua New Guinean officers in the teaching force.
J. Mendzela had obviously convinced himself that his complaints about inspection procedures were correct. After his rating had been changed, he stood firmer on this and continued to challenge the procedures used by Simpson and the integrity of the inspector. He displayed unsound reasoning when discussing those topics.

I had quoted the secretary's instructions. What, pray tell, was unsound about *my* reasoning?

> *E. Mendzela was hard-working and concerned for students.*
> *However, she had lured the rest of English department into*
> *attacking her Subject Department Head. She was convinced*
> *that Tolley had made verbal comments about her to Simpson,*
> *because she believed Tolley had previously made indecent*
> *remarks to her.*

Total nonsense! Toady Tolley had generated smokescreens to cover up his incompetence.

> *B. Doubek would not recognise proper authority within his*
> *department. He told the committee that 'he would not accept*
> *advice from incompetent people and would teach what he*
> *thought was right'. Other witnesses had commented that he was*
> *influencing national staff, and in particular had lured Luther*
> *Tomba into behaving the same way as him.*

That was what *really* frightened them. We had set a firm professional example for national staff. And, of course, Toady Tolley was the 'proper authority' on teaching English.

> *4) Colleges Division to play a more effective management role*
> *Several teachers told the committee that they felt out of touch*
> *with headquarters* [and] *did not receive full and timely infor-*
> *mation on administrative matters.*

Just waffle.

> *5) Secretary for Education to write to all concerned, informing*
> *them of recommendations.*

The secretary certainly didn't act on that.

> *Recommendations: Normal Action*
> *6) Rewrite and re-stamp J. Mendzela's inspection report, and*
> *destroy old copies with two stamps*
> *Mendzela had complained about two stamps on his report.*
> *This action should satisfy complainant.*

How nice of them to care.

> *7) Review and reissue policy guidelines and inspection*
> *procedures*
> *Present procedures are too vague, and not clear to all staff....*
> *contributed to misunderstandings.... Procedures should be*
> *rewritten so as to have a more satisfactory flavour.*

Well, the chairman had certainly done that, rewriting procedures even *before* his committee recommended that should happen. What an outstanding professional.

> *8) Future college staff to be recruited from provincial high*
> *school staff*
> *Provincial high school work is less demanding and easier to*
> *adjust to.... New recruits would find it easier to fit in... and*
> *only those found suitable would be transferred to colleges.*

Totally impractical. It was the colleges that needed more highly skilled expatriate staff, who would hardly be willing to work at lower levels in high schools first.

> *9) Re-examine recruitment procedures with a view to ensuring*
> *that criteria are such that only top-quality personnel are*
> *recruited*

Criteria should be studied and changed as necessary to elimi-
nate unsuitable recruits.... recognised that it isn't always
possible to detect dangerous attitudes at recruitment, because
these attitudes may only become apparent after recruitment
when tasks are set.

'Dangerous attitudes'... They must be referring to the reaction from ethical professionals who discover they are working in a corrupt system.

10) Close watch to be kept on all expatriate teachers, and repa-
triation for those who display damaging attitudes and influ-
ences detrimental to the system
Inspectors to be instructed to keep a close watch over each expa-
triate officer... recommend repatriation if anyone is found
getting out of line.... Keravat staff now in local provincial high
schools had made inspectors feel unwelcome... and this attitude
could spread to national staff.

Yes, it must be those characters with dangerous attitudes again, 'getting out of line' and 'making inspectors feel unwelcome'! But where did that stuff on provincial high schools come from?

11) Legal action to be taken against G. Drysdale for damaging
PNG's image overseas
Suspected that Drysdale had used college time and resources for
private purposes... clear that exhibition had not given true
picture of his work in Keravat, damaging PNG.

Only *suspected*? Really? And how on earth did they propose to take legal action? And why spread bad publicity about PNG even further?

I checked my watch. Just nine minutes left to review the attachments.

The first attachment listed those interviewed by name, date, place and duration. The list began with 10 Keravat staff, ending with Isobel and Townsend. Next it listed Christine at her school, followed by her principal Boone (so *that* was where the comments about provincial high schools came from). Miller's name was there too — no wonder Elisa's comprehensive report on Tolley to our new inspector had been ignored. The list ended with the headquarters gang, who had been given far more time than anyone at the college. And they had conveniently been in Rabaul on other official business at the time — what a coincidence!

Next came a lengthy report signed by Isobel and Townsend, presented as a chronology. Descriptions of events before Townsend's appointment were mostly factual enough. But this year's 'events' mixed in Townsend's unsupported opinions and insinuations.

> *'Mendzela and Doubek decide to use changed ratings to attack the national education system ... 1981 gets off to a good start ... Gale dies.... Mendzela becomes emotionally disturbed... Townsend announces Simpson will be coming to inspect Keravat.... Continuing staff seek support for their opposition to Simpson from new staff.... Committee of Inquiry arrives.'*

Their report ended with a negative assessment of every individual who had spoken to the committee.

> *'Mendzela emotionally disturbed... Hoban displayed very strong anti-homosexual feeling ... Doubek very insecure'.*

A thorough smear campaign that pretended to be objective and had enough factual context to seem credible. Clever!

Time was almost up. The further attachments looked like unimportant paperwork that I could just flick through. But then came the surprise — a letter from former Keravat principal James Beckham, sent from Australia and addressed directly to the Secretary for Education.

> *Dear Philip*
> *...I agree with Mr Simpson's assessment of Mendzela.... I*
> *know Mendzela has .22 rifle, and may be dangerous.... It*
> *would be possible to terminate Mendzela's contract on psychi-*
> *atric grounds..... Doubek may be under Mendzela's influ-*
> *ence.... Available to answer further questions by telephone....*

Simpson didn't know I had a rifle. So it was *James* who took the initiative to libel me to the committee. In a society living by payback, it could seem plausible that I would swear vengeance for the death of my best friend. Ingenious and unscrupulous.

It was six minutes to one o'clock. Must close before Vince gets back.

I replaced the report on Vince's desk in exactly the position I had found it and tucked my notes into my briefcase. By the time Vince unlocked the outside door at precisely one o'clock, I was reading the newspaper. But my pulse was still racing.

Vince bustled cheerfully into the inner office. He looked first at me, and then at his desk with the report sitting on it. 'I hope you were comfortable while I was out.' He smiled. 'Let's finish the interview.'

Over the next 50 minutes, Vince asked detailed questions from a handwritten list — about professional inspection procedures here and overseas, about our interactions with Simpson and Tolley in the previous year, and about how Christine's letter first came to us. He nodded a lot and took fulsome notes. I gradually relaxed.

Finally, Vince sat back. 'That's it for today. Thanks a lot.'

I started to speak. Vince beat me to it. 'You're wondering what happens from here? Well, we continue the investigation and start to develop our findings. We'll check all the background facts thoroughly, including everything in the Committee of Inquiry report. Then we'll start thinking about recommendations. I'll want to talk to you again in a week or so. Our office will call you.'

Vince looked thoughtful again. 'I know you've been through a lot, and more waiting won't be easy.' Then he grinned broadly at me. 'Don't worry, we'll get to the truth. Just hang in there!'

I thanked Vince and exited, blinking in the harsh sunlight. My thoughts whirled as I drove home.

40. Media Negotiations (Elisa)

SOON AFTER JOHN left for his interview with the Ombudsman Commission in Rabaul, Bohdan arrived. 'Have you seen *this*?' he demanded. 'This' was a copy of *The Times*, an English-language weekly that had started up just months previously. *The Times* came out at the weekend and carried more features than news. It had already printed a long article on 'What Really Happened at Keravat?' that began with the published review of explicitly sexual art and outlined the events leading to the Education Department's Committee of Inquiry. Another article, titled 'No teachers, no classes, no exams', had highlighted the impacts on students. *The Times* hadn't printed anything about Keravat since, apart from a few terse facts in their round-up of the week's news. All fine from our point of view.

But this latest issue carried a hostile editorial. The tone and approach completely contradicted the line taken by other media and their own earlier feature. *The Times* editor seemed to have been given the Committee of Inquiry report that none of us had seen. He explained that the committee had found no evidence against the inspector and characterised the sacked teachers as troublemakers who were indulging in 'petty quarrels' and 'minor obsessions'. I read the editor's conclusion out loud. 'The inspector of colleges has borne the brunt of a campaign to discredit him personally and professionally, which has not produced a shred of real evidence.'

'Looks as though one of Simpson's friends wrote that!' I suggested. 'Don't worry about it. I'll show the paper to John when he gets back.' We chatted a while before Bohdan departed for his interview with the Ombudsman Commission.

John returned a few hours later. 'Well, how did it go?' I asked eagerly as he walked in.

John sat down heavily. He paused before replying. 'Well, now I know how that so-called "Committee of Inquiry" set us up for the sack. I'm a dangerous lunatic, you're wrecking your department, and Bohdan's stirring up the national staff. So, of course, we had to go!'

John described the start of his interview and Vince's decision to circumvent his investigation protocols. 'That was brave. We must never say or do anything to compromise him. Everything I tell you now must stay just between the two of us — we can't even tell Bohdan.'

We worked through John's notes from the report. He added a few points as my questions sparked further recollections. Finally, John sat back, looking exhausted. I realised why. 'Don't tell me you haven't eaten all day!' He nodded. I made a quick meal and we went to bed early. I didn't dare show John the story in *The Times*.

To bed, but not to sleep. John tossed and turned sleeplessly for the entire night but gallantly tried not to wake me. I pretended to sleep, but I was awake most of the time. Then our neighbourhood rooster enthusiastically announced dawn, just outside our window. We both jumped up with a start.

'Well, so much for lying in. Let's get up and have breakfast,' I suggested.

John looked haggard but determined. 'Those bastards have tried to ruin my career, and yours. They will fail. I could tell from Vince's comments at the end that he'll do a thorough job and demand hard facts from them, which they won't be able to come up with. And our evidence on everything else is rock-solid; remember what Bernard from the PSC team said about that.'

Over breakfast, we planned our day. We would visit with our friends but keep what we knew about the Committee of Inquiry's report strictly to ourselves. John relaxed and grew cheerful. I decided to show him the story in *The Times* before someone else did.

John surprised me. Instead of getting angry, he laughed. 'Cheeky buggers, aren't they? Nice try, leaking the report. But bad timing. I've seen the report myself now. I'll fix them. Let's go find a phone!'

'To call Peter, so he can do what he did with the radio people?' I cautiously enquired.

'No. I can do this myself.'

An hour later, June, Bohdan, Mark and I listened as John spoke by telephone to the editor of *The Times*. We could only hear one side of the conversation, but it was still a great spectator experience.

John sparkled with energetic outrage. 'Yes, that's right. A defamation suit. And that's just for starters. The Ombudsman Commission investigation is under way now, and I can assure you they will find plenty of evidence to report on. You're going to look not just biased but stupid! And maybe the Commission will sue you for pre-empting their investigation.'

The telephone had a long cord from the wall. John walked up and down holding the phone to his ear for several minutes as the editor responded. He winked at us before continuing. 'Who on earth did you talk to before writing that story? What did they show you? And what did you think they were up to?'

Another long pause and another wink. 'All right, I believe you. You've been deceived,' John said more sympathetically. 'But you've defamed us. The question now is what will you do about that?'

Another long response that we couldn't hear followed. John took notes. Finally, he spoke again. 'I'll have to speak to the others about that. They're right here — we were ready to head to our lawyer's office. Wait a minute please.'

John covered the phone. 'Will we be satisfied with a retraction and an apology, plus a new feature article that will cover the entire Keravat affair in depth and criticise the Education Department? All that to appear in next week's edition?' Absolutely we would! John waited a few minutes before resuming the phone conversation and then confirmed the deal in a positive tone — it was good to have cleared up this 'misunderstanding' with their new commitments 'as I have noted and read back to you'. He hung up grinning from ear to ear, and we celebrated with Bohdan's favourite drink of cafe cognac.

The rest of the week passed cheerfully too. The Ombudsman Commission investigation dropped out of the headlines, but the *Post-Courier* and even *Niugini Nius* printed letters from teachers and students at other educational institutions, all of them supporting us. Some openly declared that the problems exposed at Keravat were widespread in the education system. Meanwhile the pidgin weekly roundly condemned the Education Department's action to send the students home and thereby further damage their studies. To anyone following the story, the Education Department's silence could only be a guilty plea.

The courts, acting swiftly for once, scheduled charges against 230 students to be heard not long after their exams. That sparked yet another round of public outrage and media comment. Why were the students still being victimised for their justified protests?

Despite all the positive news, John and I felt uncertain about our future. Could we be reinstated? If so, should we stay? Or should we pack up to leave? And if we left, where would we go? With his contract almost expired anyway, Bohdan had already started looking for work opportunities in other countries. Should we start looking too?

We waited edgily for the promised call from the Ombudsman Commission. That finally came late Friday afternoon. John would see Vince again on Monday. The weekend's *Times* arrived too, with everything printed precisely as the editor had promised.

41. A Deal Emerges (John)

THE OMBUDSMAN COMMISSION's outer office was no longer engulfed in papers. Instead, a pile of labelled boxes stood in the corner. Staff packed another box while I waited. Everyone was friendly, but they conveyed an air of winding down and moving on.

Vince called me into his office. We shook hands, and one of his team brought coffee. Vince's desk was clear this time. He began informally, wearing a big smile. 'Well, how are you? And how's Elisa?'

I'd gone in resolved to demand a quick result. 'We're okay, I guess. Thanks for asking. But we've waited a long time for an outcome. What happens now?'

Vince kept smiling. 'Okay, I can understand your impatience. But I must complete our investigation properly. Our team still has more research and interviewing to do, back in Moresby and in other places around the country too. Then we've got to write up a report. At this stage, I can't disclose the likely outcome of our investigation.'

My resolve crumbled. I spoke haltingly. 'Vince, we've behaved professionally and put our careers on the line to protect our students. And for that, the Education Department tried to ruin us.' Embarrassing tears threatened my eyes. 'Please help.'

Vince didn't stop smiling. 'I know you've been through a lot. I didn't say I can't *talk* about the likely outcome. In fact, provided you agree to keep our discussion confidential, I want to do that.'

I mustered control and agreed.

Vince explained his intentions. 'This is a special investigation under our constitutional statute, and that demands a full public report to parliament. Our commission wants to recommend practical and conclusive outcomes. We are willing for the Secretary for Education — who after all did the right things originally — to personally emerge in the clear, as someone who put things right after being misled by his subordinates. That will bring him onto our side.

'We can and will comprehensively discredit the Education Department's Committee of Inquiry, which wrongly advised the secretary. And we will identify those responsible for that. Faced with all the evidence, the inspector will either resign and leave PNG or face sacking and criminal charges.'

Vince leaned forward and looked at me. 'But our biggest challenge concerns the three of you. We can conclude that your contract terminations were certainly not "in the best interests" of the students or the nation. And we will conclude that. Then you could take legal action to overturn the sackings or even sue for damages. But that's an uncertain path, and it would certainly take a long time.

'Or....' He paused. 'You could accept our conclusions as restoring your reputation and accept new one-year contracts from the Education Department to eliminate your potential financial loss. And you would have to serve out those contracts someplace else, not at Keravat. I think we could negotiate that outcome with the secretary. I hope you can accept it. If you won't, then I'm not sure we can negotiate the rest of the package either. It's your call.'

I looked down silently for a while. What did we really want? To be right and principled or to achieve a positive outcome? What did winning mean? What would Gus do?

When I raised my head, Vince was still looking at me. I looked back and nodded. 'We'll agree to what you propose. I need to check that with Elisa, and especially with Bohdan. But let's assume we have a deal. What do the three of us do while your investigation and report play out?'

Vince spoke decisively. 'You must get away from Keravat before the students come back for the last term. Far away. Too many things could go wrong if you stay there, and plenty of people might try to make that happen. Move out of your houses, put your personal stuff in storage, and take a holiday for two or three weeks while we sort everything out. Don't leave PNG though — you might have trouble getting back in.'

I drove home jubilant. Elisa soon shared my triumph and agreed to accept the deal Vince was offering. 'Just one thing though, John. What happens with Toady Tolley? Firstly, he's incompetent and, secondly, he's supported corruption. And for that matter, what about Townsend and Isobel? They should all go. Especially Luten, that oaf who chaired the Committee of Inquiry!'

'I don't know what will happen with them. Vince is focused on ousting Simpson and vindicating the three of us. He won't discuss outcomes for anyone else with me, and I can't insist. We need to confirm our deal with Vince now and leave the rest for him to pursue later.'

We went to see Bohdan. To our surprise, he baulked. 'I want to sue them! It's different for you two. I am still rated "Unsatisfactory" —

that could ruin my career. And I want to know what the Committee of Inquiry report said about us. Vince wouldn't even show that to me!'

I couldn't disclose that I knew what was in the report. I quoted Vince's statement that under his investigation protocols he couldn't show it to us. Yes, we could probably sue the Education Department and get that report exposed in court. But, I argued, to refuse the deal Vince was offering and take legal action surely wasn't a better option. 'How much more money would we have to put in? And how long would it take? And the Education Department would probably take no action against Simpson or do anything else. Bohdan, I'm sure Peter as our lawyer would advise us to accept what Vince is offering. We can call him tomorrow morning to check.'

Next morning, Peter did indeed advise us to accept the deal on offer. Bohdan had slept on the matter and was happy to take that advice. I immediately drove into town to see Vince, who was about to leave for Moresby. As I expected, he still wouldn't answer questions about other individuals. 'John, to get the secretary on our side, I need to negotiate three simple bottom lines: injustice occurred, new contracts for you three, and the inspector goes. And while our Commission negotiates that, you three must maintain a low profile, leave the area and stay away from the students. That's what you're agreeing to. Do we have a deal?'

We did. I thanked Vince. I assured him we would leave Keravat within a week and take a holiday away from students while he finished the investigation. And I looked intently at Vince as I promised that 'everything I learned in your office will stay confidential, even from our friends'.

42. Escape by Sea (Elisa)

A BUSY WEEK BEGAN. Students would start returning for term four in just 10 days.

We decided to put all our bulky gear and our car in storage, to await further instructions. There was a lot to pack up and catalogue — including the infamous .22 rifle. But with no work commitments, our preparations didn't take too long.

It was even easier for Bohdan, who had fewer personal possessions. He soon sold his vehicle and arranged a holiday. 'I'm going to the next province, to stay in a village. One of my students invited me.'

I didn't like the sound of that. 'Bohdan, do you think that's smart? We agreed to stay away from students. We have a lot of enemies, watching for anything they can use to smear us.'

Bohdan waved my concerns away. 'Don't worry, her father invited me. I met him in town earlier this year. It won't look out of place.'

John joined in. '*Her*? You mean a female student? Don't be an idiot!

You're putting us all at risk. We *must* stay away from the students until the commission reports publicly. I'm sure Vince told you that.'

Bohdan wouldn't budge. 'What if he did? It's my business, not yours. Don't tell me what to do. If it wasn't for me, you'd be gone from here weeks ago, with your reputations ruined.'

John was implacable. More angry words followed from both of them. Eventually the argument wound down.

I tried to play peacemaker. 'Okay, Bohdan. Do what you want. But we've come too far together to mess up now. Please be careful and apply good judgement.'

He promised he would.

Our next problem was where to go and when. We could make our international flight bookings open-dated and we could stay with friends on the mainland while Vince negotiated a deal. But we still had to get to Moresby at some stage. And we knew that airline staff in Rabaul would gossip — someone would be sure to keep the Education Department gang informed. That was not just undesirable; it might be dangerous. Violent 'incidents' often occurred in Moresby, and our foes must be getting desperate.

We visited a bustling Rabaul harbour to sort out storage of our effects. John ploughed through the paperwork with a shipping agent, in an office near the docks. I wasn't needed, so I ambled around to enjoy the motley assortment of ships and boats and take in the stunning harbour views. I had loved ships and the sea ever since I was a child visiting my grandmother in southern Italy. I would sit on the beach there and watch huge vessels plough through the Straits of Messina. I was impressed by how those gigantic and sometimes dilapidated behemoths, adorned with exotic flags and names, passed within spitting distance of me sitting on the sandy shore. I marvelled at how they could forge a path across the wild and distant oceans. What freedom of movement the sea gave them! Ever after I had pictured the sea not as a barrier but as a pathway to anywhere in the world.

Inspiration struck. Why not leave by *sea*? Cargo ships plied the waters between here and the mainland, on regular timetables. Surely some of them might also carry passengers.

Excited by that idea, I hurried back to the shipping agency. John was about to finish up there and it was easy to start a casual conversation about regional shipping. Why yes, the agent told me. Cargo ships sometimes ferried passengers between their ports of call. Usually passengers just sat on deck, but some ships had cabins. We left his office without saying any more.

John gratefully adopted my suggestion to leave by sea. We checked timetables and made enquiries. Yes, a cargo ship leaving in a few days could take us to Lae. And it had two passenger cabins. Their larger cabin was already booked, but we could reserve a small two-bunk cabin for a modest price. The booking clerk looked at us doubtfully. He explained that the cabin wasn't very comfortable, the trip was 'a little slow' (three days and two nights), and the passage through open seas to the mainland could be 'plenty rough'. No worries, we said, and booked passage under our alias of 'Mr and Mrs Portman'.

Back home, we followed Vince's advice to keep a low profile. We told only Mark about our departure plans, after first swearing him to secrecy. Surreptitiously, we telephoned friends on the mainland and arranged for them to meet us off the ship in Lae. A couple of trips to town sufficed to drop off our chattels for storage.

The day before departure brought an unexpected visitor — Isaac, our traditional carver. As usual, he had a couple of carvings with him.

Isaac knew enough about recent events to realise that with our future still uncertain we weren't buying anything more right now. No worries, he told us, he was not selling anything today. Instead he had brought us a gift. 'Mi save yu mas go pinis nau. Dispela samting i ken kisim yutupela long kantri bilong me gen. Olsem long narapela ples ating' (I know you must leave now. This can bring you back to my country. But maybe to a different place).

His gift was a simple but elegantly carved black walking stick, sized for someone my five-foot-zero height. Isaac explained that he had not carved the walking stick but inherited it from his father. We were touched — and heartened — by his generous gift and parting good wishes.

That afternoon we drove to our familiar local beach for a last swim and to watch the sunset. We felt sad as the huge red sun slid into the sea. Our life at Keravat was setting too, and we would probably never see this beach, our dear friends, or our students again. As we drove away, several other staff arrived and called out to us — we just waved and pretended to be in a rush.

Packing our on-board luggage was easy, since we didn't have much gear left. The biggest item was John's immense pile of paperwork.

Bohdan came to see us that evening, in a grumpy mood. The Ombudsman Commission had been in touch with him again, by phone. Vince was unhappy about Bohdan's holiday plans. 'It's not their business where I go in my free time! Who do they think they are?'

I gingerly probed. What was their specific concern?

'You already know. They don't like me going to a village to visit students. Someone's already making trouble about that, from the last time. Now the Commission wants to interview me again in Moresby!'

We were stunned. What last time?

The full story slowly emerged. During a previous term break, Bohdan had visited — and stayed in — the home village of a female student. Someone had told the Ombudsman Commission about that visit, and it was now part of their collected evidence. I was appalled. John was horrified. And furious. 'Can't you see this could wreck everything? What a bloody idiot you can be!' The two of them wrangled furiously for a while.

Eventually I calmed them down. 'We need to focus. What happens from here?' We swapped plans. Bohdan would leave the day after tomorrow for his village visit and then see the Ombudsman Commission again in Port Moresby before flying overseas. He was still angry. 'I'll be busy when you leave tomorrow, delivering my car and packing. Let's say goodbye now.' Our farewells were stiff and uncomfortable, and we went to bed unhappy.

We faced another sad task in the morning. When Aipat arrived to start his chores, we sat him down. I explained that we were sorry to say we would leave the house soon, so we wouldn't need him to work for us anymore. John gave Aipat a month's extra pay — a small fortune in his terms — and a written reference. He could remain in his small house at the back for now at least and maybe work for the new occupants later. Aipat had seen the house emptying and expressed no surprise. He accepted the situation stoically and said he would miss us. And we would certainly miss him.

Next afternoon we drove into town and added our car to the rest of our gear, to be held in storage and shipped out later. Then we boarded our temporary maritime home. The cargo ship, a 40-metre-long veteran, badly needed a coat of paint. As we'd been warned, our cabin was cramped and uncomfortable: two bunks, a small wardrobe and a dilapidated sink. No air conditioning or fan. The small scratched and discoloured porthole didn't open. A sailor delivered our luggage and told us that dinner would be served after we were well out of the harbour — the captain would be busy with piloting until then.

We unpacked and went out on deck for a last look at Rabaul. Neither of us said anything, but I could tell John was, like me, feeling glum and uncertain. The ship's engine throbbed noisily and the whistle sounded. Sailors pulled up the gangway and untied mooring ropes.

A familiar voice called from the wharf. It was Mark and a group of our supporters from the college, shouting and waving! Surprised and delighted, we shouted and waved back. They wished us luck. We all promised to stay in touch and keep fighting the good fight. John pretended to chastise Mark — 'so much for our secret departure!' — but our happiness and gratitude was obvious. And as we moved out of earshot, Bohdan joined the group of waving well-wishers — he'd come too!

The ship chugged away from the wharf. With a final wave, our friends turned away. Feeling much happier, we stayed on deck to farewell Rabaul. The stunning beauty around us felt poignant. We would probably never again see the magnificent drowned caldera of the harbour or sniff its competing smells of frangipani, coconut and sulphur. Worse, we might never again see our dear friends and students — people who had stood by us at great personal risk.

Dinner at the captain's table followed an hour later. The fare was simple and hearty. Our fellow passengers from the large cabin turned out to be a family of Scandinavian missionaries travelling to the mainland for a new posting there. They readily accepted our bland explanation of our journey as 'a short break to do something different'. But the captain and his two officers were a different story. Our vague statements about 'working for government in Rabaul' just whetted their curiosity. Our unfamiliarity with people who should in that small town have been mutual acquaintances first puzzled and then annoyed them. To escape their questions, we pleaded need for an early night. But we wondered what they might say amongst themselves.

43. Unmasked! (John)

THE NIGHT PASSED UNEVENTFULLY. Our vessel hugged the north coastline of New Britain, in a calm sea. Elisa and I slept long and well. Over a hearty breakfast, taken after everyone else had finished, we watched our ship chug into Kimbe, its first port of call. The captain called us over. 'The ship will stay in Kimbe for five hours, until 4 p.m. So you have plenty of time to go ashore. Just don't be late back.' Keen to stretch our legs, we set out on foot to explore the wharf area and the small town beyond.

To our surprise, Kimbe explored us back. As we strolled down the main street, many nationals gazed at us curiously. Several expats stared hard. And it was growing too hot to walk around. 'I guess they don't get many expat visitors here,' Elisa observed. 'Let's find a cold drink somewhere.'

A small supermarket offered a basic snack bar, which to our surprise was already selling today's daily papers. Great — we had become keen newshounds. We might see a new story or letter on the Keravat affair.

We sat down with a juice and tried to ignore the obvious interest in us from other patrons. Elisa opened the *Post-Courier*. I scanned *Niugini Nius*. Nothing in that. I looked up and saw Elisa reading carefully. She seemed surprised. 'Something in the *Post-Courier*?' I said impatiently.

Elisa looked at me archly and passed over the paper. 'Take a look at page seven.'

The full-page feature that rumbled our clandestine sea escape (Post-Courier)

Page seven was a full-page feature, headed by a large photo of the two of us under the headline 'Sacked — The Conflict that Set the Campus Alight'. I read eagerly. The article first reminded readers about the hundreds of Keravat students arrested. Then it explained the background to that crisis with fresh details. The story described Gus as the man originally 'at the centre of the controversy that led to those recent dramatic events, who would have been on the deportation list too'. The story moved on to praise us. We had 'courageously carried on the fight against unethical behaviour and suffered severe penalties for doing that'. The feature ended with a reference to the Ombudsman Commission investigation now in progress, which would (the writer hoped) finally reveal the full truth. Another story on the facing page talked of many stranded Keravat students unable to fly back for the upcoming start of term four, despite a demand from the Prime Minister to 'Get Students Back!'

I leaned back in my chair, pensive. 'Remember when Simon took that photo of us and said he was thinking about a feature? We urged him to recognise Gus's role, not just ours. But that was weeks ago, before the students even began their boycott. With all that's happened since, I thought the idea was forgotten!'

'Well, clearly it wasn't.' Elisa replied. 'And that's great. But now we know why people are staring at us.' She frowned. 'What do we tell them back at the ship? The captain won't like being lied to. Probably he'll tell us to leave.' We decided to return right away and explain our deception before the captain learned about it from someone else.

The captain didn't seem fazed by our request for a private discussion. He listened attentively as we used the newspaper story to explain ourselves, emphasising the *official advice* we had from the Ombudsman Commission to keep a low profile. 'We certainly owe you an apology for giving you a false name and humbugging

everyone at dinner last night. But I hope you can understand why we
needed to do that.'

The captain looked stern for a moment. Then he laughed. 'Oh, the
boys and me knew you were humbugging. We just didn't know why.
We thought you were probably running off together from some
husband or wife — maybe from both. We planned to find out more
at dinner tonight.'

He continued more thoughtfully. 'I wasn't surprised to read about
the troubles at Keravat. A lot of that stuff goes on. It's almost a tradition now for expat homosexuals to recruit their overseas friends into
jobs here. Rabaul's full of them. We've even had them sneaking
around the boat a couple of times, looking for targets. The crew
threw one guy in the harbour!'

He laughed at the memory, then looked stern again. 'But I must
punish you for lying to me.' He grinned. 'I tell you what. You give us
the whole story over dinner tonight, and we'll call it even.'

We tried to mix drama and humour in our dinnertime tale. The officers enjoyed both. The missionaries, recently arrived from overseas,
listened with horror and promised to pray for our success in combat-
ting such evil. Discussion grew animated for a while. Then the
captain rapped on the table. 'Until now we've been sailing on the
sheltered side of New Britain. But later tonight we move into open
water. Heavy seas are likely there. I suggest an early night for
everyone.'

We quickly complied and soon fell asleep. But not for long. The ship
began to pitch and roll. Elisa became seriously seasick. Loud prayers
from the next cabin, interrupted by retching noises, told us our new
missionary friends were suffering too. Feeling queasy myself, I went
out to spend the rest of the night on deck. Holding tightly to a stair-

well, the swell didn't seem too bad. It just tossed the ship up and down in an unpredictable way, without breaking over the deck. We were uncomfortable, not endangered. But Gus would have been in serious peril traversing these waters back to Rabaul in a small yacht.

By mid-morning the sea had calmed enough to allow breakfast, though I was the sole passenger at the table. Our friends collected us off the wharf at lunchtime and announced their diversion plan. They would drive us a long way into the hills and then head off elsewhere on business. We could spend two nights quietly at an empty house there and fly into Moresby from a totally unexpected direction under our pseudonyms.

Forty-eight hours later, we landed at the capital's domestic air terminal. There we bumped into Anthony, an Education Department expat whom we knew slightly. He had just seen someone off.

Anthony stared at us with amazement. 'I didn't know there was a flight from Rabaul this afternoon!'

We enjoyed his surprise. 'There isn't. We didn't come from there.' Anthony was eager to gossip. We stayed tight-lipped. 'Sorry to seem rude, Anthony, but we're here on confidential business.'

'Can I drop you somewhere?' Anthony persisted.

We couldn't easily refuse. 'Sure, thank you. We'll be staying at the old Papuan Hotel in the town centre.' We fended off his persistent attempts to pump us and soon reached the hotel.

We checked in and confirmed we could extend our reservation as long as necessary. After unpacking, we ambled down to the piano bar for a drink. The bar was busy with people coming and going, but there was no one there we knew. We enjoyed our anonymity for a while, certain that it wouldn't last long. Soon enough, I noticed the door from the corridor opening quietly but without anyone coming in. Then a familiar face appeared, peering earnestly around the bar. It was Superintendent of Operations Bruce Hawthorne from Colleges Division! Catching my gaze, his face quickly disappeared. We strolled to dinner laughing.

44. Triumph and Departure (Elisa)

EARLY THE NEXT MORNING, we took a taxi to the head office of the Ombudsman Commission to keep the appointment we made before flying to the capital. We briefly met the Chief Ombudsman — an impressive national with a legal and religious background — and proceeded to Vince's office for a briefing.

The news wasn't as good as we'd hoped. Vince explained the situation. 'We still have a few loose ends to tie up before we can close the investigation. Our main recommendations are clear already, but it may be weeks before we can formally report to parliament. It's crucial that you stay in PNG until we finish.'

John was unhappy. 'Look, Vince, that's just not fair. We stayed on after our contracts were terminated and fought for justice. But we've already spent a lot of money doing that, and now we're living in a hotel. That's expensive! And psychologically, we really need to get away from all this.'

Vince was sympathetic but firm. 'Sorry, but that's how it is. And it could be worse. Bohdan almost compromised everything. I interviewed him again yesterday, right here. I explained that the commission couldn't support his complaint about the Education Department and criticise officers there for dubious ethical conduct, after hearing that he spent time with female students in their home villages. And worse, we were told female students sometimes visited his house on the campus too and spent time alone with him there.'

We looked at one another, dismayed. Vince continued. 'So, I formally asked Bohdan to withdraw his complaint and let the commission focus on putting *your* situation right.'

We looked at one another again. I spoke first. 'And Bohdan wouldn't withdraw?'

Vince grew pensive. 'Not at first. He just got angry with me, and he didn't seem happy with you two either. He assured me — on his honour — that nothing sexual had occurred with female students. I agreed we had no evidence of that. And no one had directly accused him. However, his conduct looked wrong, and the commission has a duty to publish all the facts. It would be harder for us to make any positive recommendation about your contracts, and the public report might damage his future career prospects. Therefore, I explained, it would be in his own best interests, not just yours, to withdraw.'

Vince shook his head. 'That sobered him. He asked me what would happen with his new contract if he withdrew.

'I explained that was now out of our hands. He had already been paid to the end of his contract. No one has any right to contract renewal. And after what we've learned, we can't press for that. The most he was likely to get from the Education Department was an apology.'

Vince brightened. 'Bohdan got the message in the end and withdrew his complaint. It was hard work though. And he seems to bear you two a grudge, for no good reason that I can see. I doubt you'll hear from him again.'

We thanked Vince profusely. Saddened, we returned to discussing next steps for us. Surely there was some way to speed up the process.

Vince outlined a possible path forward. The commission could negotiate for our contract reinstatement only, as an initial step. It should be feasible to issue a preliminary report privately to the Secretary for Education, who could gracefully accept that recommendation. Then we could safely leave the country while the wider issues were fully investigated and reported to parliament. 'But you will still need to sit tight here until we negotiate that interim outcome.'

The days passed slowly. Law and order was always problematic in Moresby, especially after dark. So we couldn't go out much. For energetic people, sitting by the near-deserted pool like idle vacationers wasn't much fun. There were only so many lengths we could swim. Without our friends and students, we felt isolated — confined to barracks, not on holiday. And we were under orders not to discuss our situation with anyone. To spin out funds, we lived frugally by shopping outside for snack food and dining in the hotel restaurant only every second night.

Continuing controversy in the newspapers helped counter our anxiety and boredom:

- Term four at Keravat started with a majority of students still
  to return. Concerned parents and politicians publicly
  bewailed the past and continuing disruption to studies
  caused by the Education Department's wrongful actions
  and its attempts to cover those up.

- 'Tavarek Rebel' (a student anonymously spelling Keravat backwards) outlined how the students had been lied to. He lamented the damage to college property and student prospects: 'All this would not have happened if you, Mr Secretary, had just flown over and answered our questions. Questions and answers, very simple.'

- 'Gay n Clean' opined that 'Male educators who muck around with boy students are just as guilty of professional misconduct as their male colleagues who muck around with girl students. They should be sacked!'

- 'Experienced Expat' took an opposite stance. The sacked teachers 'had ruined the careers of senior officers and... embittered and disrupted the schooling of students'. He concluded that 'The decision has been made to get rid of these three people. In all justice, let it be carried out immediately.'

Ten days after briefing us, on Friday morning, Vince finally called our hotel room to explain the interim outcome he had negotiated with the Secretary for Education.

John handled the conversation while I listened in. 'John, the secretary will call you shortly. He will accept and act on our commission's recommendation that you both be given new one-year contracts *provided that* you and Elisa accept that outcome as full legal settlement of your complaint. The Education Department will find you a new posting for next year, outside the college system and well away from Keravat. And you already understand the wider background to that deal. Our report to parliament will present the secretary himself in a favourable light, as someone trying to do the proper thing but being misled by his officers. Then he can be seen publicly to "put things right". It's the best outcome that we can get for you quickly. So, whatever you might feel about it all, please be gracious!'

John concurred. Vince reminded us again about the need to keep everything confidential until the commission formally reported to parliament. Then he hung up.

Five minutes later, the phone rang again. John picked it up. An unfamiliar voice spoke. 'This is Philip Manu, the Secretary for Education. Am I speaking with Mr John Mendzela? I believe you are expecting my call?'

'This is John Mendzela, Mr Manu. Yes, I was advised you would call.'

The secretary was official and precise. 'Mr Mendzela, the Ombudsman Commission has made me aware of a number of new facts concerning Keravat College and your personal situation. I understand that you have spoken with the commission about its potential recommendation concerning you and your wife?'

John was equally official and precise. 'Yes, Mr Manu, I have. I can confirm to you that Mrs Mendzela and I are willing to accept new one-year contracts with the Education Department as full and final legal settlement in relation to the termination of our previous contracts.'

The secretary's tone grew more friendly. 'Then we will proceed on that basis. I am pleased to resolve this matter.' He paused. 'I hope that despite encountering various difficulties you and your wife have enjoyed your time in Papua New Guinea.'

John turned on the charm too. 'Thank you, Mr Secretary. Yes, we have greatly enjoyed working here. And we will be pleased to continue next year. But first we will take a holiday.'

The secretary chuckled. He sounded wistful. 'Yes, a holiday will be good. And thank you for your contributions to our education system and your work for our students. I am pleased to have spoken with you personally. Goodbye.'

John put the phone down and shouted. We embraced, almost disbelieving. Could it really all be over, at last? Sworn to confidentiality, we couldn't even tell anyone the good news. But we could finally relax and splash out on champagne and a celebration dinner without worrying too much about the price tag!

Next morning was Saturday. Staying cautious about our finances, we shopped for our lunch snacks outside the hotel as usual. At the supermarket checkout, an expatriate man I didn't know came up to us. 'Hi, John. Congratulations on your victory! When we met at the symposium a year ago and talked about professional ethics over drinks, I had no idea what you were involved with.'

John replied cautiously. 'Hi, Robert. This is my wife, Elisa.'

Robert shook my hand. 'Congratulations to both of you! How does it feel to be heroes?'

I was cautious too. 'Pleased to meet you, Robert. But I'm not sure what you mean.'

Robert looked astonished. 'Haven't you heard the radio? You're all over the news!'

No, we hadn't. Robert effusively explained. 'The bulletin was dramatic. Secretary for Education Manu personally announced that in response to a preliminary report from the Ombudsman Commission, he will ask the Public Service Commission to offer you new contracts. A full report to parliament will come later, with more recommendations. The announcer talked for several minutes about the arrests at Keravat College and the way reporting improper conduct to the authorities got you sacked. Like I said, you came across as real heroes! What a shame you didn't hear it.'

Robert left, still congratulating us. With the embargo on public announcements clearly ended, we felt able to call our friends in

Keravat and celebrate success. It felt good to speak to our dear friends after all this time. We could hear the glow of happiness in their voices.

In the afternoon, we walked cautiously down the hill to Ela Beach. The police band was giving a concert. Their brassy numbers elated us and a solo bagpiper was a real treat. The concert closed with the national anthem:

> *O arise all you sons of this land*
> *Let us sing of our joy to be free,*
> *Praising God and rejoicing to be*
> *Papua New Guinea*
> *Shout our name from the mountains to the seas*
> *Papua New Guinea;*
> *Let us raise our voices and proclaim*
> *Papua New Guinea*
> *Now give thanks to the good Lord above*
> *For His kindness, His Wisdom and love*
> *For this land of our fathers so free*
> *Papua New Guinea*
> *Shout again for the whole world to hear*
> *Papua New Guinea*
> *We're independent and we're free,*
> *Papua New Guinea*

The last verse — 'we're independent and we're free' — spoke directly to us. We sang along heartily.

On Monday morning, Vince explained our Saturday surprise. 'The public announcement was the secretary's initiative, not ours. I think Manu wanted to get the news out and make himself look good before facing the rest of it. Our preliminary report didn't pull any punches about how his Committee of Inquiry became a deliberate cover-up to protect senior officials in the Education Department. And we are still working on who those people are and what should happen to them. But your own situation can be sorted out quickly now. I suggest you book a flight out for next week while that happens.'

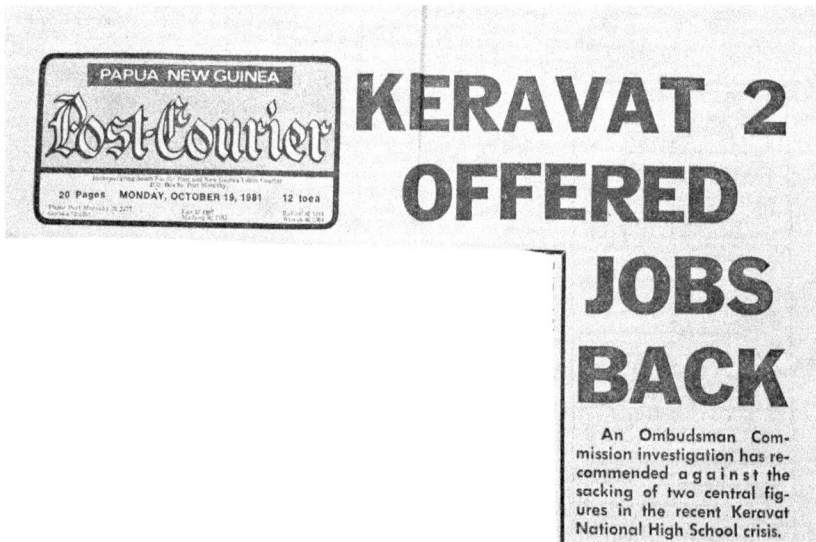

PAPUA NEW GUINEA

Post-Courier

20 Pages   MONDAY, OCTOBER 19, 1981   12 toea

KERAVAT 2 OFFERED JOBS BACK

An Ombudsman Commission investigation has recommended a g a i n s t the sacking of two central figures in the recent Keravat National High School crisis.

Finally, after five investigations, the front page says we've won.... (Post-Courier)

We enjoyed a pleasant week as more events unfolded through the newspapers. The front page of Monday's *Post-Courier* echoed the radio news — 'Keravat 2 Offered Jobs Back'. An official announcement from the Public Service Commission that they would offer us new contracts 'at the recommendation of the Secretary for Education' ended the initial story.

Next day came the headline we had worked so hard and long for: 'Keravat Man Quits'. Simpson — cautiously described only as 'the inspector whose conduct had been questioned by the terminated teachers' — had resigned and would leave the country. Claiming he was 'the victim of unsubstantiated allegations', Simpson refused to comment further. So did the Education Department. The flow of news wound down with the Chief Ombudsman's statement that his Commission was 'continuing its investigations into other related issues and would present a full report to parliament later this year'.

... and next day the inspector resigns (Post-Courier)

Media criticism of the Education Department rumbled on though. The *Post-Courier* thundered that 'to reinstate the sacked Keravat teachers is only the first small move. Whose interests were best served? That judgement can only follow public disclosure of the facts.' Even *Niugini Nius* ran a strong editorial. 'The students have been the pawns in this sad game. They protested, believing in the innocence of the teachers. For their troubles, they were charged and valuable schooling was lost. For the teachers, who believed they were doing the Education Department a service, the sack was their reward. This nation cannot afford to have the future careers of these students destroyed by heavy-handed, irresponsible bureaucracy.'

Fresh controversy emerged too. The Prime Minister demanded that the charges against Keravat students be dropped. The Minister of Police refused, citing his constitutional independence. The charges would remain and the court hearings would proceed.

We received an invitation to attend the offices of the Public Service Commission. They even sent a car. A genial official welcomed us into his office. He explained (again) that yes, the Public Service

Commission was the formal employer for expatriates working in government, but naturally they needed to rely on the recommendations of the departments where those officers worked. It was certainly not *their* fault that our contracts had been wrongly terminated. Fortunately, they could now act on the recommendation of the Secretary for Education and offer us a new contract. We would be re-recruited (from England this time) 'in due course'.

'Why not sign up the contract now?' John demanded.

The official was expecting that question. Still genial, he explained that it was necessary for the Ombudsman Commission to finish its investigation and issue its formal report and recommendations. Then the Education Department would organise its staffing for next year and formally request our re-employment, and *then* his commission would issue a contract offer. All those things would naturally take a little time. But there would be 'no worries' about it. In the meantime, we could leave PNG and enjoy a holiday.

We were expecting that answer. And we didn't intend to meekly accept it. 'I see,' John nodded. 'That will be fine — provided you give us a duly authorised letter from the Public Service Commission to confirm that you will make that contract offer.'

The official's geniality level dropped. He explained that would not be normal procedure. Their commitment had already been made publicly, and we could rely on their good faith.

We were tempted to ask what had mysteriously happened to their own investigation. But we would not jeopardise Ovea and Bernard any further, so citing that example of the Public Service Commission's bad faith was off limits. Instead, we explained that because we would be leaving PNG for several months we would 'feel more comfortable' with a confirmation letter. And we were sure that in all the circumstances the Ombudsman Commission would support that reasonable request, publicly if necessary. So, would he please oblige us?

The official's geniality level dropped further. He would need to refer to 'higher authority'. Perhaps we could come back tomorrow? No, we preferred to deal conclusively with the matter *today*. We would be happy to wait here while he sorted out the paperwork. The now-not-very-genial-at-all official huffily asked us to wait in reception. Two hours later, he emerged with a letter. 'I trust you will now be satisfied of our good faith,' he sniffed. We read the brief letter confirming the contract offer would be made and our visas issued in UK "as a matter of formality", signed by one of the commissioners. We soothingly assured our huffy official that of course we had *never* doubted the Commission's good faith and cordially left the office.

As we left the building, John said hello to someone entering. 'It's the guy from the Prime Minister's Department, the security intelligence guy I met with in Rabaul,' he whispered. We all shook hands. 'I followed the news about you,' the man said with a smile. 'I am happy to see that your problem has been resolved. Excuse me, I must go now.' He hurried off. Had he been involved in resolving our battles? We would never know.

It was time to fly out. John wrote polite thank-you letters to the Ombudsman Commission and the Secretary for Education, and a letter to the PNG High Commission in London to alert them about our agreed re-recruitment from England. We would reward ourselves with an itinerary-of-a-lifetime of famous tourist destinations through Asia, Africa and Europe before arriving in England to see my parents for the first time in four years. We arranged for the Ombudsman Commission's final report to parliament, the offer of new contracts when that came through, and any other correspondence to be forwarded to their address.

Packing brought problems. John insisted on taking all his papers with us — most of one suitcase. And we had another challenge. June had asked us to take Gus's ashes back to England, meet his son from a previous marriage there, and help scatter the ashes at a spot that had held special memories for Gus. We had readily agreed, proud to undertake that last service for our friend. But the heavy sealed hardwood box took up space and weight. And what might happen at customs as we travelled from country to country? What if they broke open the box? We decided to wrap the box inside a towel, never declare it, and deal with problems if and when they came up. Luckily, they never did. (Years later we discovered that transporting human remains internationally required a special permit. None of us had understood the potential pitfalls of June's request.)

To our delight, Father Luke phoned the hotel to say he would be flying to Australia on leave the same day we would fly out to Hong Kong, and he would overnight in Moresby first. Could we meet up?

Over a celebration dinner, the three of us recalled high and low points from our battles. Father Luke had fresh news too. He had been formally reprimanded by his bishop for getting involved in matters outside his parish. 'Don't worry, I didn't mind the reprimand. I did the right thing. But John, you didn't need to make me swear that night — the bishop gave me a heavy penance for that!' We laughed uproariously.

The three of us visited the Ombudsman Commission next morning for thanks and farewells before our afternoon flights. Their office was located in a building that housed other government agencies. After a brief but jubilant 'morning tea' at the commission, John disappeared outside to collect travellers' cheques from the nearby bank. Deep in conversation, Father Luke and I strolled up and down the long and narrow air-conditioned foyer.

Someone walking towards us looked familiar. Oh my God! It was Martin Simpson! Stunned, I stopped as he drew near. Looking up startled, he stopped too.

Simpson recovered first. 'Fancy seeing you here,' he said sarcastically. 'I suppose you're flying out soon. So am I. I'm *so* pleased to have this chance to say goodbye.'

Flustered, I replied as coolly as I could. 'Likewise, Inspector. Or should that be *former* inspector?'

'Former is right, thanks mainly to your husband. He's a lucky man you know. Last week he walked out onto the street right in front of my car. It would have been easy to run him down.' Simpson looked hard at me for a moment. 'I decided not to.' He stalked off.

Father Luke gasped. 'Oh, my goodness! That was just like running into the devil. My heart jumped right into my mouth! It's a good thing John wasn't here.'

But John was sorry to have missed the encounter. 'I don't know what I would have said. He was smart as well as ruthless, and I respected him for that. Early on, I actually liked him.'

After a fond farewell to Father Luke, we — and Gus's ashes — set off on our travels.

45. Home and Free (John)

It had been a long, exciting journey to England. We visited archaeological sites, natural wonders and busy cities in a dozen countries. It felt good to be just having fun. Apart from sending a few postcards, we had no communication with anyone in PNG.

A short stopover in London with friend Doug demonstrated how out of touch we had become over the past two years. What at first looked like a rash of new bookstores, full of colourful volumes, turned out to be a boom in video rental shops. Christmas shopping in full swing bewildered us. Where did all those people come from? Why did such a frenzy of consumption grip them? After living in remote PNG and surviving the dramas of Keravat, we felt adrift and anonymous in a busy crowded world.

We rented a car and drove north to spend Christmas with Elisa's parents. They were delighted to see us but couldn't really grasp what we had experienced. That was no surprise, so we just emphasised the positive final outcome and talked of other things. The large box of forwarded correspondence they had collected for us stayed closed during a plentiful and happy Christmas dinner.

Afterwards, I unpacked that box while Elisa sorted our luggage. Most of the contents were from PNG — we had a lot to catch up on. Mark had diligently sent several packets of newspaper clippings. I read them aloud in date order.

The court cases against Keravat students began just a week after we left PNG. The prosecution was eager to proceed with charges of 'riotous assembly', damage to property and disobedience of police orders. But the defence attorney requested deferrals. The Ombudsman Commission report hadn't been released yet, he told the court. It might contain important evidence. After legal wrangling, all hearings were deferred until after that report.

Next came the front-page stories when the Ombudsman Commission's report was tabled in parliament. Not much was said about us — we were old news now. Instead, lengthy quotes appeared under headlines like 'Evidence Falsified' and 'Ombudsman Blames Department for Cover-Up'. We savoured each reported statement:

- The Committee of Inquiry's report was 'a biased, dishonest and untruthful document'.
- Its proceedings were manipulated 'by senior officers friendly toward the inspector'.
- One Keravat colleague (Kevin Maitland) had faced 'outright intimidation by Superintendent of Operations Bruce Hawthorne', who threatened him with non-renewal of contract. The report recommended renewal of Kevin's contract and termination of Hawthorne's.
- Colleges Division was 'an authoritarian regime more concerned with protecting those loyal to it than with guaranteeing competence and ensuring ethical values'.
- Our 'professional complaints against the inspector were in fact justified'.

And best of all:

- 'After discussions about the Commission's findings, the inspector resigned'.

Victory at last!

Newspaper stories had continued over ensuing days. In a lively debate, parliament endorsed the report and condemned the Education Department. One sober speech referred to 'unwanted foreigners who wrongfully influence our young, educated people' to make them into 'immoral creatures'. Another speaker more colourfully called on the Education Minister to get rid of the culprits in his department, yelling that 'I am not going to pay a lot of money to send my children to school when they only go to get their trousers pulled off by these queers!'

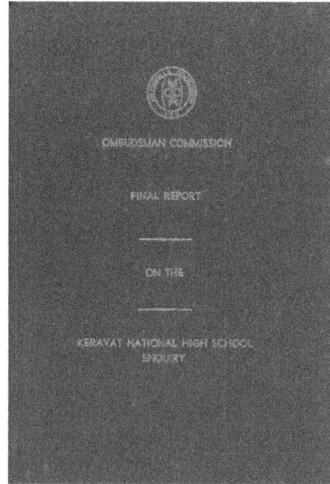

While we travelled, the Ombudsman Commission reported to parliament...

```
We find that the termination of Mr. and Mrs.
Mondzella served only the "best interests" of
those who sought to prevent misconduct, abuse,
and incompetence from being exposed.  It
certainly was not in the best interests of
the education of our children.
```

... and firmly concluded who had served whose "best interests"

Media opinion took a firm line too. The report vindicated the student protests and strongly criticised the Education Department for involving police in efforts to cover up its own wrongdoing. *Post-Courier* editorials concluded that 'reinstating the sacked teachers is only the first small move' and demanded that the Education Department "Clean Out the Closets" to restore public confidence in the teaching profession and its administration.' *The Times* and even the *Niugini Nius* bemoaned the disruption to their studies that Keravat students had wrongly suffered and echoed the *Post-Courier*'s call for comprehensive reform.

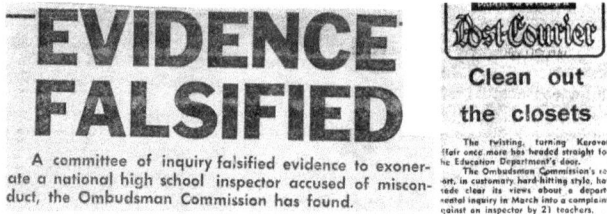

EVIDENCE FALSIFIED

A committee of inquiry falsified evidence to exonerate a national high school inspector accused of misconduct, the Ombudsman Commission has found.

Post-Courier

Clean out the closets

The twisting, turning Keravat Affair once more has headed straight for the Education Department's door.
The Ombudsman Commission's report, in customary hard-hitting style, has made clear its views about a departmental inquiry in March into a complaint against an inspector by 21 teachers.

Front page news again as the Department is publicly castigated

But then, responding under the headline 'Inquiry Men Clean', Secretary for Education Manu publicly defended his Committee of Inquiry team. He stated that he did not hold them responsible for distorting evidence. And instead of sacking Hawthorne, Manu had merely asked for a written explanation of his conduct. Proper process? Or just playing for time? We wondered.

More front-page stories followed. The Police Minister and the Public Solicitor rejected calls from MPs and others to drop charges against the Keravat students. The first seven cases were heard in court. Deputy Principal Isobel, as main prosecution witness, testified that groups of students were shouting and throwing stones. But she could not conclusively swear that any of the particular *individuals* charged had thrown a stone: 'I can't remember the names, they were part of the large group.' 'I was too busy dodging stones.' 'My memory is blurred.'

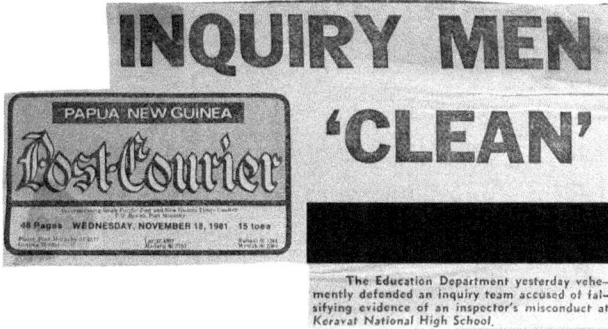

The Education Department denies its cover-up (Post-Courier)

The magistrate found the state had not proven its charges and acquitted all seven defendants. Next day, the prosecution dropped all the remaining cases. Our students were pictured smiling as they left the courthouse, arms raised in victory.

A feature on the discharged students described them as 'free at last'. And the students were far from repentant. 'We had a peaceful boycott, and all the time we knew there was something wrong. But nobody would tell us the reasons for the teachers being sacked. All the problems were started by police provocation.'

Criminal charges against the students are at last dropped (The Times)

The newspaper clippings and Mark's covering letters rumbled on. Not all the news was good:

- 'Hawthorne Denies Intimidating Teacher'. He also disclaimed responsibility for the recommendation that Kevin Maitland's contract not be renewed.
- The Keravat administrators criticised in the Ombudsman Commission's report had been transferred and promoted. 'Keravat Principal Joins Inspectors' — Townsend would now be an inspector himself. 'Deputy Principal Isobel Barnes appointed headmistress' — she would now head another educational institution.
- Safe in Australia, James Beckham had not been interviewed by the Ombudsman Commission. But he wrote to *The Times* from there to defend 'two outstanding educationists, Martin Simpson and Graeme Drysdale, who have been subjected to a totally malicious and misguided attack. Both are totally professional in outlook and approach, and indefatigable hard workers.' He proclaimed his neutrality and called for the Ombudsman Commission report to be 'viewed sceptically'.
- Several staff from Keravat — people who had taken our side — had not had their contracts renewed. The Education Department 'refused to comment on individual contracts'.
- Ovea lost his job at the Public Service Commission, supposedly in 'a routine restructuring'. But Mark felt sure that was payback for going public when his investigation was blocked.
- Keravat students had done badly in their national exams. Complaints about unfairness failed as the Education Department decided results 'could not be adjusted'. Some had lost future education and work opportunities they might otherwise have won.

Victory had come at a price. And far from 'cleaning out the closets', the Education Department was still signalling that loyalty to the system would be rewarded while dissent would be punished.

Keravat principal joins inspectors

Keravat principal Townsend, heavily criticized by the Ombudsman Commission, gets promoted (Post-Courier)

Mark's final letter explained that the whole story had petered out, in the public domain at least. We c onsoled ourselves that we had done everything we could.

Near the bottom of our pile of mail we found two official-looking envelopes from PNG. The first one, from the Education Department, contained my replacement inspection report. I enjoyed seeing the new and official 'Satisfactory' stamp on that.

I passed the letter inside the second envelope to Elisa. 'Look at this! It's our copy of a letter from the Public Service Commission to the Prime Minister himself. It advises him "that to achieve the intent of the Ombudsman Commission recommendations the Mendzelas will be offered a one-year contract as though they were new recruits". They won't dare mess us around after that!' We guessed our friend in the Prime Minister's Department had generated that letter.

We left until last our bound copies of the Ombudsman Commission's report to parliament. Vince's team had been thorough. A foreword explained that the Commission had taken testimony under oath not just from relevant people at Keravat and at the Education Department but also from 'numerous other public officials and private citizens' around PNG. Eighty-three pages of findings and recommendations followed. We each took a copy and settled down to read.

The introduction didn't mince words: 'On Wednesday 26 August 1981 three teachers at Keravat College were called from their class-rooms and notified that they had been sacked. The only explanation given for their termination was that it was "in the best interests of Papua New Guinea". The sackings came at the end of a long-standing struggle by a number of Keravat teachers and a Catholic priest to get the Education Department to recognise their grievances and concerns.' The introduction went on to attack the Education Department's 'heavy-handed administrative control, which was arbi-trary, abusive and unfair; which protected incompetence in those loyal to it; and which covered up immoral practices'.

After a 'Summary of Findings and Recommendations', already explained in Mark's letters, the main report outlined the events that culminated in the Education Department's Committee of Inquiry. Next the report described in full detail the intimidation, manipula-tion, falsification, bias and omissions of that committee. That malpractice hadn't just happened to us. First, Simpson had person-ally approached our former school captain Helen, urging her to with-draw the statement she had given Gus. Then the committee of inquiry had interviewed Helen and Felicity about the written state-ments they gave to Gus — but *reversed* what the students actually told them and characterised Gus as a bully who extorted those state-ments from them. The Ombudsman Commission's report explained how, contrary to the committee's findings, all of our complaints about inspection procedures were in fact justified professionally and by the PNG Education Department's own rules.

The report then castigated the Committee of Inquiry for failing to investigate allegations of improper sexual activities as its terms of reference required. Instead, it had attacked us.

Over many pages, the report demolished every one of the committee's allegations and recommendations about us. I was especially glad to read its annihilation of the slanders and libels about my alleged murderous intentions. Those were 'deliberately designed to discredit Mr Mendzela'. And the report conclusively vindicated Elisa's alleged 'troublemaking' in the English department. It documented Tolley's incompetence and his evasive responses to the commission's questions and directly linked the Education Department's failure to inspect him to the testimony given by Tolley himself and others that he was a 'loyal supporter of the administration'. Principal Townsend's actions and omissions were heavily criticised too, directly in detail and more broadly for creating a leadership vacuum that other staff had to fill.

The report documented and dissected the improper actions of Drysdale and Simpson. Drysdale's intimate relationship with a student 'had violated his *in loco parentis* responsibilities' and 'was a serious breach of ethics'. The inspector had 'violated his position of trust and failed to fulfil his public duties and responsibilities'. Simpson's resignation seemed to be a negotiated closure of the sensitive topic of homosexual abuse of students, and the report merely referred to 'additional findings' that were not appropriate for discussion in a public document and had been presented to the Secretary for Education. The report instead emphasised the 'widespread evidence' that the Education Department operated an 'authoritarian regime' more concerned with protecting those 'loyal to the system' than with guaranteeing competence and 'ensuring that ethical values are passed on to our children'.

I finished reading first and couldn't resist interrupting Elisa. 'Sorry, but I just have to read this out loud. Listen: "We believe that this country needs teachers like the Mendzelas. We find that the termination of Mr. and Mrs. Mendzela served only the 'best interests' of those who sought to prevent misconduct, abuse, and incompetence from being exposed. It was certainly not in the best interests of the young people they were working with."'

The last section of the report discussed events on campus when the police moved in. The text reconstructed those two days in detail, commending the actions of college staff and student leaders who had acted courageously to prevent a potentially fatal catastrophe. It condemned the principal and the Education Department for unnecessarily bringing in police and criticised the police for bringing arms onto the campus. The students didn't escape criticism, especially for damaging property after the first police invasion. But their fundamental actions to demand an explanation for the terminated contracts, and boycott classes when they didn't get one, were 'reasonable in the circumstances'.

I turned back to the introduction and the summary. Bohdan's involvement had received no comment at all, just a footnote in the introduction that 'the case of the third sacked teacher has been closed and he subsequently left PNG'.

The summary merited rereading. Vince's investigation had extended well beyond our own rehabilitation. He had nailed Bruce Hawthorne for his intimidation of Kevin Maitland at the time of the Committee of Inquiry, and his subsequent 'payback' of recommending against renewal of Kevin's contract. The Ombudsman Commission had recommended Hawthorne's contract be terminated just as ours were. Its report also recommended that fair and proper disciplinary processes be established for expatriates on contract.

The report commended the Secretary for Education. 'The record shows that he has corrected injustices when they were brought to his attention.... We believe that he has been the victim of ill-advice by some subversive subordinates rather than a protagonist.... We have been impressed that when confronted with the findings of our Preliminary Report, the secretary did not delay or find excuses but made the decisions necessary to implement our recommendations.' Maybe so. But he had also sent in the police to quell the students and publicly backed his corrupt and incompetent 'Committee of Inquiry' *after* they were exposed.

The deal we had done had been delivered, on the public record. But where the Education Department would go from here remained to be seen.

We had a lot to digest that night, in more ways than one.

46. The Deal Unravels (Elisa)

THE NEW TEACHING year in PNG didn't start until February. We had time to catch up with relations and old friends after our years away.

We even met up with two Keravat staff who were back in England on annual leave. Tim and Joy Roberts had been new in 1981 but had actively supported us and the students. They related how the college year had stumbled to a conclusion through our announced reinstatement, the Ombudsman Commission report, student court cases, fill-in teachers and national exams. 'The English department ran true to form. The internal assessment papers Tolley prepared were a complete mess and had to be redone. Isobel Barnes showed little leadership and lost everyone's respect. Maths head Grant Riddell became acting deputy principal and just fumbled around. The students found it hard to concentrate for the external exams. Many of them wouldn't even attend the graduation ceremony. Everyone felt relieved when the end of the year arrived.'

Tim related how the Education Department continued to blatantly reward its supporters and punish those who had supported the students. 'Our Governing Council was reconstituted, and it recommended Mark Hoban as the new head of the maths department. No way would Colleges Division accept that; they are recruiting a new expat instead. They wouldn't engage Joy — a qualified chemist and teacher — for the chemistry role and have just left that vacant. And when the Council demanded that Isobel Barnes and Bill Tolley leave the college, the Education Department helped them find new jobs. Isobel will become a high school principal, and Toady Tolley will apparently become an expert on adult education!'

Tim's sad tales did include some laughs: 'To celebrate his promotion and new contract for next year, Toady Tolley hosted a memorable farewell party at the Travelodge. He ended up thumping a guest in the jaw. His wife left in disgust and drove home by herself. Tolley spent the night on the floor of the hotel.'

John undertook the painful duty to meet Gus's son and help scatter Gus's ashes in a remote part of Norfolk. That had been an adventure too, John explained. 'I was really upset when we parted. I still found it hard to come to terms with Gus's death and the pointless and frenzied busyness of England. Driving in a congested country, with a profusion of roads to everywhere, bewildered me. I set off for Doug's place in London without planning the route properly. I got lost amongst the identikit towns with yellow bollards everywhere. At one point, I backed up in the darkness and reversed into a pole, then got lost again. By the time I got to the road tunnel under the river Thames I could hear a clanking noise. Turned out I was dragging the bumper along amid a shower of sparks!'

We expected our new contracts to arrive in good time. But when mid-January came and went with no paperwork arriving, we grew suspicious. Unless we took the initiative, nothing might happen. John got busy on the telephone, making calls late at night to coincide with office hours in PNG.

The Ombudsman Commission, his first stop, wasn't as helpful as we hoped. The Commission's report had been published, recommendations had been made and accepted, and our complaint had been closed. Now it was up to us and the Education Department to follow up through normal channels.

John's next call was to the Public Service Commission. They were polite and formal. Yes, they intended to issue us with new contracts. But they had to wait for the Education Department to determine a posting and make a request, and so far, they hadn't received any information. As soon as they did, they would contact us and send contracts to the PNG High Commission in London. Then the High Commission could issue our work visas and air tickets.

John tried the Education Department next. The secretary's office of course knew about us, and assured John that instructions to determine our posting had been issued weeks previously. Two days of telephone tag around various offices and individuals within the department revealed that everyone was somehow waiting for information from someone else about what posts were available. What would happen if all suitable posts were already filled, or if the new year started before information came through? Nobody seemed to know. Or if they did, they weren't telling.

Costly phone calls to the other side of the planet were getting us nowhere. We decided on direct action. John called the PNG High Commission in London and explained our situation and intentions to the High Commissioner's secretary. We would come in person to the High Commission in London in two days' time to process our contracts. If no contract had arrived by then we would expect to see the High Commissioner. That message should be passed on to him urgently please.

An 'Assistant to the Commissioner' called us back an hour later. Polite, but frosty, he explained that they could not take any action until the contracts arrived. Furthermore, the High Commissioner did not get involved in individual contract matters. We should wait for the contracts to arrive and for the High Commission to call us.

John interrupted before the other side could hang up. 'I understand how that would apply in normal circumstances. But these are not normal circumstances. I am sure you get copies of PNG newspapers. Please read these papers from last year, to help you understand our situation better.' He gave details of a few key stories. 'Thank you for your help. We look forward to meeting you at the High Commission on Thursday. Goodbye.'

Two days later we entered the High Commission office in London. A receptionist received us politely, and a few minutes later brought out the officer we had spoken to on the telephone. He looked curiously at us and spoke neutrally. 'Oh, you really have come. The High Commissioner is busy right now, but if you wait a little bit, he may see you.'

We waited patiently. John looked impressively calm with his large briefcase full of documents, but I could tell he was nervous. No refreshments were offered.

After more than an hour, we were ushered into the High Commissioner's office. The High Commissioner was an unusually tall national with a deep voice. He introduced himself and sat us down. 'Your case is interesting, so I decided to meet you personally. But I can only advise that no contracts have arrived for you, and no message either. You must understand that we cannot issue work visas until contracts have been signed. And without visas, you won't be admitted into PNG.'

John was conciliatory. 'High Commissioner, I understand your position. But you must also please understand ours. We were treated very badly by the Education Department. So were our students. That became a major scandal, and we needed help from the Ombudsman Commission to put things right. The commission made a full report to parliament. I have that with me if you would like to read it. And here is a copy of a letter to the Prime Minister, confirming that the Public Service Commission will offer us new contracts. It was sent to us personally, here in England.'

The High Commissioner read the letter and smiled. 'You have important friends!' He paused, thoughtfully. 'And I remember my niece telling me there were some wrong people working in the education system when she went to college. I respect what you did.' He looked at us shrewdly. 'But tell me, why do you want to go back to PNG? Surely you can find work in England or New Zealand. Why return to a place where you had so much trouble? I even believe you lost a good friend there.'

I spoke up. 'Yes, we could work somewhere else and forget about all that trouble. But that would break faith with our students and the other people who stood by us. And with the friend we lost. You know our story, and now you have met us. So please help. I'm sure you can.'

He deliberated for a moment, then came to a decision. 'All right. Here is what I can do. I will make direct enquiries about your contracts, based on the information in this letter. Give me a few days for that. I will contact you as soon as the contracts arrive. If you receive any relevant communication in the meantime, then please call me right away. Here is my card.'

We thanked the High Commissioner and cheerfully took the train back to my parents' home in the north of England.

A week later, we were still waiting. John called the High Commissioner's office and enquired politely whether the contracts had arrived yet. 'Yes, I'll hold on. Thank you.' He covered the phone and spoke to me. 'They're checking.' A few minutes later he spoke again, into the phone. 'Hello High Commissioner. Thank you for following up on our behalf.' Then he listened for several minutes. 'I see. Yes, I understand. Thank you for your efforts. Goodbye.'

John hung up the phone and frowned. 'Well, the High Commissioner certainly tried. He sent three telexes — to Education, PSC and PM's Department. No reply from any of them.' He sighed heavily. 'Maybe we should just forget about it all. The new education year is about to start, so it's probably too late for us to go anyway.'

I wasn't buying that. 'If we give up now, they've won. Let's try the Ombudsman Commission again.'

It took several 2 a.m. phone calls to get a response. John was persistent and persuasive. 'Yes, I know our complaint is closed, and constitutionally you have no further jurisdiction. But Vince, these are government agencies that publicly accepted your recommendations. Now they are ignoring them. If you let that happen, you might as well close down.'

Finally, we were promised action. And that promise was delivered on. Three days later, the High Commission called to say they had contracts from the Education Department waiting for us, on condition that we take up department head posts at Kiunga High School — apparently those were 'the only postings left' at our contract level. And because the school year had already started, we would need to visit the High Commission *tomorrow* and then fly out immediately.

Did we accept the offer? John said he would confer with me and call back in an hour.

'Where's Kiunga? Do I know that name from somewhere?' he asked.

'Don't you remember?' I replied. 'When we were doing our induction, that English guy Derek was going there. Everyone felt sorry for him because it was so remote and had the worst malaria in the country. He wrote to us once, saying how poor and unhealthy the place was and how the malaria there was a dangerous type, immune to drugs. The Education Department is making an offer they know we will refuse, so they can close the file and win.'

John grinned. 'Then let's not refuse! Are we going?'

I grinned back. We were.

After 24 hours of feverish activity — and tearful farewells to my mum and dad, who understood nothing of it all and thought us deranged — we were back at the High Commission. They had been busy too. All the paperwork was ready for signature, visas were quickly stamped into our passports, and we received air tickets for that evening. The High Commissioner came out to personally see us off. 'Like I said, you have important friends!' he said jovially. 'It has been good to meet you. I wish you luck.'

As we headed to the airport, I had a sudden thought. 'John, shouldn't we call Mark and tell him we're coming?'

John considered for a moment. 'No, better not. We don't know what's gone on behind the scenes, and we won't be able to talk to him without others finding out too. Let's get there and see Vince first.'

That sobered us. Until now, frantic activity had displaced concerns about safety. Yes, John had as a sensible precaution left copies of key documents with my parents and asked a good friend to take action on them if he didn't hear from us. But amongst all the excitement, it hadn't registered that we were walking back into a potentially dangerous situation. Not to mention the risks of an isolated and hot malarial location with few modern facilities, set deep in the jungle.

It was too late to reconsider. And anyway, we didn't want to. We were committed.

Three flights and 36 hours later, we landed in Port Moresby on a sunny weekday morning.

47. Another Adventure (John)

WE FELT nervous going through immigration. We needn't have. With our one-year work visas in order, we got a quick stamp and a friendly smile. A professionally dressed national waited for us on the other side. Julius introduced himself as from the 'Planning Office' of the Education Department. He seemed genuinely pleased to see us.

Julius explained the arrangements that had been made. We would overnight at a basic hotel here and fly out to remote Kiunga early the next morning. The high school there awaited our arrival. Furnished accommodation would be waiting for us too.

Julius handed us air tickets and other documents. 'You are entitled to a remote duty allowance to buy immediate essentials — get what you need at this store and pay with this purchase order. And we will ship your vehicle and stored goods from Rabaul to Kiunga. Just sign these authorisations.'

How much Julius knew about us he didn't say, and we didn't ask. But he couldn't have been more helpful. He gave us a car and driver to help with the afternoon's shopping. Anticipating only basic accommodation and limited local supplies in Kiunga, we bought bed linen, lots of candles, a supply of toiletries and a few 'treat' drinks and foodstuffs that wouldn't spoil. Plentiful insect repellent and mosquito coils too. Weight, not cost, was the most important consideration — our luggage allowance on a light aircraft would be small indeed!

We took advantage of our transport to visit the Ombudsman Commission, but everyone we knew there was out. Leaving a message was all we could do. And the telephone at hotel reception would not be private. Our priority now was a good night's sleep.

The alarm woke us before dawn. A car and driver were waiting. So was our plane — an 18-seater propeller plane that would take four hours with a refuelling stop to reach remote Kiunga. Our luggage and shopping filled much of the small cargo hold. Extra freight for 15 kg was personally payable. Never mind — we would surely value those comforts over the next 10 months.

The plane droned over a stunning tropical-green coastline for two hours. Coral reefs studded a brilliant blue sea. White sandy beaches alternated with chocolate-brown river estuaries. Finally, we landed at Daru, capital of the huge Western Province that included Kiunga. Daru comprised a small town and a gravel airstrip, perched on a low muddy island bordered by mangrove swamps.

It felt good to stretch our legs. But not good to hear that 'due to operational requirements' we would have to change to a smaller plane for the final 800 kilometres up the Fly River. And we would have to wait several hours for that plane to arrive.

I decided to turn delay into opportunity. After quiet persuasion, the airport staff let me use their telephone to 'discuss our arrival arrangements'. I called Keravat College instead. To my delight, the secretary there remembered us. She quickly located Mark. I brought him up to date.

Mark shared my delight. 'John, it's terrific to know that you and Elisa have made it back! Simpson's gone of course, and the college is operating professionally again. But Colleges Division helped find *promotions* elsewhere for Townsend and Isobel and it selected their replacements for principal and deputy. We have a new inspector who is their man too. Basically, the same old gang remains in charge. They're weeding out all the staff who took our side, as their contracts expire. The story went around that you wouldn't be returning. I'll enjoy putting that right!'

We couldn't talk long. I promised to call again when I could. In the meantime, we would keep in touch by letter. Heartened, we settled down for our long hot wait.

Finally, our onward flight was ready to depart. We squeezed into an old eight-seater aircraft with a single engine. As usual, I was given the co-pilot seat in the cockpit. (The enduring PNG belief that an expat male might be able to fly the plane if something went wrong was entirely untrue in my case, but I never argued against getting the best seat.) Elisa crammed into the back with three other passengers and our oversized luggage.

The young Australian pilot was chatty. He motioned me to put headphones on so we could talk over the noisy propeller. He explained that a lot was happening in Kiunga. 'The Ok Tedi mine project in the mountains is driving big changes.' He pointed to a huge barge on the river below. 'See that? They're barging equipment and supplies upriver to Kiunga. First challenge is to construct a new road for over 100 miles, from Kiunga to the mountains. Until that road's finished, everything that travels to the mine site has to go in by helicopter. It's a giant project — billions of dollars being invested! How come you didn't know about it?'

Warily, I explained that we had been recruited from Britain at short notice (true), and implied that we were here in PNG for the first time (not true). Keen to know more, I asked questions. I learned that the mine's development timetable coincided with our contract. The road should be finished by mid-year. Money was already flowing through Kiunga as the mine company brought in skilled workers and built new infrastructure. There were even plans to start a provincial airline that would fly directly to and from Port Moresby. Kiunga might not be as quiet and remote as we had been expecting.

Our plane began to descend. Ahead, I spotted a break in the endless green below.

48. Red Earth (Elisa)

WE HAD SPENT four days inside planes or waiting for them. But this was the worst yet. The crowded interior was hot and airless. Propeller noise made conversation impossible. I could peer out a small window, but there was little to see. Jungle stretched to every horizon, broken only by the massive brown and winding Fly River and the many swamps and lakes the river had created over time. No human habitation was evident.

Finally, the pitch of the propellers changed and we began to descend. The pilot banked, and our destination rolled into my field of view. There still wasn't much to see though. A patch of blood-red earth broke the green of the jungle. Kiunga 'town' comprised a few dozen low buildings, scattered along a dirt road that led out into the jungle and then disappeared. A short dirt runway ran at right angles to the road. My heart sank. Keravat had seemed remote at first, but there we had Rabaul town not far away, offering most modern comforts. We wouldn't enjoy that luxury here.

Our plane landed smoothly and taxied back down the runway. Clouds of red dust billowed all around us. The pilot switched off the engines and waited for the dust to disperse. Then he climbed out, opened our door and folded down the steps. I clambered out, along with the three national passengers. John carefully lowered himself from the cockpit over the wing. Unsure what to do next, we stood in the hot late-afternoon sun and looked around.

A young national man with an impressive Afro hairstyle walked up to us from the edge of the runway. His unprepossessing dress of crumpled shirt and shorts was understandable in the heat and dust of the airstrip. He hesitantly introduced himself as Michael Maino, principal of Kiunga High School.

We shook hands with our new boss. Michael ushered us to what he called 'the school car' — the only vehicle around apart from a few trucks. The rusting utility van had once been white. Now the remains of its faded paintwork merged with patches of rust, red soil splashes and a layer of red dust to create effective camouflage.

We helped unload the plane and stowed our luggage and supplies in the open back of the van. Then we all three squeezed onto the front (and only) seat and rumbled slowly down the rutted dirt road.

We had decided to pitch ourselves as new UK recruits, not old hands. So we said nothing about our PNG history. Michael didn't either. Instead, he cheerfully pointed out the sights as we drove to the school a few kilometres away at the other end of the township. Apart from the airstrip, there was a river port (mostly out of sight down a steep bank), the trade store (run by a religious mission) and the town's administration building (flying a limp and dusty flag). 'The admin building is our post office and courthouse too,' Michael informed us. A dozen small houses of the familiar government fibreboard straggled along the earth road and punctuated locally built wooden and thatch habitations. *Everything* was covered in a thick layer of red dust.

The school campus looked more promising. Fibreboard buildings dotted tidy grounds planted out in green grass and neat hedges of colourful variegated shrubs. Michael stopped the van and explained the layout: administration block, classrooms, student dormitories, a mess hall, staff houses around the periphery, and a few assorted service buildings. Even a small library!

A delegation waited in Michael's office to greet us. We shook hands with his deputy Lami and several senior staff. The school secretary served tea and sandwiches while a fan vainly fought the afternoon heat. Henry, the senior department head, welcomed us warmly. 'It's great you're here. We were struggling — two weeks in, no head of English, and no head of Science. Now we've got everybody!'

John looked puzzled. 'You mean English and Maths, don't you? I'll be head of Maths.'

It was Michael's turn to look puzzled. 'No, we already have a head of Maths. That's Henry. They told us you would be head of Science.'

John explained he had some background in science, but not enough to head the subject. There had been a mistake. An uncomfortable silence descended. Then Michael became quietly persuasive about what the school and its students hoped for from us. Keen to keep everything positive, John agreed to take up his unexpected new role. Much relieved, Michael said that other work matters could wait until tomorrow morning — we should get settled in before dark in case the town generator failed. Once again no one had referred to our PNG history, so once again we didn't mention it either.

Back in the van, we rumbled past the roadside girls' dormitory towards fields where the pupils grew their own food. Bumping overland, we approached a cluster of three houses from the rear. They rose high on poles. Stairways climbed to a front porch and a back door. A large water tank squatted beneath each house. The middle house would be our new home.

Michael led us in, helped unload our luggage onto the porch, and said he would arrange for two senior girls to 'help you clean up and settle in'. Did we need any provisions to make dinner? Pointing to our supplies, we assured him we didn't. Before driving off, Michael warmly welcomed us again. 'Just come to my office tomorrow after the morning bell. And if you need anything, just ask.'

We explored our new home. The house had obviously been disused for a while, and it badly needed cleaning. Furnishings resembled those we had in Keravat, though they were even more dilapidated (something I hadn't thought possible). But we would enjoy running water, electricity, and a stove fed by bottled gas. I felt certain I could make the house feel like home for the 10 months until the school year ended.

It was the first day in Keravat all over again — the same cold-water shower, mould-stained mattresses and pillows, and sticky discoloured foam cushions. But we had learned from that experience. Our supplies included tools, cutlery, sheets, pillowcases, and curtains. Not everything could be easily remedied though. We would wash our clothes by hand ourselves, not with a machine and a houseboy. And the rotten-fish smell that inhabited the refrigerator would be hard to eradicate.

Soon we had the stove working and everything packed away. A gentle knock at the door introduced two female students who helped me scrub linoleum floors and painted walls. Meanwhile John checked the fly wire on windows and doors to repair small gaps, and systematically doused each room with insecticide.

With our new home in reasonable order, we retired early and enjoyed the sleep of exhaustion. A loud noise woke us — a pipe banging on an empty gas bottle. That 'bell' was the signal for students to rise and start their day. And the signal for us to tackle the work timetable that Michael would give us. We just had time for a hasty breakfast of cereal and tea, both made with 'long life' irradiated milk (it would be that or milk powder from now on).

My first day at work began. English was naturally the most important teaching subject and had the largest staff. Michael introduced me to two contract employees from Canada (Jimmy and Gerald) and one national lady (Sarah). All were young. None had much teaching experience, but they welcomed me and showed plenty of enthusiasm.

Teaching materials were limited too. The 'department resource room' beneath one classroom had a dark and damp earth floor. Instead of walls, rusted fly screens dangled from the building's frame. A perimeter of crude freestanding wooden shelves would probably come crashing down in an earthquake. A single dim light bulb achieved little against the gloom.

The shelves housed a motley collection of textbooks, reading book sets and paper worksheets. Many worksheets had stuck together in the damp and could no longer be pried apart. Most of the reading books appeared to be only partial sets, or in poor condition, or both. As I moved around the shelving, I discovered additional copies of some books buried beneath other items or scattered about the room. I could not easily gauge what the resource room actually held. I resolved to change that, starting with a good clean-up at the next work parade.

I introduced myself to my own classes of 'Grade 10s' — the most senior students — and began teaching. Those who had started primary school at the official age were now 15 or 16 years old, but some were much older than that. The contrast between the many tiny twig-like youngsters and a couple of huge, muscular and fully mature males startled me. The older 'boys' needed to be masterful contortionists to squeeze their limbs into the diminutive one-piece desk and bench furniture. But they showed no signs of discomfort or self-consciousness. Without exception, the students were welcoming, enthusiastic and industrious. I knew they would be a joy to teach.

Classes over for the day, John and I compared notes at home. (Thankfully, the roster for other staff duties didn't include us until next week.) John's experience of the students had been equally positive. He would teach science to the more senior students while a sole Sri Lankan contractor covered the rest (his full Sri Lankan name ran on at great length, so everyone just called him Buna). Books, equipment and teaching materials for science were sparse but adequate, and John's predecessor had been a missionary nun who kept everything in good order. John could confidently handle the parts of the curriculum that fell under physics, but his experience with practical chemistry was weak and he had never even studied biology, let alone taught it. He would have major gaps to close — on the run!

That evening we dined on chicken curry and rice, hosted by my two Canadian staff. Once again no one spoke of our history, and we kept the conversation to local topics. We learned that the 400-plus students here mostly came from poor villages that subsisted on gardening, hunting and fishing. Cash was scarce. The modest-sounding school fee for a single student could, in reality, stretch the meagre financial resources of an entire village. Over 70 percent of our students were boys, who were seen as a better investment than girls. Apart from a few town families, our students were boarders who might travel for days by foot or canoe to reach Kiunga. They felt proud and privileged to gain a secondary education and happily worked hard not just on their studies but also to grow food and manage the school. Sixteen staff (counting us) worked hard too. Class sizes averaged close to 40. The social highlights of the week were church on Sunday mornings and (electricity supply permitting) an open-air movie on Friday nights.

Next day was Saturday and the local market day. We knew we had to start living on local food supplies, so we resolved to walk down the road to town and do some shopping.

After heavy overnight rain, that wasn't easy. The sun beat down and humidity was intense. Deep ruts ploughed into the red dirt road were filled with water. Mud sprayed from several large trucks that slowly ground by and coated the straggly roadside vegetation. We missed our footing more than once, and our white gym shoes quickly turned red. Other pedestrians, mostly barefoot villagers dressed in ragged clothes, smiled and said hello. Some politely struggled not to laugh at our clumsy progress.

Kiunga's market comprised a few sad-looking people selling tiny amounts of food. Scrawny vegetables and limp greens that I had never encountered before sat in front of the vendors on bare ground. What would one do with them, I wondered? We came away empty-handed.

Our colleagues had told us anything available from the market could be purchased more conveniently (if more expensively) at the trade store. Retreating to that small barn of a building, we introduced ourselves to proprietor Jerome, a hearty Australian missionary for an evangelical church. We looked around at his stock.

There wasn't much to see. Many of the rough-hewn wooden shelves were empty. Jerome explained that most people in Kiunga could barely afford a little corned beef or canned fish to add to their boiled rice. Fresh food was always in short supply and right now he had none.

We realised that we too would have to eat mainly from packets and cans: the local staple of government-subsidised rice, supplemented by uninspiring fare like water crackers, canned corned beef, canned tuna fish and even canned cheese of an ugly pink colour. The only 'luxury' item available was a plentiful supply of mango chutney, probably left on the shelf because no one knew what it was. We made our selections and Jerome quickly filled a bag of groceries for each of us.

As we left, a scrawny and toothless old man approached us. 'Cigaret long mi?' he asked. I replied that we didn't smoke sorry, and he stepped away. Jerome stepped outside to explain. 'He's not really a beggar, more a freeloader. No one's sure how old he is. Maybe 70 at most. That's far older than the age most people around here live to, so as far as the locals are concerned, he's *always* been here. That's convinced many of them that he's a sorcerer, so they give him small gifts to be on the safe side!'

Dismayed and depressed, we trudged home through the mud with our shopping. It might be only 10 months to the end of the year, but without any fresh food or other 'basics' we had taken for granted in Keravat, that time wasn't likely to fly by.

49. Knuckling Down (John)

ON SUNDAY MORNING we sat down to take stock of our situation. We had come to remote Kiunga to finish the three-year PNG contract we had always planned, and to keep faith with the sacrifices that Gus and many others had made to help us win our professional battles at Keravat.

We discussed the upside first. We had ample time to plan ahead for a future back in New Zealand or England. We couldn't spend much, so saving would be easy. Our teaching work would be pleasant and fulfilling. Living conditions weren't great, but 10 months until the school year and our contract ended wasn't a long time. And with luck, our car and chattels would arrive soon to make life more comfortable.

But on the downside, we had two big worries. First, we had vindictive enemies in Moresby and elsewhere in PNG. We might want to quietly serve out our contracts, but would they somehow make trouble for us? So far no one here had even mentioned our struggles of the past two years, but it was hard to believe they knew nothing about them. We decided never to mention those past experiences. Instead, we would do our jobs well and maintain a low profile.

Health was a greater concern. We were living at the edge of the jungle on dubious food and water. Kiunga was notoriously malarial, and the preventive pills we could take might not work. Having had one serious bout of dengue fever and a tropical ulcer, I knew there were plenty of other threats too. So we would apply strict protective routines — boil all our drinking water, keep doors and windows closed or screened at all times, wear insect repellent all day, and burn mosquito coils all night. No sitting outside to watch the sunset from the spacious elevated veranda that was the most attractive feature of our house.

Kiunga students with school campus and buildings behind

The school's new timetable — a heavy load for all staff, including department heads — clicked into place and kept us busy. The curriculum was simple and well-structured. Learning was tested by national exams for graduating classes near the end of the year. Kiunga High School had only been founded five years previously, and its first graduating class a year earlier had scored near bottom nationally in every subject except science. And even there Kiunga had only outscored 20 percent of the other schools.

During the first weeks, we set tangible goals to improve student performance and leave our departments in better shape for our successors. Elisa's main challenge was professional leadership. The English department had never been run well, as a succession of new teachers came and went each year or even during a school year. Her staff had become accustomed to going their own way, for better or worse, with scanty resources and limited oversight.

Elisa established high and consistent professional standards and mobilised her colleagues to attain them. She insisted resources and skills were systematically developed, catalogued and shared. Elisa actively monitored and assisted each member of her team. That generated grumbling at times, but she combined personal energy, long hours and a firm hand to deliver improved outcomes.

I faced different challenges. Science teaching mixed factual learning with experiments. Both had to be delivered competently and confidently. The curriculum bounced around between physics, chemistry, and biology. I had no background at all in many topics. My colleague Buna was far from expert himself and, anyway, I was reluctant to confess too much inadequacy.

I needed to spend evenings and weekends in my office and laboratory, just to stay a day or two ahead of my classes. I resolved to convert that problem into an opportunity. I found that the students enjoyed my fresh approaches to novel subject matter and tolerated my occasional check back to the textbook. We often all tackled a new topic together for the first time and made that trite phrase 'shared excitement of learning' a reality. Hard work but fun. And several of the older students — Matthew, Patrick and Gulu — displayed real scientific talent.

Running a remote school with 400 student boarders wasn't simple. School maintenance was done by teaching staff, or not at all. Limited cash funds needed careful conservation. Our dilapidated old utility car coughed and spluttered whenever it collected the erratic supply deliveries from Jerome's store or the airport.

Food stocks depended heavily on what could be grown in the school's own fields. Students collected firewood and cooked over open fires under a corrugated iron roof. Large cauldrons boiled up sweet potato or rice to mix with small amounts of tinned fish or corned beef, and perhaps some local greens. On good days fresh chicken or fruit might be added to the menu. The duty class for the week served meals on wooden tables with benches, in the open air under another iron roof.

With no telephone, school organisation was tough. Our principal Michael regularly visited the town's 'administration office' (just a rough wooden shed with a hatch that opened to serve customers), where he queued patiently in all weathers for the single telephone line there. Sorting out purchase orders and drawing some of the limited cash available for local purchasing was wearisome. Postal mail and newspapers — eagerly awaited by everyone — arrived only twice a week.

After our late start, the end of term one came quickly. And it brought a surprise! A *Post-Courier* story 'Keravat Man Was Re-Hired' revealed that Bruce Hawthorne, the Colleges Division superintendent recommended for termination by the Ombudsman Commission, instead had his contract renewed by the Secretary for Education himself. That had been done *after* the secretary had received the Commission's report and promised to investigate him. The Education Department had been caught out. But who had blown the whistle to the newspaper, and why?

Education Department caught out renewing the superintendent of Colleges Division who should have been dismissed. (Post-Courier)

That *Post-Courier* story sparked another round of published letters from concerned teachers and students. 'Disaffected Teacher' complained, 'There's something wrong when our independent politicians sit at the feet of these expatriates while they run the Education Department like their own club.' Another writer warned him that 'his letter will enrage and ignite again the fears of senior education bureaucrats. When wounded elephants rampage, it is the grass which suffers.' A third letter spoke of 'secret files' being used to 'pressure and bully teachers' and a fourth encouraged students and parents to report past sexual abuses. Not to be outdone, the weekly *Times* publicised how those Keravat teachers who had supported their students were still being weeded out while administration supporters like principal Townsend had been promoted.

Then came another twist. The *Post-Courier*'s front page — 'Keravat Scandal Figure Gets Axe' — announced that Bruce Hawthorne's contract renewal had been overturned. He had been sacked by the Public Services Commission, in accordance with the original recommendation from the Ombudsman Commission. 'We looked at the evidence and decided he had to go,' a PSC spokesman said.

Education Department chicanery overruled — great news! But how had all that happened? And what might happen next?

Superintendent's renewal reversed, as front-page news
(Niugini Nius)

I badly wanted to talk to Mark, even if I had to do that with someone listening. After classes one afternoon, I walked down to the town administration office and asked to use their telephone for a personal call. I would pay for the call, of course. I knew others did that occasionally. Everything seemed fine until the secretary wrote down my name. She looked up at me. 'Excuse me sir, but I cannot let *you* use the telephone.' Her emphasis seemed meaningful.

'Why not?' I said in surprise. 'Other people do. Check with your boss if you like.'

She did. He came out to see me. 'Mr John Mendzela, yes?' he asked, struggling to pronounce my name. 'I regret to inform you that I have a specific instruction that you and your wife may not use our telephone. If you have a personal emergency or you need to make an official call, then please make arrangements through the school principal.'

I persisted with my request but couldn't shift him. He 'had his instruction and must obey it'. And I didn't want to involve Michael.

Elisa had a sharp idea. 'Jerome has a radio on the mission network at his trade store. Maybe we could use that?'

It took several days to enlist Jerome, relay requests through the mission network, and finally get Mark lined up on another radio near Keravat College. And of course, I first had to explain our full background to Jerome, swearing him to secrecy about that. But finally, we were connected.

'Hello Mark! How are you all? What's going on at Keravat, and in the Education Department?'

Hearing Mark's voice again made me realise how isolated we had become. A simple personal call felt like cause for jubilation! We enthusiastically updated each other. But in truth Mark couldn't offer much information beyond the media stories. 'John, no one here knows much about it. The *Post-Courier* protects its sources and the identities of letter-writers. I think nationals are feeling encouraged by our example at Keravat to speak out. But the name "Mendzela" is a buzzword around here, so the Education Department will probably think you're somehow behind it all. Watch your backs!' We signed off.

Jerome was more reassuring. 'A lot of people will remember what happened to you and admire how you fought back and won. Some really bad eggs are deeply entrenched in PNG, but there are plenty of good people around too. In my position, I can't afford to get openly involved. But if you need to communicate urgently with anyone, come round again.'

We decided to continue our local silence about our past, act on Mark's advice to watch our backs, and keep Jerome's offer in mind.

The flow of newspaper stories and letters about the Education Department dried up. With term two under way, our attention returned to more local issues.

50. Drying Out (Elisa)

We settled into familiar daily routines for teaching, administration and work parade. We also had rostered morning and evening duties once a week. Morning duty demanded rising in the dark to walk across the campus, ring the 'bell' and start the school day. The students would rise, wash, dress and attend to their rostered duties: sweep out the dorm, sort the food supplies, fill the cauldrons and light the fires, make breakfast, serve everyone, and clear up. After classes came work parade, dinner and study hall. Then evening duty demanded a check around the dormitories and other buildings to ensure everyone was where they should be and lights went out for the night.

John was no early riser, so I performed morning duties for both of us while he did all our evening duties. Making my way down the narrow dirt path to the bell, I nervously shone my flashlight to watch out for 'death adders' — poisonous snakes that lay in camouflaged ambush, waited for something to move near them, and struck without warning. John's evening duty walks around the grounds, when snakes were more active after the day's heat, were even more nerve-wracking.

We didn't enjoy the rain and mud of our early weeks in Kiunga. Constant washing, cleaning and drying became dreary and difficult chores, and keeping clear of the many mosquitoes wasn't easy. At first, we welcomed a period of dry weather. Baking dry heat felt much more comfortable than Kiunga's normal regime of high heat *plus* high humidity.

But as term two progressed, the rain stayed away. Within weeks, the river level fell sharply, and supply barges could no longer forge upstream. The Fly River was our town's main supply line to the outside world, especially for heavy goods like rice and fuel. And it was a critical lifeline for the gold mine taking shape in the distant hills, essential to ship in bulk supplies and large items.

To counter the loss of river transport, the mining company flew in crucial supplies on a chartered Hercules aircraft. Kiunga's dirt airstrip, cut from the jungle, possessed no lighting, control tower or navigational aids. Four times a day, the huge plane landed in an impossibly short space, braking hard to nuzzle just outside the jungle wall. Once relieved of its 20 tons of cargo, the behemoth lifted off with an impressive roar, almost vertically it seemed. Each take-off and landing stirred up huge clouds of fine red dust that drifted over the town for hours. Despite my constant cleaning, everything — floors, furniture, even our mattress and sheets — looked and felt gritty. Electricity became intermittent as the town generator struggled for fuel supplies and repeatedly broke down. And the occasional outdated newspaper that still reached us grimly advised that this drought was an unusual and widespread regional phenomenon, forecast to last for months.

To add to our dismay, our car and chattels had literally missed the boat. As so often in PNG, a lot of prodding from our friends in Rabaul had been needed before the shipment finally got started. Now everything was stranded 500 miles away at the river mouth. We would have to manage with what we had. Most seriously of all, the dwindling river would become our only source of fresh water once our water tanks and the town's small reservoir ran out.

Drought did offer one compensation. We could now safely sit on the veranda in the parched evenings and watch impressive red sunsets over the western jungle, with no fear of mosquitoes and the diseases they carried. Sitting outside was cooler and we could invite visitors there to chat.

The town's tiny expat community was friendly and sociable. Russell was an Australian doctor who ran Kiunga's hospital — really just an outpatient clinic with a dozen beds for serious cases. Nigel, an aid worker from England, had an impressive brief to encourage local business development — no easy task in a community where cash for employment was a new concept. Garth was a visiting American anthropologist who resided in town for some weeks before disappearing into the jungle to live in a distant village and gather material for his PhD.

Friday nights sometimes found us at a house overlooking the river, where Gerhard the German mechanic and jack-of-all-trades (another aid worker) lived with his pet cockatoo. But the noisy activity we watched on our first visit there as villagers washed and swam in the Fly River soon stopped. As the river's tributaries dried up, crocodiles moved into the main channel. Several barges, stranded in our primitive river port by low water, tilted precariously on massive mudbanks. A foul smell emanated from rotting vegetation on the newly extended shoreline.

The town reservoir dropped fast. Showers became a forgotten luxury. Newer houses not yet connected to the town reservoir fared worst as their roof-water tanks ran dry. Nigel occupied one, and he was forced to carry water in by hand for drinking and an occasional bucket wash. Then the town administration, generously funded and equipped by the mining company, pumped river water into his tank from a small truck. Nigel's initial relief became puzzlement and then alarm when his replenished water tank sounded occasional thumps. Opening the tank, he discovered by torchlight not only much plant life but also several small turtles feeding on that.

We suppressed any tendency to grumble because we knew things were far worse for our students. The vegetables, greens and fruits sourced from the school garden and surrounding forest quickly declined in quantity and quality. The student diet grew completely monotonous — just glutinous rice with token traces of canned fish or meat. And the students did not have our facilities to boil or refrigerate drinking water.

Sunsets from our veranda became a source of upset as we watched local people and our students hunt for edible plants, animals and birds. They would burn down trees to (as they hoped) 'bring back the rain' and reduce cover for anything edible that might hide in the vegetation. Day by day, bare red earth extended its reach. As the jungle around us retreated we decided to declare our backyard, with its single hardwood tree, a nature reserve. To protect its resident pair of kingfishers, we chased away boys with home-made (but deadly accurate) slings and arrows.

Despite the drought, professional work progressed well. Our days were busy and productive. We enjoyed seeing our students study hard and sometimes make startling progress. John returned to his laboratory most evenings to plan and prepare ahead, while I spread out on our sole table at home to work on marking, resources and administration.

51. The Department Attacks (John)

TERM TWO BROUGHT MORE than drought. A routine circular posted in the staffroom announced that Philip Manu was no longer Secretary for Education. He had been sent on 'overseas study'. The new Secretary for Education would be the same man who had sent an intimidating letter to Gus two years previously, when we had first objected to Simpson's inspection procedures. Worse, Gai Luten, chairman of the department's publicly disgraced Committee of Inquiry, had been advanced to Deputy Secretary. The puppets who had actively covered up for corrupt expats were being promoted. So much for any chance of real reform.

Then came a bombshell. At a routine staff meeting, Michael announced arrangements for our school's upcoming inspection visit. He read out the names of staff to be inspected this year. That list ended with Elisa and me.

Conscious the whole staff was listening, I raised my hand. 'Michael, the Education Department has issued clear secretary's instructions about inspections. Those instructions say that staff already rated "Satisfactory" at their working level, like Elisa and me, will normally not be inspected. I don't think there have been any concerns about our work. So why are we on the inspection list?'

Michael shrugged. 'John, I don't know the story there. All I have is the list of staff to be inspected. I will follow up your question with the inspector when I telephone him tomorrow morning.' The meeting moved on.

We spent a worried evening. The Education Department gang was up to something. They would harass us here in Kiunga and might find a way to damage our future career prospects. We decided to fight. We would do whatever was necessary to keep them away from us.

Next afternoon, I went to see Michael. 'What did the inspector say when you phoned him?'

'Well, John, he seemed ready for the question. Apparently, you and Elisa are to be inspected at the specific request of Mr Embahi, the superintendent in charge of education for our province. Mr Embahi's request was approved by Mr Hobson, who is the Superintendent for Inspections nationwide. I agree with you that the inspection seems unnecessary, so I asked for a copy of the request. The inspector said he "couldn't supply that". And he wouldn't discuss what might have sparked the request.

'That means the decision is out of my hands. But I'm happy with your work here, so no worries, right? Let's just go along with the inspection process.'

It was time to come clean. I took a deep breath. 'Michael, Elisa and I won't just go along, because inspection of us would not be professional. It would be payback. Let me explain.'

I outlined the key events from Keravat, and how we had come to work in Kiunga. 'I'm sorry we didn't tell you or any of the other staff about this before. But we hoped for a quiet year, not more trouble. I know it's bad for the school for us to have a fight with headquarters, but we won't just go along with their payback.'

Michael looked at me quizzically for a moment. Then a beaming smile lit up his face. 'Did you *really* think I didn't know about your background? We all saw the headlines last year! When the Education Department offered me you two to fill vacancies here, I think they expected me to say no. But that would not be in the best interests of our students, so I said yes. That's why you're here now.'

I was startled. 'But you didn't say anything! And all the other staff act like they knew nothing about our history.'

'Well, we discussed that at a staff meeting before you came. We decided you might want a completely fresh start. If you didn't want to talk about your past experiences, then we wouldn't either.'

It was my turn to smile. 'Michael, thank you. For your support, and for your discretion.' I took another deep breath. 'But we still have the problem of this so-called inspection.'

Michael frowned. 'Leave that to me for now. I'll see if I can get the inspection called off. In the meantime, just cooperate with the inspector when he comes next week. He won't formally inspect staff during this first visit anyway — that comes later. You can meet him and see what you think. With any luck there won't be a problem. And don't talk to other staff about this, or about your past experiences at Keravat. Do we have a deal?'

We did.

The inspector's visit was a study in diplomacy. A relative newcomer to the country, from England not Australia, Roland Bennett seemed professional and affable. While other staff were present, Elisa and I cordially cooperated with him. At Michael's invitation, Roland called in briefly and informally at every classroom during lessons. Just before he departed, Elisa and I saw the inspector together at our request 'to confidentially discuss a professional matter'.

Bennett opened the discussion, a little curtly. 'Why did you want to see me together? I will inspect you individually in your own areas, on my next visit. It's a simple and normal process.'

We had planned for Elisa to kick off, in a friendly manner. 'Roland, there is nothing simple or normal about inspecting us. You know those inspections have been especially ordered, contrary to normal practice. And I expect you know something about our background.'

The inspector bristled. 'Yes, I've been specifically instructed to inspect you both. I'll perform that duty in a fully professional manner, and I will of course expect your cooperation. What I know or don't know about your background is irrelevant.'

I took over. 'Roland, we appreciate and respect your position. And we have no reason to doubt your professionalism. But there is no valid reason to inspect us.' I read the relevant sentences from the secretary's instructions.

Bennett was getting testy. 'I know all that. But for whatever reason, you're on my list. Perhaps the department is thinking ahead in case you take up another contract. Anyway, if you are doing your work here well, as I trust you are, then everything will be fine.'

Elisa spotted an opening. 'Oh, so that's the concern? We can give you a letter to verify that we don't want another contract and wouldn't accept one. Then you can take us off the list.'

Bennett wasn't having any of it. 'That's not within my discretion. All you need to know is that I will inspect you both on my next visit, as my superiors require me to do.'

I took over and spoke coldly. 'No, Mr Bennett. All *you* need to know is that you will *not* be inspecting either of us. And you can tell your superiors that. If you're concerned for the best interests of this school and its students, then let's avoid unnecessary disputes. Just take us off that list please.'

The inspector was angry now. 'That won't be possible. You are challenging my instructions and therefore the authority of the department. Be assured that I *will* inspect you next term!'

After Bennett's departure, I reported our discussion with him to the principal. 'Michael, we are not giving in. There will be trouble. I'm sorry to drag you and the school into it.'

Michael wasn't fazed. 'No wonder he looked cranky when I drove him to the airstrip. Leave it with me a little longer. I'm still checking on it, and I don't like what I'm finding out. This school is *my* responsibility, and *I* will decide what serves the best interests of my staff and students.'

Next day I gave Michael a letter to verify that we would not seek or accept a further contract, plus copies of our inspection reports from Keravat stamped 'Satisfactory'. We agreed that Elisa and I would continue to sit tight, stay silent about our past, and take no other action without consulting him first.

52. Rats! (Elisa)

TERM TWO MARCHED ON. Teaching and administration kept staff busy. Our students studied diligently and worked hard to meet the challenges of our deteriorating school logistics. 'Greens' for the mess no longer grew in our desiccated fields and had to be laboriously gathered from the retreating jungle. The protein available to add to the monotonous daily rice ration dwindled. The growing water shortage created extra work on many fronts and made daily life — even basic hygiene — more and more difficult.

Meanwhile the mining company redoubled its efforts to cut a viable land supply road through to the mine site 170 kilometres away. The first 50 kilometres had long existed as a narrow dirt track, but that track needed widening and a hard gravel base to serve heavy vehicles and survive rainy conditions. Further on, work teams cut a new route from scratch through virgin jungle and swamp. An array of bulldozers, six-wheel drive trucks and specialised logging and digging machines trundled off the Hercules aircraft and drove through town and out. Local people who until recently had been isolated from the twentieth century stood in their traditional (and minimal) bush clothing to watch in amazement. We felt like people living in a documentary.

Just as forecast, the drought persisted. The town reservoir was now almost empty, and everyone made strenuous efforts to conserve what little water was left. Students carried water a kilometre from the river just to wash. No matter how hard I tried, a depressing layer of red dust settled over everything at work and home. That included us, as bathing became perfunctory for everyone. Student rations were cut and then cut again. Fuel for the town generator ran short, and power cuts from 8 p.m. to 6 a.m. darkened each night. The candles we had purchased in Port Moresby now came in handy.

Water quality could not be trusted. Luckily John, as head of science, still had a supply of gas bottles, and he made sure staff could boil enough water for drinking and cooking. Our less fortunate students had to gather firewood for that purpose, from further and further away.

Our personal food supply suffered. Rice was compulsorily supplied by air under a government-controlled scheme. But otherwise, the limited space available in the few small commercial planes that still arrived was devoted to high-margin items like liquor. Our diet grew steadily more monotonous as the trade store's shelves grew bare and our few remaining 'treats' like canned salmon and long-life milk ran out. Feeling short of fresh produce, we began to worry about our health. Reluctantly, we asked Father Luke to send us vitamin and mineral supplements in the mail.

Social habits worsened as everyone grew stressed. Michael had always tried to enforce moderation and keep noise down during the fortnightly 'payday-Friday' staff drinking sessions. John and I had consciously set a personal example of 'two beers and go home'. But intermittent loud noise and the dark glasses everyone wore the next day revealed that the more typical PNG practice of 'drink until it's gone' took hold after we left.

Sometimes outcomes were funny. On one occasion deafening disco music woke me at three in the morning. Following the music back to its source with my flashlight, I came upon my principal and deputy principal happily practising disco moves. I had intended to be angry but instead burst out laughing. They spotted me in the shadows and sheepishly turned off the music, while I slipped quietly away. We never spoke of that incident.

Sometimes outcomes weren't funny. The school captain came to our door late one Saturday morning to tell us that no one had unlocked the ration store for breakfast. The students had gone hungry. Could we please obtain the key and unlock the ration store for lunch? We found both the duty teacher and the deputy principal (backup for the key) sleeping off hangovers. Handing over the key, we lamely explained to the students that staff were under a lot of stress.

Fighting and domestic violence within a few staff families grew more frequent and audible. Most had 'wantoks' (relatives or other people from the same ethnic group) living with them, not always peacefully. More than once, we invented an excuse to knock at a door to interrupt the proceedings.

Tensions were not confined to campus. Men at the mining camp sought their own forms of stress relief. They drank heavily, drove around aggressively, and pursued local women at every opportunity. Relations with nearby villages grew fraught. One hill near the campus became an ambush site where local youths regularly stoned company trucks.

Unlike us, the mining camp ate well. In fact, it generated a volume of edible waste too large to easily burn. Black ship rats had arrived in town on supply barges earlier in the year. A plague of rats soon infested the camp's rubbish dump and spread outwards from there.

Rats invaded our roof space for the first time. Even our living quarters felt insecure. One night, responding to my scream, John chased off an especially bold specimen that was tearing fly wire off the bedroom window.

At the trade store, we asked Jerome about rat remedies. He offered a novel solution. 'Of course, what with storing rice and other foodstuffs, I've always had to deal with rats. You just need a couple of pythons inside the roof. You can borrow one of mine if you like!' I firmly vetoed that approach, and we settled for conventional traps instead. After we caught two grotesquely large rats and several smaller ones on the steps outside, our ceilings grew quiet again.

The campus faced similar problems. But our students were more than capable of fighting back. I took over responsibility for the campus aid post, which had over several years degenerated into a sadly neglected state. Now hordes of rats had taken up residence there. I enlisted a squad of students to help me clean and renovate. Taking the field with rocks and small catapults, my army surrounded their target. As skirmishers moved in with sticks and brooms, the main body formed a perimeter and gleefully mowed down any rodent fugitives that made a run for it. The battle ended swiftly as my keen commandos mopped up the holdouts by hand (literally). Our final tally was 67 black rats, tidily trucked away in three wheelbarrows for burial.

Indeed, our students were a little too capable. Familiar with hunting edible bush rats and other small animals, many routinely supplemented their school rations from the jungle. Now truly hungry, they were naturally inclined to see plump black rats as a wonderful new food source to toast over open fires and enjoy. John called a special assembly to explain that these black rats were different and *not* safe to eat, and to urge them to thoroughly cook *all* food from whatever source.

By term end, Kiunga High School faced a dire situation. To spin out food supplies, Michael sent all the younger students home and extended their term break to three weeks. Many faced a week's walk to reach the nearest villages they had kin connections with. We admired the fortitude of these youngsters — some only 11 or 12 years old — as they set off on foot with two days' slim rations. Only our Grade 10 students, who faced graduation exams at year-end and needed all their study time, stayed on.

Oh, how everyone wished it would rain.

Soldiering through the drought

53. Turning Points (John)

O<small>UR YOUNGER STUDENTS RETURNED</small>. Term three began. Michael called me into his office. 'I complained to my contacts at provincial headquarters about the proposed inspections — on behalf of my school, not you personally.' He grinned. 'Two of them — both nationals — went to see that expat Joseph Hobson who heads up the inspectors. They showed him your inspection reports from last year and your letter about no contract renewal and told him that as principal I didn't want inspections of you two to proceed. Hobson claimed he had only been responding to the request of the provincial superintendent and had to agree there is no reason to inspect you and Elisa. He said he will contact Mr Embahi and ask him to withdraw that request.' Delighted, I rushed to share the news with Elisa.

But that was just a personal victory. The school and our students still needed a major turnaround in the weather.

Short of personal reading material, I explored the school library. One corner harboured old reports and documents dating back to colonial days in the 1920s and 1930s. Several published anthropological studies proved fascinating. One study outlined living conditions for the small village settlements scattered sparsely through the province's swampy jungle. It noted how nutrition was often barely enough to survive and how settlements often disappeared completely in bad seasons when their inhabitants died out or moved elsewhere. Life expectancy within the population was estimated to be in the mid-twenties. Another study looked at local customs and included the revelation that village men routinely 'shared' their wives with the occasional hunting party that might pass through — a sensible way to counter inbreeding, the writer concluded.

The baked red earth was still parched and desperate for rain. So was the whole population. Brief and sparse raindrops had spattered a few times to tantalise us during the term break, but not even a shower had broken the drought. Michael developed a contingency plan to close the school for the rest of the year if nothing changed within the next month.

Hoping to repair relations with the local community, the mining company had undertaken several charitable initiatives around town and donated a brand-new utility vehicle to the school. Just in time — the ancient 'school car' that had collected us at the airport finally died. The company donated sporting equipment too, and I began teaching softball to a group of students. Softball bats and gloves and even the game itself were entirely new concepts that they took up enthusiastically. We aimed to develop a team that could enter an upcoming competition at the mining camp.

The softball diamond near the camp was several kilometres from the school. I proudly drove our spanking new utility there, packed with students for our first practice game. At the end of the dirt access road, I parked the utility in a bare depression at the foot of a steep hill. We climbed the hill to the diamond on foot, split into two teams, and started play.

Driven by a strong wind, black clouds approached from the horizon and loomed over us. At first that just made the air pleasantly cool. But then lightning split the sky and torrential rain bucketed down. Visibility disappeared. The dry earth of the diamond melted into a sticky red soup. Gathering our equipment, we scurried back downhill towards our vehicle.

But our brand-new utility now stood in a gully that was rapidly filling with water. Rain drummed noisily from the heavens and foamed down the steep hill, scouring the channel deeper. Our utility already stood at an ugly angle, part-submerged in muddy water. I waded to the cab, jumped in and gunned the engine. The car rocked but went nowhere. I tried several more times. No result. The rear wheels couldn't gain enough traction to climb the steepening bank, and just spun helplessly. The foaming water would soon drown our prized new vehicle.

The students looked at me from the banks of the new-born torrent with fear and expectation. I was an expatriate, and a scientist to boot — surely I knew what to do!

I didn't. But I had to try. Shouting calmly over the downpour to show confidence (that I wasn't feeling), I ordered the biggest boys to wade through the now knee-high water and sit on the back edge of the utility over the wheels. Bravely, they complied. It was now or never! I started the engine again, put the gearstick into neutral, and revved the engine almost to a scream. Then I jabbed the gear lever into first. We lurched a little, then a little more, and slowly clawed and yawed up the muddy slope to safety.

Ten minutes later, we watched from a safe distance as the torrent overtopped the gully. Several metres deep at least! For the next few days, I basked in glory as the legend grew in the telling. No one (except Elisa of course) asked me why I had stupidly parked in such a vulnerable place to begin with.

.   .   .

That storm broke the drought. Two weeks of heavy downpours turned the town's fortunes around. The air felt pleasantly cool and the plague of red dust vanished. The stranded empty supply barges below Gerhard's house floated down the rapidly filling river. Their fully laden replacements mainly brought equipment for the mining company but still had ample room for food supplies. And — to our amazement and delight — the third barge to arrive had on board our four-wheel-drive car and our other chattels from Rabaul!

We luxuriated in long-forgotten comforts, from familiar crockery to taped music. A barrel of diesel fuel bought from the mining camp and a jump-started battery gave us independent mobility again. We celebrated by driving ourselves, our colleagues and our students around town on any excuse. No more walks down to the trade store in the mud!

And of course, my infamous .22 rifle arrived with everything else. I confidentially explained to Michael what had happened at Keravat and he quickly made sure it was relicensed for its new location. I kept the rifle well hidden, for more reasons than one. We weren't far from the border with Indonesia, and a few of our students were refugees from a low-level insurrection there. One morning we watched a company of armed PNG soldiers march through town to discourage any border incursions.

Invigorated by our pluvial turnaround, I enjoyed my work more than ever. A week teaching the basics of sex education to younger students was a novel experience. The students, most just 12 or 13 years old, received the information with dignified attention and asked thoughtful questions. Even my cautious outline of contraceptive methods proceeded without a single giggle or smutty joke.

The next week, it was time to demonstrate microbes to my older students. Reading just a lesson or two ahead as usual, I diligently filled petri dishes with a nutrient soup of agar solution. Under my guidance, students added plant particles, insect corpses, soil, spit, or nothing at all to each dish. We sealed the dishes and stored them in a warm cupboard. Each day for two weeks we noted the unchanged appearance of those dishes where nothing had been added and marvelled at the strange multicoloured growths that appeared in all the others. Microbes must be everywhere in the environment, we all agreed.

Flushed with my beginner's luck as a biologist, I turned to the back of the textbook to find instructions for disposal of our results. Bold type there warned me of the serious health dangers to plants, animals and even humans that might have evolved in those sealed dishes. So before opening the dishes, I must heat them in an autoclave (a special high-temperature oven) for 24 hours. I frowned — I had no such equipment. I read further. The text explained that I must not open the dishes to the air (spores might escape), or bury them (contaminating soil), or let their contents enter water supplies (microbes could breed). Nor could I do nothing and leave them around, I read despondently, since the seals on the dishes would inevitably deteriorate.

I felt like Dr Frankenstein after his monster ran amok. What had I done? What to do now? After two worried nights, I decided to open the dishes underwater in sinks that ran into our septic tanks, while wearing gloves and masks. Then we would clean the empty glassware with boiling water. Speaking with a confidence I didn't feel, I explained the need for great care to the three student volunteers who assisted me with laboratory work. Loyally, they helped me destroy the colourful results of our successful but unwise microbiology experiment. And to my great relief no problems emerged.

No running track or shoes for sports day. Our car is next to the "reviewing stand".

54. Development Challenges (Elisa)

WITH THE RIVER OPEN AGAIN, Kiunga evolved rapidly. People and equipment for the start-up of actual mining poured in and shuttled up to the mine site. A regular air service began too — small planes operated by newly formed Cloudlands Airways flew daily to the provincial capital and connected to onward flights. Jerome's trade store faced competition when a nationwide company ambitiously opened a small self-service supermarket. We luxuriated in new food options.

Anthropologist Garth returned from his village sojourn for a short stopover in town before flying home. He proudly showed us gifts the villagers had given him and related many exciting discoveries about tribal culture and customs that he would include in his anthropology PhD. Some of those discoveries sounded dubious, and a few seemed downright wrong even from our limited local knowledge. But whenever challenged about his findings, Garth rebutted scepticism with copious notes and even tape recordings. After he flew out, our local doctor, Russell, enlightened us. 'He's not the first anthropologist to leave here with false information that will make an exciting academic paper. Some villagers are happy to tell tall tales to outsiders, especially those who give them cigarettes or money.'

Economically, it probably made sense for our new supermarket to get in on the ground floor. But culturally, its business model didn't work. Under local custom, goods left on display had normally been gifts made available to others, usually from a temporary food surplus, to be reciprocated in due course when fortunes reversed. And local security guards would not stop their village friends walking out with whatever they desired. Those trophies included food, clothing and even electrical appliances (to be proudly displayed in villages without electricity!). After heavy 'shrinkage', the supermarket reverted to a traditional trade store layout where only shop assistants and not customers enjoyed direct access to the shelves.

Economic development increased social tension. Weary of attacks on its vehicles, the mining company demanded police protection for them. The government flew in a squad of riot police to safeguard the road. That cure soon proved worse than the disease. The bored policemen — all from distant tribes — applied their off-duty time to rival mine company employees in dedicated drinking and pursuit of local women. Worse, the police were armed and quick to wave pistols around or even fire into the air to terrorise any complainants. It was only a matter of time before someone got seriously hurt.

But the locals struck first. The police squad had rehabilitated an old weatherboard house, set in a once gracious garden, for their barracks. An informal drinking club sprang up in the spacious grassed area surrounded by a waist-high hedge. Late one night, without warning, a flurry of long arrows whizzed in from the intense darkness beyond that hedge. Carousing ended abruptly. Two policemen went down, one with a leg wound and another with an arrow embedded deep in his abdomen. Their colleagues drew pistols and blazed away into the night. With no impact — the raiders were long gone.

With his basic medical facilities, Russell couldn't do much for the seriously wounded policeman; he was evacuated by helicopter at dawn. We feared reprisals against locals would follow the night attack. But after tense consultations between the police commander, village leaders, the mine company and government authorities, sanity prevailed. As a peace offering, the mining company created a special fund to develop community amenities. The riot squad was withdrawn and attacks on vehicles ceased.

To our glee, Kiunga High School qualified for the new community amenity fund. Each department head suddenly had a large budget to spend before the end of the year. John ordered science equipment (including an autoclave). I planned replacement of our dilapidated English texts and could add modern encyclopaedias and many other books to our small library.

Unfortunately, our campus developed its own social tension. Michael grimly announced that Panau, a maths teacher who acted as the school bursar and lived in the house next to ours, had run away after being caught raiding the school's cash funds. His replacement Torasu was a stocky bearded highlander. Torasu arrived trailing a large noisy family plus some disturbing rumours. Apparently, he had seriously assaulted a fellow teacher at his last post and was available to us at mid-term only because he was still serving probation for that offence. Torasu moved into Panau's house. We now had a potentially dangerous new neighbour.

A taciturn man who didn't mix much with other staff, Torasu did indeed seem dangerous. A few days after his arrival he was sitting on the ground near our house when he spotted a bird high in one of the few tall trees still standing close to the campus. Torasu stood up and hurled a stone 40 metres with astounding speed and accuracy, just missing the bird. He saw us watching from our neighbouring veranda and grinned with pride in his prowess. Not a man to tangle with.

Torasu's house and family were noisy at the best of times. Problems worsened when he began to entertain fellow tribesmen who worked for the mine company. They drank long and loud over a nocturnal outside fire. Our sleep patterns soon became erratic. We had to do something, and I knew that, as a woman, I would make little impression on a highlander. So one noisy night John went out to speak with them. Their uproar died abruptly, and John returned out of the dark. 'How did it go?' I asked.

'Not well, I'm afraid.' He looked unhappy. 'I tried to explain that I had come to see him personally about too much noise, instead of complaining to the principal. But Torasu interpreted that as a threat, not a friendly gesture. And I think I embarrassed him in front of his friends. Anyway, they promised to go elsewhere in future so that night noise should stop.'

And stop it did. But more than once over the next few weeks I saw Torasu glaring at John. He would seek payback for sure.

55. Two Wins and A Loss (John)

TERM THREE WAS ENDING. Our inspector Roland Bennett finished his second visit, complete with a rerun of our previous stand-off with him. He coolly informed Elisa and me that he would return early in term four to prepare inspection reports for the teachers on his list, including us. 'It's your call. You can either cooperate fully with me or face disciplinary action under the regulations.' Our principal Michael still thought we would be taken off the inspector's list, but we were getting worried again.

Michael drew me aside one morning. 'John, I have to prepare the school accounts for an audit that happens every three years. An auditor is coming here in two weeks, and we have a problem. Panau was never replaced as bursar, and I don't know how to do the annual reconciliation that regulations require. Also, each income and expense item in our accounts should be checked and countersigned by someone else, not me. I remember you said you studied accounting. Can you help?'

I agreed to do what I could. I spent a long evening in the school office cross-checking three years of bank statements and neatly written cashbooks against a large box of supporting receipts and cheque stubs. The records had been kept surprisingly well. I found only three anomalous items. Each was a cash cheque for 'returned school fees' made out to some individual. The corresponding payments were missing from the bank statements. So those cheques had never been cashed. They were two years old now, so legally they could no longer be presented for payment.

Michael remembered the unpresented cheques. He had dispatched them to distant villages when students unexpectedly withdrew from school. 'It wasn't safe to refund school fees in cash, so I gave each departing student a cheque for his parent or guardian to cash at the admin office in town. Maybe the cheques never got there, or maybe those people never came to town. Anyway, it was all done according to regulations.'

'That's fine then,' I assured Michael. 'The school has *more* money in its account than the records show. Those people might ask for a replacement cheque at some stage, or maybe the auditor will just reverse the transaction. Either way, no problem.'

The next night I turned to the reconciliations. With all cashbook entries correct, the prior year's reconciliation should be simple. I just needed to repeat whatever format Panau had used for the previous two years.

But that task turned out not to be simple at all. The first year's reconciliation occupied many pages. Panau hadn't known how to reconcile accounts. Unpresented cheques hadn't been allowed for. Totals and balances for various items wandered back and forth in the cashbook as he vainly struggled to create two matching amounts. Finally, Panau had grasped that subtractions created smaller numbers. He had repeatedly deducted two declining column totals from one another to eventually, and inevitably, reach a difference of zero.

'Reconciliation complete' was triumphantly written in large letters under that outcome!

The Year 2 presentation was much shorter. Panau had applied his novel and undeniably successful reconciliation technique right from the outset.

I didn't know exactly what a genuine reconciliation should look like, but from the cashbook and bank statements it was easy enough to develop supporting calculations that harmonised totals and highlighted the unpresented cheques. Next morning, I showed Michael reconciliations for the previous year and right up to the last month, with footnotes to explain the unpresented cheques and the correspondingly higher bank balance. 'Michael, the auditor will criticise Panau's reconciliations for the two previous years. You might want to phone the provincial office and advise that there were some discrepancies in the accounts that have now been resolved.'

Two days later, on Thursday, Michael drew me aside again. He looked worried. 'The auditor is coming tomorrow, and Mr Embahi the head of provincial education is coming with him. They had recent problems with stolen funds at other schools. I tried to explain that no funds were missing here and that the accounting discrepancies meant we had more money not less, but Embahi didn't seem to understand. He wants a formal meeting with you, me and the auditor after the accounts have been inspected.' I reassured Michael that the outcome would be fine.

Embahi arrived at lunchtime, auditor in tow. Sure enough, the auditor quickly grasped the situation and confirmed my checking and analysis. At the formal meeting that followed, he explained that the accounts were fully in order with no funds missing. In fact, a small extra surplus could now be recognised. The auditor left the room to write up his report.

Embahi's previously stern face relaxed. He looked at me quizzically. 'You know, I didn't really think there was a problem with the accounts. I had another reason to come here today. Michael told me you have a concern about your inspection. I don't know much about what happened at Keravat last year, and I wanted to meet you before making my mind up about that. The school here is very happy with your work. Why do you object to being inspected?'

I took a deep breath. 'For two reasons. Firstly, it's pointless, because the school is happy with our work and we will leave PNG at the end of the year. You've seen our letter to say so. But more fundamentally, what they really want is payback for what happened at Keravat.'

I outlined the key issues and outcomes there. 'So you can see, Mr Embahi, that in our case an inspection would not be genuine. It would just be an opportunity to invent criticisms and put them on record. The inspectors at the Ratings Conference — who will be mostly the same people who backed Simpson two years ago — can then rate us "Unsatisfactory". We need to protect our professional reputation for the future, and we will fight to do that. Your request to have Mrs Mendzela and me inspected is not in the best interests of this school or its students. Please withdraw it.'

Embahi looked thoughtful. 'Yes, I did make that request. But it was not *my* idea. It was Mr Hobson's idea. *He* recommended to *me* that you should be inspected. Mr Hobson gave several reasons why that should happen in the best interests of the Education Department, especially with your background. And he showed me your report on file at headquarters, with two different stamps on it. I naturally acted on his advice.'

He turned to Michael. 'Now that I know more, I accept the advice of your principal instead. I will telex Mr Hobson tomorrow and withdraw my request. You won't hear any more about it.'

He stood up and offered his hand. 'John, I thank you and Elisa for your work here in our province and for what you have done for our country. Good luck for the future!'

I reported gleefully to Elisa. Two wins in one day, for the school and for us! I banged off a letter to Education Department headquarters to point out that the copy of my report on their file had apparently never been retyped and restamped as promised. Then we celebrated with a tasty dinner and a bottle of wine.

Our mood changed abruptly next morning. An early knock at the door woke us up. Elisa answered and talked with someone in low tones for a few minutes. She returned to the bedroom looking tearful. 'Matthew is dead.'

It took me a moment to understand. One of our teaching colleagues was called Matthew. Had there been an accident? Then it hit me.

The Matthew who had died was one of my top Grade 10 students. He had been taken to Russell's 'hospital' for examination several weeks earlier, suffering from a severe cough. That was nothing unusual. Students often returned from their villages with ailments that were endemic there, and coughs and colds could spread rapidly through the dormitories. We had used exactly those examples in my science classes to help explain how bacteria and viruses reproduced and spread.

But Matthew's problem grew more serious. His condition didn't improve under the routine treatments he received. In fact, it got worse. A second examination and blood tests followed a few days later, and he was admitted to the hospital for observation. Russell told me that it looked like a case of early tuberculosis, probably caught in his home village. 'TB is common up there in the mountains, where it's cold and damp a lot of the time. We can give him antibiotics to treat that, and it's probably not highly contagious at this stage. But to be sure, I'll isolate him here at the hospital until the test results come back from Moresby.'

I visited Matthew in the hospital a few days later. He looked dreadfully wasted and had an intravenous drip attached to his arm. I was shocked but determined to be cheerful. 'Well, Matthew, from our studies you understand sickness better than most people. The medicines here have already stopped the coughing. When the doctor gets the test results back, he will know exactly how to fight the microbes that are making you sick.'

Matthew shook his head sadly. 'I know about that science, Mr Mendzela. And it is true. But this is a different problem. My father is a good leader of our village, but he has enemies in other villages nearby. Someone in one of those villages is using a sorcerer to kill me, to hurt my father.'

I was stunned. 'Matthew, you don't believe that, do you? There is a scientific explanation for your illness.' Matthew looked down and didn't argue, but he clearly disagreed.

I saw Russell on the way out and recounted our conversation. He shook his head. 'John, I'm sure of my diagnosis of TB. But our routine treatments for that aren't helping like they should. Matthew is deteriorating fast. I can't tell why. I think it's because he believes he's going to die. And he might if something doesn't change. I will try it his way too and get in a traditional healer. Someone who is a good fellow and has a strong reputation around here. Maybe he can work some counter-magic.'

I visited again a few days later. Matthew looked terrible, even worse than last time. He spoke slowly and quietly like someone resigned to his fate. I talked breezily about what the class was studying and when he would return to lessons. Matthew played along, but I could tell he was just humouring me.

I confronted Russell. Harassed by many demands, he was unusually brusque. 'Yes, I got in the healer, and he did his magic rituals. Then the two of them talked quietly for a while. I spoke with the healer before he left. Matthew told him who the sorcerer was. His own magic apparently isn't strong enough to combat that more powerful person. And he explained that Matthew is happy to die as compensation, to end the feud back in his home area.'

I exploded. 'Okay, I accept all that cultural belief stuff. But what about the medical diagnosis? You're a doctor!'

Russell shook his head. 'I don't have anything left to try. I've sent off three sets of test results, and the results come back negative each time, for tuberculosis and for anything else I can think of. But don't worry, he's not in immediate danger yet.'

That had been four days earlier. I'd heard nothing more until now. And now there would be nothing more to hear.

Elisa explained that the mining company had offered to fly Matthew's body back to the airstrip nearest his village. The mission network would send a runner from the nearest radio to get a message to his family.

A sombre procession left campus that afternoon. The school's utility led the way to the airstrip, driving slowly. Matthew's body rested on the back under a simple white sheet. The entire staff and student body followed on foot, in silence. The tiny four-seater plane waiting at the airstrip didn't have a cargo compartment large enough for a body, so friends stretched Matthew's body over two of the seats and covered it with the sheet. Another student from his local area took the remaining seat. The plane buzzed down the dirt runway and disappeared into the distance.

I caught up with Russell a few days later. I was still angry, and I found what had happened hard to accept. Surely our science and medicine were strong enough to overcome superstitious fears. And surely Matthew didn't really want to die.

Russell was philosophical. 'I've had things like this happen a few times now. I don't try to explain it anymore. I just do the best I can with what I've got. All I can tell you is that I talked with him several times before the end. You're right that he didn't *want* to die. But he believed that he *should* die, and that he *would* die. So he did.'

56. Fresh Battles (Elisa)

JUST TERM FOUR left now before our contract ended. The weather settled into a benign pattern of regular moderate rainfall, ending my dust problems. And we had our car and our home comforts. Life was looking up.

Then a new story in the weekly *Times* revived the Keravat affair. One historical photo showed the Keravat students under arrest. A familiar face jumped out of another: Luther Tomba, my former English department colleague at Keravat, raking over the saga from a fresh angle. He explained that while a few specific expatriate villains had been removed, the wider cultural and administrative changes to the Education Department recommended by the Ombudsman Commission had not occurred. Luther attacked the Department's discredited Committee of Inquiry, especially its decision to terminate us 'on the absolute knowledge of the damaging influence these officers are capable of embedding'. That allegation 'made by our PNG brothers at headquarters' was 'insulting, degrading and morale-shattering. It implied that PNG teachers are unable to think for themselves and...incapable of judging wrong and right.'

Luther bemoaned the departure of national teachers from Keravat (including himself) and detailed by name the individual outcomes for a number of expatriates. His list included us. Luther protested against a corrupted Education Department: 'If education is left in the hands of unscrupulous expatriates and their national stooges...this country is doomed.' But it was far from clear to readers that — unlike all the others Luther named — John and I here in Kiunga were not amongst those stooges. And he said nothing at all about our role in fighting corruption.

The Keravat affair refuses to die, as nationals begin to speak out (The Times)

John and I discussed how to correct those false impressions without too much fuss. We decided to send a short factual letter to *The Times* to clarify the confusion in Luther's article without attacking the Education Department. That would come from me, not John. *The Times* happily set the record straight in its next issue, quoting the

Ombudsman Commission's finding that 'the termination of Mr and Mrs Mendzela served only the best interests of those who sought to prevent misconduct, abuse, and incompetence from being exposed'. And their correction went further, to emphasise that 'the other transferred expatriates mentioned in the article were involved on the other side of the struggle'.

After several letters of support for Luther, publicity about the Education Department died away. John received a letter from department headquarters confirming our end-of-contract arrangements. The letter also promised to retype his report and invited him to inspect his corrected file 'in the presence of a senior officer, if you so wish'. Battle over, we decided.

News reached us that road construction had broken through to the mine site, so we could now drive up there. And we had plenty of fuel left in our barrel of diesel. We had learned by trial and error — and a few unpleasant mouthfuls — how to siphon that fuel into our tank.

It would be a long round trip of over 300 kilometres into the Star Mountains. We thought it wise to wait a few weeks while finishing touches were applied to the entirely new part of the road. To do a test run first, we decided to drive just the first 50 kilometres to the previous roadhead at the Catholic mission station. That first section had long been a dirt track of sorts along relatively flat land, and the widened road with a new gravel base should be easily passable to that point.

We took company along. We had warned John's science colleague Buna and his wife that the trip might be uncomfortable. They were keen to see the countryside outside Kiunga and our warning didn't deter them. But they soon looked deeply unhappy hanging on to the roof from sideways bench seats as John drifted back and forth across the dirt road to hug bends and avoid ruts. Buna's polite question 'Excuse me, John, but which side of the road do they drive on in New Zealand?' came as light relief. John slowed down to reduce their discomfort.

A priest and three nuns at the mission made us most welcome. As usual when meeting missionaries, we felt embarrassed at first. Their matter-of-fact descriptions of long treks through leech-infested jungle and swamp, to reach remote villages and treat horrific medical conditions, humbled us. Compared to them, we were paid well and enjoyed comfortable work conditions. But they told us not to feel guilty — it was their vocation to labour here. And they gratefully accepted our cash donation, which would be put to good use. And best of all — being a *French* religious order — they kept a wine cellar. A fine red wine became the best beverage we'd enjoyed in months.

As we chatted, an amazing coincidence emerged. One nun was English not French. She had grown up near me, in England near Manchester, and we even had a few acquaintances in common. Talking privately after a refreshing swim in the river, I drew Sister Edith out a little further. At Kiunga's high school, we had girls leaving at age 11 to get married. Wasn't early and excessive child-bearing a key health and social problem here? I left unspoken my implicit criticism of Roman Catholic doctrines against contraception and abortion.

Sister Edith laughed. 'I know what you're thinking. I can tell you that I routinely distribute contraception information in the villages. It's the right thing to do, and I don't care what the Pope thinks about it.' She related how she had personally taken part in key conclaves in Rome during the brief flowering of Vatican II, when many dogmas had been overturned and the concept of 'liberation theology' had emerged. Perhaps, like us, she too had been exiled to the remote jungle for her principles? And here in extreme conditions she still did what she thought was right, without making a fuss about it. A remarkable woman.

Two weeks later, John and I set off for the mine site. This time we went alone and raced along the first section at dawn to tackle the entirely new road early. That track climbed at amazing angles, plunged down steep slopes, and looped around on itself to avoid the swampiest terrain. Ruts, mud and loose gravel often slowed us to a crawl. But John managed the hours of tortuous driving to the mine site, where (as their first outside visitors to arrive by road) we received a hearty welcome and a guided tour. The scale of the operation to first extract the mountain's 'gold cap' of valuable gold deposits and then mine deeper for rich copper ore staggered us.

Enjoying ourselves, we forgot how quickly tropical darkness would descend and stayed too long. Driving back became a race against nightfall. As we skittered at high speed along a rare straight stretch of road between two walls of jungle, John slammed the brakes on. Remarkably, the car stayed on the gravel as it screeched to a halt in a cloud of dust. And the seat belts we had installed two years ago kept us strapped in.

I was furious. 'What did you do that for?' I demanded.

John just pointed ahead. A few metres further on, a monitor lizard the size of an adolescent crocodile stood in the centre of the road staring at us. 'I guess he's not used to the road yet. And he's big enough that hitting him would not be good for any of us.' Well, it was *his* habitat not ours. The lizard gazed at us disdainfully a while longer, flicked its long tongue, and lumbered off into the jungle.

Back at work, Michael posted the schedule for the upcoming inspection visit. As Mr Embahi had promised, we were no longer on the list of teachers to be inspected.

When Roland Bennett arrived at the staffroom a few days later to begin his final visit, he looked pale and flustered. We wondered why. The inspector completed his formal inspections of the staff on his list. Keen not to gloat, we had only minimal contact with him.

It wasn't until that evening that a colleague enlightened us further. 'It wasn't you two getting off his list that upset him. As Deputy Principal, Lami collected Roland at the airport. Lami's wife came along too, and while Lami was driving them here, she pulled a knife out and started shouting. Why was she, a hard-working classroom teacher, being inspected while her husband the deputy principal who drank too much and abused her was not? Roland had to talk her out of stabbing Lami on the spot!'

We wondered what her inspection report would say.

57. Road Rage (John)

WITH THE ROAD OPEN, individual trucks and convoys could shuttle equipment and supplies all the way from riverhead to mine site. Traffic volumes climbed dramatically. That brought new problems. Our girls' dormitory was prudently situated well away from the three dormitories for boys, but that located it next to the road. Truck drivers started finding excuses to stop outside the dorm to chat with the girls and offer them treats like chocolate bars. We knew some of the drivers hoped the girls would offer something in return.

Quiet persuasion from staff failed to stamp out those assignations. Our girls were being tempted into misconduct that would compromise their own futures and the investments their villages had made in them. Michael appealed to the town administrator and the police chief. Surely the trucks could follow a longer route around past the airstrip.

No, they couldn't, the mine company responded. Supply schedules were tight, and time was money. The road was a legal right of way, the trucks had every right to use it, and they would keep on doing that. The town administrator and police chief backed the company's stand.

Michael threatened to physically close the road. He was told in no uncertain terms that would be illegal. But as Michael informed the staff, he wasn't giving up so easily. At work parade, Michael assigned a squad of boys to dig a deep trench across the road. We could still travel back and forth into town using a rudimentary track through the bush behind the campus, but a through road passable by large trucks would no longer exist. Michael, deputy Lami and senior master Henry headed off to town to explain what they had done. That left me in charge of the school, worried about what might happen next.

Michael had instructed the digging squad to defend the trench until he came back. The boys, several just spindly chest-high youngsters, dutifully took turns on guard duty behind the trench. Devoted to their mission, they held bush knives aloft like bayonets at the ready.

During the first hour, several trucks individually drove up the road and stopped at the trench. Each one ultimately turned around, but only after threats and shouts. Two hours on, a convoy of three police vehicles arrived. Several policemen emerged to talk to the boys stationed behind the trench. The police seemed to be ordering the boys to do something, and the boys appeared to be resisting. Voices got louder.

It was time to intervene. I felt like a colonial officer heading to the battle lines, lacking only a red jacket and a white pith helmet. Trying to look composed and authoritative, I approached the policeman who seemed to be their leader. 'I'm Mr Mendzela, head of science. I'm in charge of the school at the moment, officer. What seems to be the problem?'

To my surprise, he was quite deferential. 'Hello, sir. I have an official letter to deliver.'

I was taken aback. What could be in the letter? Was it a legal document? Was Michael's team being held hostage?

I retreated a little way to read the missive. It bore an impressive letterhead. And it was from an official source alright. But its content was innocuous, indeed hilarious in the circumstances. The school's senior staff were 'invited to afternoon tea with the Australian High Commissioner' when he visited our town and the mine site next week. Would we RSVP please?

Smiling broadly, I returned to the officer. 'Thank you, please say we will attend.' Then I broached what had worried me. 'Why did you come here in *three* vehicles?'

He laughed. 'Oh, we just wanted to see the trench. Your boss is with the chief now, talking about that. They will have another meeting tomorrow. I think you will be there. Goodbye sir!'

Michael returned soon after and sought me out. He explained that no agreement had been reached with the authorities. There would be a further meeting at nine tomorrow morning in the school library. Would I act as facilitator please? 'Of course,' I agreed, 'if that would help.'

The morning meeting assembled bang on time — a rarity in itself! The participants walked up the stairs and into the library. They settled unsmilingly on opposite sides of a table. Michael, Lami and Henry faced the town administrator, the Police Chief and another senior police officer. I sat 'in the chair' at the head of the table. A ceiling fan in the middle of the room spun lazily and all the louvre windows were wide open. But oppressive heat prevailed even at that early hour.

I convened the meeting and explained that my role was to help them reach a mutually acceptable solution to the road problem. I first wanted each side to state their concerns and the areas of disagreement as they perceived them. Resisting temptation to flip a referee's coin, I asked Michael's group as the home side to kick off. Impressive rhetoric followed from the three members of the school team. They emphasised the duty of the school to protect the girls under its care. They expressed dismay and great sadness that the town authorities would hide behind legal technicalities, rather than support their principled defence of the girls' virtue.

In reply, the town administrator authoritatively explained that he had no power to prevent people legally and peacefully using public roads. If our girls encouraged company drivers to stop or socialised with them in some way, then that was a problem for the school and not for him. The Police Chief spoke next. He curtly stated that the school had illegally blocked a public road. He was obliged to prevent such criminal action. If necessary, police would arrest and jail the people responsible. His supporting officer — a bulky and imposing uniformed figure — confirmed his men would make those arrests.

'Thank you all for the clear statement of our shared problem,' I pronounced with maximum dignity. 'But now I want you to suggest what we could do next, as a solution that might be acceptable to everyone. Let's hear from the town authorities first this time.'

That didn't take long. The solution, as those authorities saw it, was to remove all obstacles from the road and allow traffic to proceed. And that must happen immediately — the mine company had already made a formal complaint and the law would be enforced. The rejoinder from the school team was equally firm. The road past the school would remain blocked. The mine company could use the longer route around past the airstrip and stay away from the school.

Anticipating impasse, I had jotted notes on tentative solutions the night before. But as I prepared to speak, movement outside distracted me. Fifty metres away, a small woman walked briskly towards the library at a speed rarely seen in torrid Kiunga. She carried a large wooden stick. I stared curiously for a moment. Following my gaze, the other meeting participants stared too.

I returned my attention to the job at hand. But before I could say anything, the second police officer started fidgeting. He now looked decidedly nervous, and not imposing at all. Abruptly, he stood up and bolted wordlessly for the exit. The door slammed. We heard the officer clump rapidly down the stairs as he passed out of our view. But he had left his escape run too late.

A woman's voice reached us from underneath the building. 'You liar!' Whack! The unmistakable sound of her wooden stick meeting uniformed flesh. '*You* are the one who is going to see those girls, every night in your car!' Another whack! '*That* is why they must close the road.' After a short pause, a more distant whack followed. And at increasing distance and attenuating volume, more accusations. And more whacks. 'How can you go to church on Sunday?' Whack! 'How can you wear your uniform?' Whack! 'Get home and pray for your soul!' Whack!

I started to laugh but saw that all the other faces around the table remained utterly serious. Stifling my mirth, I explained a range of solutions that had been applied to similar situations in other countries. The town side, embarrassed to see one of their team humiliated, became conciliatory. The administrator mused that while people must be free to travel on the roads, they should *travel* and not stop without a good reason. The Police Chief conceded that the main issue at stake was that vehicles must be able to *travel* the road; there was no need to let drivers stop at the school unless they were on school business. Within an hour, with technical guidance from their facilitator, everyone expressed satisfaction with a freshly minted town ordinance that created a 'no stopping' zone for the stretch of public road that bordered the school grounds.

We all met again a few days later over afternoon tea with the Australian High Commissioner. Even the Police Chief was grinning.

58. Closing Clashes (Elisa)

OUR LAST TERM was racing by. Michael had already arranged the paperwork for our final payments, travel vouchers and shipment of effects. For the first time in years, we could plan our future with confidence. We would fly out to Asia for five weeks of holiday while our possessions travelled by river barge, coastal trader and freight liner to New Zealand. There John would complete his interrupted business studies and I could work freely.

The closing news from our friends at Keravat was less positive. Letters from Mark, Father Luke and Tim (now our main correspondent) had documented the steady erosion of our supporters there: June had been allowed to 'go finish' early with health problems, Glen went back to Australia after his marriage broke up, Gabriel resigned to leave for Zimbabwe, and all the national staff had left. Every expat staff member who had backed us and the students had been denied contract renewal. Their protests to the Public Service Commission and the Ombudsman Commission achieved nothing as the Education Department applied its 'discretion'. By year-end, just one of the 21 signatories of the staff letter to the secretary would remain, and none of the students who had known us. Father Luke, described by Tim as subdued and world-weary, would soon return to Australia to serve a parish there. His church altarpiece that had once been Gus's hand-carved table would soon be the only concrete remnant of our struggle.

The college year had been despondent, with unhappy staff, low student morale and disappointing exam results. A new principal had little impact, while the English department operating under his wife continued to be the weakest link academically. A new inspector had replaced Miller, but like most others with long service in the Education Department he sided firmly with the administration to muffle any and all concerns raised by students or staff.

As part of a routine tour of the provinces, the Chief Ombudsman had visited Keravat and addressed the student body there. But he avoided speaking about past events at the college and, Tim told us, he seemed discouraged. We couldn't blame him. He might be able to help right some individual wrongs, but he had not changed the Education Department's abusive power structures.

Our days flew by as year-end approached. We worked hard to prepare graduating students for their exams and to improve the resources we would leave behind for our successors. We applied the mine company's cash grant to order teaching materials and equipment for the next year, and even received some early deliveries. The school administration block now boasted a phone and a fax machine, which greatly simplified communications with the wider world.

John had a novel problem. 'What do I do about the chemical cupboard? A circular with new safety regulations came around. It lists all the potentially dangerous chemicals that I should destroy. But there are some I can't dispose of, like that huge jar of potassium cyanide that's been there since God knows when. We don't have the equipment or the locations to follow the instructions in the circular!' In the end, all he could do was put the forbidden chemicals in a box vividly labelled 'DANGER!' and leave them for his successor with an apologetic note.

The national examination papers arrived by air in securely sealed boxes. Kiunga High School's first-ever graduates had done badly last year — hardly surprising given the school's newness, its difficult working conditions, and the remote origins of most students. But while expectations for this year might not be high, effort was. Everyone cooperated to make the school a quiet and effective place for the Grade 10 students to concentrate. The campus grew hushed as examinations proceeded under tight supervision. After an intense week, the completed exam papers were securely sent off to the provincial capital Daru for marking. John soon followed them to join a regional marking panel there.

Left to myself for several days, I deferred packing until John returned. We would have end-of-contract admin to sort out then anyway, especially the logistics for shipping our car and chattels out to New Zealand. After cleaning out the freezer and fridge one evening, I sat down to relax with a backlog of newspapers. And got a surprise.

Under the headline 'Airport Watch for Teacher', the *Post-Courier* had run a dramatic story about a fugitive in the highlands: 'Police are watching airports for an expatriate school principal alleged to have engaged in homosexual conduct with at least four students aged between 14 and 16. Warrants for the man's arrest have been issued. The matter was brought to the attention of the police after the school's 640 students went on strike.' The story went on to cite four similar abuse incidents at other schools, and to recall the tale of our own sacking and later reinstatement. At least our battle was still encouraging others to challenge abusive behaviour!

The article went on to cite four similar abuses elsewhere by others and to recall the "Keravat affair" (Post-Courier)

I followed the story through the next few issues. The fugitive — a crony of the headquarters gang whom we knew about but had never encountered — was dramatically arrested two days later as he boarded a plane and immediately appeared in court. The *Post-Courier* investigated further. It revealed that he had been re-recruited by the Education Department, *after* a previous criminal charge of 'carnal knowledge with a male against the order of nature' had led to cancellation of his work permit. Then *Niugini Nius* created confusion with its competing headline: 'Ex-Keravat Man on Carnal Charge'. In fact, the accused wasn't from Keravat at all.

EX-KERAVAT MAN ON CARNAL CHARGE

*Niugini Nius linked those recent events back to the Keravat
scandal and cover-up (Niugini Nius)*

Not only was Keravat in the news again, but in *The Times* the Education Department belatedly replied to Luther's criticisms published there weeks before. The new secretary accused Luther of being a mouthpiece for 'the previously sacked teachers who were still stirring up trouble'. And he publicly named the Mendzelas as disaffected teachers who were using the media to 'keep the pot boiling'. So much for our efforts to let bygones be bygones and keep a low profile.

Furious, I composed a rebuttal and immediately faxed it to the editor. 'The secretary implied that my husband and I are attempting "to resurrect the controversy surrounding Keravat". On the contrary, Mr Secretary, we have been getting on with a professional job in a remote part of the country, from where communication is not easy (as you are no doubt aware). The reason why the Keravat affair continues to feature in the press is because moral corruption is still rife in the Education Department.' After a series of rhetorical questions, I concluded that 'if it wasn't for our stand against moral and professional corruption in 1981, the activities of homosexuals in schools would have gone unmentioned in 1982. Why does the secretary want secrecy and silence to return?' *The Times* editor was so keen to publish my letter that he faxed me back the next issue's proofs before lunchtime.

Belatedly, I wondered whether I should have consulted John before rushing into print. But when he returned from the marking panel, John congratulated me on my letter. '*They* came after *us* this year, remember? You were right to fire that parting shot. Your rhetorical questions were clever — far more effective than statements.' He grinned. 'And I've found one more shot we should fire. Mr Embahi's secretary asked one of her colleagues in Moresby to check what's on our headquarters files there in case someone like a future employer requests information about us. And sure enough, they *still* have never got around to retyping and restamping the copy of my inspection report that's on file there. I've arranged with Michael that we can fly to Moresby a day early. I can attend to some school business there for him. That will give me time and opportunity to visit headquarters, take up their invitation to inspect my file in the presence of a senior officer, and get that correction made.'

I was delighted. 'Sounds good! But what about Gus's file? It's probably the same. I know it doesn't matter for any practical purpose now that he is dead, but it would be great to restore his reputation on paper at least. I hate to think those corrupt bastards can get away with not setting the record straight.'

'I thought of that. I feel the same. But for privacy reasons they probably won't let me see someone else's file. Fair enough, I suppose. Anyway, I'll have a go when I visit them.'

My rebuttal letter was far from the last word on Keravat. The Education Department had once again shot itself in the foot. Its new secretary foolishly blustered that the media 'did not serve the interests of the nation' by publishing Luther's article. That was angrily refuted by *The Times* itself: 'The Education Department would be doing the country a service by fully explaining the Keravat disturbance.'

And my letter soon had plenty of company. A flurry of news broke out.

Under the headline 'The Pot Keeps Boiling', Luther waded back into the Education Department with vigour. Other letters thundered that 'Keravat symbolises problems of homosexual exploitation of students found in schools throughout PNG' and asked, 'How can anyone involved in education have any faith left in the department hierarchy?' Gai Luten's promotion to Deputy Secretary despite his role as head of the disgraced Committee of Inquiry received renewed attention. One writer stated that 'a high proportion of senior staff are of doubtful integrity and morality' and asked the new secretary why he was persisting in 'a cover-up rather than a clean-up'.

With splendid timing, the Chief Ombudsman released his Commission's Annual Report. It reprised the Keravat saga and spoke of continuing 'improper conduct' with children by teachers. And it went further. 'The two teachers were reinstated upon our recommendation, but only after much foot-dragging and attempts to harass them. Other Keravat teachers who had been vocal against the administration also started to fall victim to retribution.' Problems extended far beyond Keravat. 'Numerous complaints are still coming to us regarding allegations of arbitrary, biased and unjust actions by the Education Department. We call upon the Minister for Education to put a stop to this and conduct a thorough housecleaning.'

Meanwhile the captured fugitive's continuing trial kept a spotlight on sexual abuse of students. The continuing critical publicity — and no doubt growing political pressure too — finally led to some concrete response. The Teaching Services Commission had always been a toothless agency operating under the thumb of the Education Department. But now headlines blazed: 'Government Tightens Moral Code for Teachers' and 'Teachers Get a Sex Lesson'. The articles explained that it was 'essential that positive steps' be taken 'to erase sexual and homosexual misconduct of teachers'. A new code of conduct that 'stemmed from the "Keravat Affair" last year' was introduced. The Teaching Services Commission would in future act directly and independently to deal severely with staff who transgressed that code. The Education Department's fortress had at last been breached.

And that wasn't all. The Public Service Commission belatedly acted on the Ombudsman Commission's earlier recommendation to establish structured disciplinary processes for expatriates on contract. Under new rules, they would receive natural justice and have the opportunity to contest any accusations made against them. Acting in secret 'in the best interests of Papua New Guinea' — as the Education Department had done with us — would no longer be possible.

After nearly three years of battling, we could feel we had achieved a real and positive long-term difference for PNG's education system. That felt good.

GOVT TIGHTENS MORAL CODE FOR TEACHERS

A new code of conduct was imposed on the Education Department to "erase sexual and homosexual misconduct of teachers" (Post-Courier)

Back in Kiunga, we still didn't know our students' exam results. Though John had been on the marking panel, he hadn't been allowed to see our own school's papers or results. Those would be announced at the school's upcoming graduation ceremony, by Mr Embahi in person.

Excitement buzzed around the campus as the students prepared for the ceremony and their departure home. It would be a special occasion for everyone. Michael had even managed to source luxury food treats for a post-graduation staff party — a big bucket of crabs and six huge lobsters flown in from Daru, hundreds of kilometres away on the coast.

Graduation was a great success. A small crowd of relatives and onlookers heard Mr Embahi proudly announce that Kiunga High School had come near the top in science, from over 150 schools. A stunning success for John's teaching. We were equally delighted by the result for English. Unlike their competitors in major towns, our Kiunga students had little exposure to English outside school. Nevertheless, Kiunga's results improved from almost bottom the previous year to well above the national average. The school's results for other subjects were less competitive, so John and I could feel we had personally made a difference during our 10-month stay.

More speeches followed, to a crowd stoic under a baking sun. Each graduating student in turn came to the veranda to collect their individual certificate. The class captains spoke, sincerely and humbly thanking the school and their teachers. To our increasing discomfort, almost every speech gave John and me special mention. Yes, we had done our jobs diligently and well, but we did find the repeated acclaim a touch embarrassing. Finally, the graduation ceremony concluded with a vigorous rendition of the school song followed by tea, biscuits and delicious fresh fruit for everyone.

We broke away from the lengthy afternoon to finish packing. John closed off his laboratories and records and checked our personal paperwork for departure next morning. I finished my own admin tasks and joined the female staff and student helpers who were preparing the staff party. The signature dish would, at my initiative, be 'Lobster Mornay'. Of course, we lacked some ingredients from the recipe, but with superb raw material and some innovative substitutes our culinary team felt confident of a good result. Early taste tests confirmed that.

The staff party began with a surprise announcement from Michael. Before dinner, we would have a knockout pool tournament, with refreshments and a trophy donated by 'our friends from the brewing company'. Play began, lubricated by copious free beer. The beer soon had adverse effects. The quality of play deteriorated. Time dragged.

Many spectators, and some competitors who had been eliminated early hungrily began to seek dinner. I decided we should add some solid food to the alarming quantities of liquor that were being put away and authorised the kitchen helpers to serve people individually as they arrived. 'But make sure to keep something back for the winning players and for ourselves, especially a little Lobster Mornay.'

I returned to watching the pool. John had reached the semi-finals, mainly by virtue of being the most sober competitor. But he looked more worried than pleased as he confided in me. 'That guy Torasu still has it in for me, and this is his last chance for revenge. He's drunk as a skunk and fighting drunk at that. See him glaring at me? If I have to play against him, I don't know what will happen.'

Sure enough, the final pitted John against Torasu. Much the worse for wear, Torasu played poorly. But John wasn't playing much better. He explained why in a whisper. 'He needs to beat me so he can feel he's won. But if I throw the match, he'll feel insulted and start trouble.' Torasu grew increasingly uncoordinated, forcing John to feign the same problem. Both missed shot after shot. Even hard-core spectators lost interest and drifted away for food and conversation elsewhere. Finally, after a skilfully contrived near-miss from John, Torasu put the last ball away. John slumped in defeat convincingly and offered his hand. 'Congratulations Mr Torasu — you are the best player!' Swaying and beaming, Torasu shook hands. He staggered off to find Michael and collect his trophy.

Relieved and hungry, John and I could at last head for dinner. At the serving table, the only remaining kitchen helper handed us plates of rice, accompanied by a few chunks of luncheon meat and some soggy greens. 'What about the Lobster Mornay?' I asked.

'So sorry, Mrs Mendzela, everyone liked it so much they came back for more, and now we have none left!' 'Well,' I thought philosophically, 'Torasu got his revenge after all.'

We munched our rice and drank a sociable beer. Then we pleaded need for a good night's sleep before our early departure the next day and slipped away to bed.

59. Setting the Record Straight (John)

MICHAEL and several other friends came to the airstrip with us. Farewells were awkward, with post-party sunglasses prominent and everyone feeling jaded. Amid our thanks to them (especially Michael), their thanks to us, and mutual promises to stay in contact, we loaded ourselves and our luggage into the 18-seater plane that flew direct to Port Moresby each day. Propellers roared as we taxied down the runway and angled into the air.

Gazing down, the dirt airstrip looked unchanged from our arrival. But Kiunga town was no longer just a few buildings straggling along a single short road. The expanded mining camp loomed large, iron roofs of other new buildings gleamed in the sun, and many new clusters of huts were evident. The narrow track north once hidden by jungle had grown into a wide gravel-grey scar surrounded by a web of raw red-earth tracks. Jungle around the town had retreated a long way, replaced by human cultivation. Elisa and I glanced at one another, thinking the same things. Was Kiunga now a better place? Would development benefit its people? Had we really achieved anything there?

A cheerful welcome greeted us at the same Port Moresby hotel that had been our home in the uncertain times of a year earlier. That evening we treated ourselves to a bottle of champagne and a fine dinner — no pink canned cheese, water crackers, or corned beef anywhere to be seen.

Next morning, I strode assertively into Education Department headquarters and made my way to Colleges Division. I told the receptionist that I was there on confidential business and needed to speak urgently to the most senior officer present. Her eyes widened at my name and she hurried into the back. I was asked to wait.

Thirty minutes later, a chubby expatriate emerged. Shaking my hand, he nervously introduced himself: 'Thomas Smith, Senior Projects Officer for the Education Department. We met when you first arrived three years ago, remember?'

'Ah yes,' I replied, trying to make him even more nervous. 'We haven't met since then, but I've *heard* quite a lot about you. Can we go to your office and speak confidentially please?'

Once safely behind his desk, Smith regained composure. 'Well,' he said brusquely, 'I checked on your situation before I came out to see you. You're going finish now and everything is in order. So why did you come here today?'

'Not quite *everything* is in order,' I replied. I explained my belief that the inspection report on my personal file had not been retyped and corrected as had been promised to me.

'Mr Mendzela, I'm sure that's not true. We take great pains to get our paperwork right.'

'Well, I certainly hope that's not true,' I smiled winningly. 'So may I please see the file?'

'Of course, of course. That's your right as a contract officer.' He left the office and returned 10 minutes later. 'Here it is.'

I skimmed through many pages of contractual and administrative records dating right back to our original job applications. I found the inspection report and sternly held it up. 'As I feared. The inspection report in this file is the original one. It still has "Unsatisfactory" stamped on it underneath the correcting stamp. Something like that could damage my future career!'

Smith blanched, then recovered. 'Mr Mendzela, I'm terribly sorry. I can't imagine how that oversight occurred. We'll get onto fixing it right away!'

We agreed that I would return in the afternoon to check the result in his presence. I stood up to leave and then halted. 'Oh, I nearly forgot.' (I hadn't.) 'You've probably made the same oversight in relation to Mr Gale's inspection report. Please let me see his file.'

Smith drew himself up stiffly. 'I can't do that. Personal files are confidential to the individual concerned and the Department. And, anyway, he's deceased.'

'Yes, that's right. He *is* deceased. And a lot of people blame the Education Department for that.' I paused to let that sink in. 'Let's make a deal. You fix his file too and let me check everything's been done right in it. And then I won't tell the newspapers about your department's — I paused again — "oversight" about our personal files. I think that would be in the best interests of everyone concerned — including your own.'

Smith shifted his gaze and shuffled his feet. Then he flashed a crocodile smile. 'Well, it's all a little irregular, but I know you were a good friend of his. It's a deal.' We limply shook on it.

I returned late in the afternoon after completing Michael's errands. I found Smith cheerfully awaiting me. 'I'm sorry to confess that Mr Gale's file was wrong too. Here are both files, all fixed as we agreed.' I paged through the files, taking particular care over Gus's. Each had a carefully retyped inspection report, freshly stamped 'Satisfactory'. And all the other paperwork appeared to be in order.

Smith held up two documents. 'And here are the previous double-stamped versions of the inspection reports, which we'll destroy.' He stuck out his hand, brightly. 'Goodbye! I wish you good luck for the future.'

I looked hard at him. 'Mr Smith, I'm not leaving until you tear up the original reports. Do that now please.'

We locked stares for some seconds. Then Smith spoke petulantly. 'Oh, all right, if you insist!' He tore the two reports in half, and then tore the pieces in half again, and then (with difficulty) tore those pieces in half once more. 'Is *that* good enough for you?'

'Thank you, Mr Smith. *My* inspection report on *your* department can now be rated "Satisfactory".' I walked out slowly and quietly. But I really wanted to whoop with delight. I had scored a small final victory, not just for myself but for Gus too.

60. A New Normal (Elisa)

I ENJOYED John's colourful account of his final visit to the Education Department. A quick trip to the Ombudsman Commission office and several phone calls to friends were gratifying too. Then we were at the airport, flying to a holiday in Asia before travelling to New Zealand.

And we would even have the last word. *The Times* editor had agreed to publish — *after* our departure — a closing letter from us to remind readers of Keravat and thank the many people who had fought on our side. 'The greatest share of the credit for this victory of justice over corruption must go to the students of Keravat. Intelligently, they took no sides at first and simply asked for an explanation. Instead, they received threats, abuse and finally armed force, followed by unjust arrest and imprisonment. Our thanks and best wishes go to them.'

We had come to Papua New Guinea seeking adventure, and we had certainly found it. Challenged on our values, we had taken a principled stand and blown the whistle on serious wrongdoing. And, by great good fortune and against the odds, we had won. So why did we feel sad, not happy, as our plane lifted from the tarmac? Because over three tumultuous years we had met many fine people and developed a love for this remarkable young nation. Given its remoteness, difficult access, and expense of travel, we didn't expect ever to return to PNG.

Adjustment to life back in New Zealand didn't come easy. When we first moved into an apartment, we found ourselves testing light switches and water taps to see what happened. It seemed strange that they always worked. Numerous road signs and complicated rules sometimes puzzled us. Grocery shopping involved far too many choices.

Socially, we didn't fit in well at the outset. To us, other people's daily concerns often seemed trivial and absurd; to them, we often seemed odd and impatient. What later became known as 'First World problems' never seemed entirely real to us, even within our personal affairs.

Busy with our new careers (now both business consultants, not teachers), PNG diminished into an intense personal memory and the stuff of dreams. Our numerous artefacts felt like dear old friends. Their rugged and unusual beauty was always a good conversation starter, but the recollections we shared with new friends and acquaintances mostly focused on descriptions of the land and its people, peppered with amusing anecdotes. Like war veterans, we learned to bottle up and cellar our stories of battle and comradeship. Experience with our families reinforced this. Most people — however hard they might try — just couldn't understand. We learned to say nothing.

The lessons we had learned in Papua New Guinea about people and organisations — and the thin dividing line of fortune between triumph and tragedy — forever shaped our lives.

And the smell of wood smoke or the ringing of a bell still evokes vivid memories.

Epilogue

OUR STRUGGLES through multiple investigations and the extensive publicity sparked by police invasion of the Keravat campus had created a rich trove of source documents. Soon after the events, we prepared a detailed chronology to comprehensively record the facts in case we ever needed professional vindication. That chronology had joined our voluminous reports, letters, photos, notes and newspaper clippings in a cupboard that we didn't open.

Seven years after leaving PNG, we received a disturbing letter from our former Keravat colleague Tim. A major British newspaper had quoted Martin Simpson as a credible professional giving his public support to claims of widespread Satanic rituals that included sacrificing thousands of babies and foetuses.

Tim's letter raised ethical questions for us. Simpson was again in a professional position that surely gave him opportunities to harm vulnerable people. And he was demonstrably using that position to fan bizarre claims. But should we intervene in his affairs again, from the other side of the world? Did we have a moral right to pursue someone with whom we no longer had any professional or personal connection?

Child abuse 'linked to satanic cults'

A TELEPHONE helpline for victims of ritual or satanic abuse receives up to 10 new cases a week, an international conference on incest heard yesterday.

██████ who founded the Safe helpline six months ago, said she was not surprised at the large number of people claiming that they had been forced since childhood to take part in abuse connected with cult rituals.

██████, aged 34, survived 16 years of physical and mental abuse. "Only yesterday I had 20 calls; we are going to get more as more people realise they have somewhere to turn."

At least 50 covens, usually spanning several generations, were known to her, and police were closing in on two. Wiltshire police say they have investigated a number of her allegations, and sent a report to the Crown Prosecution Service.

The London conference heard that covens habitually sexually abuse children or make them take part in acts of bestiality during satanic rituals. Human sacrifices included babies induced and then killed, while sometimes foetuses were eaten in ceremonies. ██████, a psychotherapist, said that in America there were an estimated 10,000 human sacrifices a year, most being specially-bred foetuses.

██████ said that she had no evidence to substantiate her claims, but insisted the practices were widespread.

██████ adds: ██████, a former local authority director of social services, told the conference on Monday that there was no stereotype child victim of abuse. "You have to listen to a wide band. I particularly want to commend what ██████ has to say," said ██████, a director of Childline, the child abuse phone service. "I will vouch for ██████."

The article that created an ethical dilemma for us, seven years after the "Keravat affair"

We decided no, to both questions. We advised Tim that it was up to him as a British resident familiar with Simpson's history to take matters further if he thought that was the right thing to do. Tim didn't take any action, and we eventually lost contact with him. The misguided public hysteria that Simpson's media statement supported, claiming thousands of babies were being killed in Satanic abuse each year, gradually died away in the absence of evidence.

With our interest in PNG reawakened, we did some research. At New Zealand's national library, John studied years of back copies of PNG newspapers. The Keravat affair had faded from view soon after our departure. Any media mentions of Keravat after that referred to later and unrelated events. Had the PNG education system really reformed, or just reverted to what it had been before our time? We couldn't tell.

Rabaul's volcanoes finally exploded again in 1994. Major eruptions devastated the hastily evacuated town and buried it under metres of ash. Keravat became a refugee camp for a time. The airport, civil administration and business activity permanently moved 30 kilometres down the coast to Kokopo. Over time, Keravat had expanded into a substantial town that still housed several important national education and research institutions on or near the college campus.

We still occasionally searched the internet for relevant posts about people and places from our time in PNG. One night we read about a history of Keravat College, compiled by none other than our former deputy principal Isobel Barnes.

We located a copy of her book at a specialist American bookshop and purchased it online. A week later, we checked the text. How did it record the tumult of 1981? How did it portray us, the sacked teachers? What did it say about the student strike? The nearly lethal police response? The extensive investigations into the Education Department? The reforms the Ombudsman Commission recommended to parliament? Our vindication and return to PNG? The fates of others who had been involved?

Fragments of the story were told, including reminiscences from several students about the police invasion. But the Education Department's senior officers and the Keravat College administration were all presented as responsible and professional throughout, while we were dismissed as teachers who 'had personal problems' and needed to go. Nothing about villains ousted, wrongs righted, or reforms achieved. So much for the 'official' history.

We decided to put the record straight and publish the full story as it really happened. The names of most of the people involved have been changed. But the roles they played have not. The events portrayed in this book can be fully validated from reports, letters, photos, notes and newspaper clippings.

Abusive behaviour by individuals working in public institutions, and harassment of 'whistleblowers' who try to stop it, continue to this day. We believe publication of the Keravat story is in the public interest. We hope our story will encourage anyone in a similar situation to act 'in the best interests', and challenge those who would abuse their official positions to exploit others or suppress the truth. Justice can, with boldness and determination (and great good luck), sometimes win through.

Acknowledgments

Throughout our story, many different individuals had opportunities to do the right thing, the wrong thing, or nothing at all. We are grateful to those who chose to do the right thing, often at personal cost and risk. Equally prominent was the key role played by reliable and respected public media. The positive role played by the National Broadcasting Commission and the *Post-Courier* brought our case to public attention, and ensured that the truth could no longer be repressed.

We thank the personal friends (listed in alphabetical order) who were our first test readers: Roger Buchanan, Mela Haughey, John Hosegood, Lindsay Mitchell, Grant Sinclair and Helen Trustrum. Each provided a different perspective. Our writing benefited from the improvement opportunities they agreed about and their occasionally opposing points of view.

Lindsay Mitchell helped us combine our sketchy geographical memories and the much-changed view from modern satellite pictures into a sketch map of Keravat.

Our manuscript assessors Dan Myers and Mikaela Nyman provided invaluable advice from their extensive writing and publishing experience. They helped us turn a highly personal story into a work of creative non-fiction that could interest a wider audience. Dan also reviewed further drafts from a critic's and reader's perspective, and generously shared many ideas and tips.

Self-publishing offers a maze of challenges. Martin Taylor has been our guide and advisor throughout the process, applying his deep experience and expertise to help us bring *In the Best Interests* into the public domain. We are also grateful to Jeroen ten Berge for a striking cover design that captured its flavour, to Brian O'Flaherty for his careful proofreading, and Penny Hartill for her tenacious work to interest reviewers and media in our story.

About the Authors

The "Keravat 2", forty years later. Few whistleblowers are so lucky!

John Mendzela was born in 1952 in England. His Polish father survived Stalin's forced labour camps in Siberia and the long walk to Iran to become a 'displaced person' in Britain after World War II. His Irish mother had left her homeland to work in Britain. John overcame a disadvantaged background to fight his way through Britain's class-driven school examination scheme and selective university system.

Elisa Hurst was born in 1953 to a working-class English father and an Italian mother (her wartime boyfriend kept his promise to return, and brought her back home). Elisa grew up on the grimy Manchester plain where her entrepreneurial father started and ran a successful bespoke tailoring shop. Inspired by nature and beauty, Elisa went to art college to undertake teacher training.

In the 1970s Elisa and John founded and led environmental action groups. They met on a slag heap being 'greened' by volunteer labour, married while still students, started work as teachers and migrated to New Zealand. *In the Best Interests* relates what happened next.

After the 'Keravat affair', John and Elisa developed new careers as independent governance and management consultants. They have worked in institutional and organisational change across a diverse range of cultures in over 30 countries, including PNG and the Pacific. In 1994, their consulting company Mendhurst was legally incorporated (unbeknownst to them) precisely on their twentieth wedding anniversary. www.mendhurst.com showcases their professional work and business writing.

John and Elisa live in New Zealand in a home and office overlooking beautiful Wellington harbour, from a native forest backdrop they have legally protected from development. They can often be found at work in the garden, on the run at the golf course or supporting local theatre. More of their narrative non-fiction can be found at 'Short Tales from Tall Orders' at www.mendhurst.com/short-tales.

www.mendhurst.com/inthebestinterests

www.ingramcontent.com/pod-product-compliance
Lightning Source LLC
Chambersburg PA
CBHW072041020426
42334CB00017B/1350